D0193945

THE CRITICAL ADVANTAGE

DEVELOPING
CRITICAL THINKING
SKILLS IN SCHOOL

William T. Gormley, Jr.

HARVARD EDUCATION PRESS
CAMBRIDGE, MASSACHUSETTS

Paperback ISBN 978-1-68253-057-3
Library Edition ISBN 978-1-68253-058-0

Library of Congress Cataloging-in-Publication Data
Names: Gormley, William T., Jr., 1950-
Title: The critical advantage : developing critical thinking skills in school /
    William T. Gormley, Jr.
Description: Cambridge, Massachusetts : Harvard Education Press, [2017]
Identifiers: LCCN 2016057511 | ISBN 9781682530573 (pbk.) |
    ISBN 9781682530580 (library edition)
Subjects: LCSH: Critical thinking. | Critical thinking—Study and teaching.
    Creative thinking. | Creative thinking—Study and teaching. | Thought
    and thinking. | Inquiry-based learning. | Teaching—Methods.
Classification: LCC LB1590.3 .G665 2017 | DDC 370.15/2—dc23
    LC record available at https://lccn.loc.gov/2016057511

Published by Harvard Education Press,
an imprint of the Harvard Education Publishing Group

Harvard Education Press
8 Story Street
Cambridge, MA 02138

Cover Design: Wilcox Design
Cover Image: I Love Photo and Apple/Moment/Getty Images

The typefaces used in this book are Palatino and Gotham.

CONTENTS

INTRODUCTION

WHEN ST. PAUL was traveling on the road to Damascus, he experienced an epiphany. It may have been divine inspiration, or perhaps just inspiration. Whatever it was, it caused him to change the course of his life profoundly. When I was thinking about education policy problems and opportunities a few years ago, I had an epiphany. It didn't lead me to unsaddle my mule, quit my job, give up my worldly goods, or do anything so dramatic. But it did convince me to switch research topics, to focus on something I had taken for granted for many years and wanted to understand better. That subject was critical thinking.

Much of my research in recent years has focused on early childhood education and its outcomes. Like other scholars, I have measured educational outcomes by using standardized tests. Although these tests have some predictive validity, they seldom tap the cognitive skills that I personally value. Standardized test scores from kindergarten or third grade can predict later test scores but not necessarily college readiness or career readiness or civic readiness. These are three goals that I really care about, and I worry that two of them (career readiness and civic readiness) don't get the attention they deserve from teachers, administrators, or public officials. My concern about college readiness is a bit different: that all children may not be adequately prepared for a goal that is closely identified with the American dream.

I also worry that many education reforms, including standardized testing requirements, performance measures for schools, lower student-teacher ratios, merit pay for teachers, school vouchers, and charter schools, distract us from the central importance of classroom teaching. The Common Core, which does focus on course content and pedagogy, is a notable exception, but it has, unfortunately, become a lightning rod for partisan criticism. My epiphany, on my road to Damascus, was to see critical thinking, when defined broadly and flexibly, as a promising pathway to college readiness, career readiness, and civic readiness. Critical thinking is the missing link between many of our most vexing societal problems and a brighter future.

What exactly is critical thinking? It is different from rote memorization, the mastery of facts without understanding their significance. It is different from what psychologists call "motivated reasoning," or biased thinking, which prefers passion to truth seeking.[1] It is different from what Daniel Kahneman calls System 1 thinking, which is quick, intuitive, and often productive but not well suited for answering really difficult questions.[2]

I argue in chapters 1 and 2 that critical thinking is an open-minded inquiry that seeks relevant evidence to analyze a question or a hypothesis. Some of the hallmarks of critical thinking are a willingness to challenge the conventional wisdom, an inclination to reconsider your own cherished beliefs, a relentless search for good evidence, an ability to draw appropriate inferences from good evidence, respect for competing points of view, and persistence when answers to important questions seem elusive. I distinguish between critical thinking and other valuable forms of thinking, such as creative thinking and problem solving. I argue that some of the best thinking on the planet is "blended thinking," which straddles these three categories. Think of it as critical thinking on steroids.

Why should we care about critical thinking? After all, there is no shortage of education issues, social issues, environmental issues, fiscal issues, and national security issues to worry about. Isn't critical thinking a bit abstract, a bit esoteric? Wouldn't it be better to focus on a more concrete, more urgent problem?

One reason to focus on critical thinking is that it is a potential cure for some of the biggest problems we face as a nation: *education deficits* that afflict many members of our society and make it difficult for them to share in the American dream; *employment deficits* that make it hard for many high school graduates and college graduates to find gainful, satisfying employment; and a *surplus of partisanship* that threatens to tear our society apart at the seams because we lack respect for our fellow citizens who have different points of view.

Education Deficits. In recent years, we have become obsessed with third-grade reading and math skills, as measured by standardized test scores. Disappointing test score results and persistent gaps between middle-class and disadvantaged students and between white students and students of color are legitimate concerns. Lackluster performances by US students on international tests are also worrisome.[3] But the more fundamental problem is that our students often learn enough to pass tests, in specific courses and in standardized testing marathons, without deeply engaging or truly mastering the subject matter. That is the real crisis in American education—that students can recall a mathematical formula without knowing when and how to apply it, that students can memorize key biological terms without understanding how living organisms actually work, that students can recall key events and personalities in history without recognizing the social movements and trends that were driving these transformations. Critical thinking can help, a lot, with these kinds of education deficits because it forces students to ask good questions, avoid glib answers, look for strong evidence, discard weak evidence, articulate a point of view, respond to feedback, and reconsider their working hypotheses. These are the kinds of intellectual skills that college admissions committees look for and the kinds of intellectual skills that will help our students excel. Incidentally, this is also our comparative advantage in education, internationally. As an exceptionally free society, we are unusually well situated to nurture and cultivate critical-thinking skills that require open inquiry to take root.

Employment Deficits. Although we managed to weather the storm when the Great Recession threatened to become a full-scale depression in 2008, our economic productivity has declined, and many Americans remain unemployed or underemployed. The technological revolution has helped create some wonderful high-skill jobs for a fraction of the workforce, but middle-skill jobs have nosedived, and low-skill jobs continue to be low-pay jobs as well.[4] The middle class has taken a hit, and our more disadvantaged citizens and families continue to suffer. Employers are frequently asked what the underlying problem is, and they consistently assert that our schools are not producing individuals who possess critical-thinking skills, communications skills, and collaborative skills.[5] When employers complain about a dearth of critical-thinking skills, it is unlikely that they are referring to high school graduates or college graduates who cannot decode a literary or historical text. Rather, they probably mean that we need to teach students how to solve complex problems, how to adapt to new situations, and how to improvise. This is very different from the kinds of critical-thinking skills we emphasize in US classrooms today because we don't really give the goal of career readiness the attention it deserves. Critical thinking can help us solve many of our economic problems, but only if critical-thinking instruction in K–12 classrooms encompasses the kinds of skills that employers value and that employees are likely to need in the workforce.

A Surplus of Partisanship. It is difficult to observe American society today without noticing a rise in partisanship, a decline in civility, a crowding out of moderate points of view, and a splintering of our mass media environments. These trends have infected our body politic like a poison, facilitating "motivated reasoning," or biased thinking. We all have our biases, of course, but motivated reasoning makes it difficult to recognize or escape them. Fortunately, there is a cure. A massive increase in critical thinking could help us become more thoughtful media consumers, more nuanced thinkers, more persuasive debaters, and better citizens. It could help us forge a truly deliberative democracy. It could help us choose our political leaders and our public policies more wisely. But isn't critical thinking part of the problem? Aren't we too critical of one another, too vicious in our rhetorical attacks, and too ready to dismiss our own critics? Yes, some of that is true. But critical thinking is not just recognizing the weaknesses of other people's arguments; it is recognizing the weaknesses in our own arguments, assumptions, and beliefs. We need to apply the same tough standards when appraising our own ideas that we do when appraising the ideas of others. That broader conception of critical thinking is the subject of this book.

For critical thinking to help solve these big problems, it must be explicitly linked to three goals: college readiness, career readiness, and civic readiness. These goals are complementary but not interchangeable. It would be a mistake to focus on only one of them (e.g., college readiness), and yet that is roughly what we have done. In practice, critical thinking is defined so narrowly that it is often viewed as the special province of high school English and history teachers, who use Socratic seminars and other devices to get their students to dissect and interpret texts with sophistication, in the hope that they will get into a good college. This is a worthy goal, and high school English and history teachers, to their credit, have a greater appreciation for critical thinking than many other teachers do. There is much that we can learn from them and their teaching methods. But critical thinking is not just a means to college readiness, and analyzing texts is not the only way to demonstrate critical thinking. Also, if we wait until students are juniors or seniors in high school to promote critical-thinking skills, then we have waited too long.

In short, we need to embrace critical thinking as a versatile analytical tool that can enhance what we know about many subjects and elevate our discussions about many subjects to a higher level. Critical-thinking instruction is not just another item on the laundry list of tasks we assign to teachers. It is best viewed not as a burden but as an opportunity. In practice, critical thinking can be liberating, for students and teachers alike, because it invites more reflection and more thoughtful deliberation than one would otherwise see in the classroom.

In conducting research for this book, I took three complementary approaches. First, I immersed myself in the literature of several different disciplines, including psychology, philosophy, economics, political science, and neuroscience. At times, this was a bracing experience, like taking a plunge into an ice-cold river. But when hunting for ducks, one should go where the ducks are. And the literature on critical thinking is scattered across multiple disciplines. Second, I developed conceptual scaffolding to illuminate the relationship between critical thinking and other useful forms of thinking and to explain the form that critical thinking takes when it is linked to different goals (college readiness, career readiness, civic readiness). Third, I visited a total of twenty schools in an effort to better understand what critical-thinking instruction looks like in different classrooms and how critical-thinking instruction can be brought to classrooms with very different demographic characteristics (see Appendix). These schools were, for the most part, located in parts of the country that I know very well—Pittsburgh, Pennsylvania, where I grew up; Arlington, Virginia, where I live; and Tulsa, Oklahoma, where I have done a good deal of education research. By visiting schools where I had relatively good access but which differed in their demographics, I hoped to shine a light on the many challenges and opportunities that teachers experience when they try to develop their students' critical-thinking skills.

In this book, I place a spotlight on critical thinking in an effort to persuade public officials and teachers to make it a high priority, to use it in multiple classrooms, to link it to multiple goals, and to introduce it early, beginning in preschool. In chapter 1, I document growing interest in critical thinking and try to explain this trend. In chapter 2, I distinguish between critical thinking and two other valuable forms of thinking—creative thinking and problem solving. When combined with critical thinking, creative thinking and problem solving can produce excellent results, including scientific discoveries, enduring systems of government, and dazzling new forms of entertainment. In chapter 3, I extract lessons about critical thinking from the growing literature on neuroscience. What does brain research tell us about the origins of critical thinking, the location of critical thinking, and how to teach critical thinking?

My central arguments can be found in chapters 4 through 6. In chapter 4, I confirm a strong connection between critical thinking and college readiness. In many ways, this is where we have made the most progress, thanks in large part to some talented, dedicated teachers. However, not all students have shared in this success. In chapter 5, I identify missed opportunities to connect critical thinking to career readiness. A key point here is that the kinds of critical-thinking skills that promote career readiness have been neglected, with unfortunate economic consequences, especially for disadvantaged students. In chapter 6, I document a civic readiness gap that seems to be worsening as we become more polarized politically. I distinguish, as others have, between participatory democracy and deliberative democracy, and I show how critical-thinking instruction can promote the latter if we choose to do so.

Throughout the book, I use vignettes from classrooms I have visited, in northeastern Oklahoma, southwestern Pennsylvania, and northern Virginia, to illustrate some exemplary efforts to promote different forms of critical thinking. In chapter 7, I draw upon these classroom visits to illuminate some promising innovations in Science, Technology, Engineering, and Math (STEM) education that combine critical thinking, creative thinking, and problem solving in productive and sometimes exciting ways. Finally, in chapter 8, I offer some practical suggestions that could help us achieve the goals of college readiness, career readiness, and civic readiness.

Before we begin our journey, I would like to state clearly what should become evident in the pages that follow, which is that I have enormous respect and affection for teachers. Like most adults, I have benefited profoundly from some outstanding teachers, who have equipped me with valuable skills, challenged my preconceptions, and pointed me in new directions. I remember a piano teacher, Mrs. McDowell, who taught me well enough that I could perform for a live audience without dissolving into a bundle of nerves—great preparation for my eventual career as a professor. I remember a high school teacher, Bruno Scuglia, who asked a question that seemed surprisingly easy at first but that proved to be deceptively hard: who is the most powerful person in the city of Pittsburgh? I remember a college professor, Samuel P. Hays, who turned my world upside down by portraying history as a bottom-up rather than a top-down phenomenon. I remember a graduate school professor, Duncan MacRae, who inspired me by shifting gears midcareer to focus on big, important questions, even though they took him outside the comfort zone of his own immediate discipline. I should also tip my hat to an elementary school principal, Sister Alberta, who allowed me and my friends to stage a production of a Shakespearean play that was astonishingly bad but also astonishingly rewarding for those of us who participated.

Throughout this book, I pay homage to many outstanding teachers who work a special kind of magic in the classroom. They are the tip of a very large iceberg. Many men and women have devoted their lives to educating the next generation and have figured out how to stimulate, how to probe, how to challenge, how to provoke, how to broaden horizons, how to introduce new ideas, and how to get students to think for themselves. Many teachers have demonstrated how much they care by working long hours and by assisting students after hours with extracurricular activities, with homework, with the ups and downs of life, and with their dreams for the future. When I make suggestions about how teachers might change their practices and their priorities, I hope it will be understood that I do so with the same constructive intent that motivated so many teachers to help me move in new directions.

I also want to emphasize that this is not just a task for teachers. If critical thinking is to occupy center stage in American education, then all of us must become involved. That includes elected officials, school administrators, teachers, business leaders, community leaders, journalists, and parents. All of us need to become critical thinkers—and advocates for critical thinking—if our educational, economic, and civic outcomes are to improve.

The Critical-Thinking Movement

IN THIS CHAPTER I try to explain the intellectual and political origins of the recent push for critical thinking in the United States. I document growing mass media interest and political interest in the subject and identify some of the manifestations of that interest, including the Common Core. All of this has taken place without a clear consensus on what critical thinking is. To explain such enthusiasm for critical thinking, despite uncertainty on what it actually is, I focus on three big goals of critical thinking—college readiness, career readiness, and civic readiness—and the corresponding deficits that critical thinking is expected to reduce. I argue that critical thinking takes different forms and requires different teaching strategies depending on which of these goals one is trying to promote.

THE RISE OF CRITICAL THINKING

In recent years, a crescendo of support for more critical thinking has arisen throughout the United States. Employers assert that they need workers who can think critically, solve problems, and respond to new challenges. Politicians argue that higher-order thinking skills are of vital importance if the United States is to compete successfully for market shares in the new global economy. The general public ranks critical thinking at the top of skills they believe schools should be teaching.[1]

Teachers' views on critical thinking are more difficult to summarize. On the one hand, they chafe at curricular fads and mandatory testing requirements that leave them with little discretion in the classroom. And they resent being blamed when testing outcomes and high school graduation rates are disappointing. On the other hand, they generally support the idea of promoting critical thinking in the classroom.[2] They also welcome changes that give them greater discretion to probe a few ideas in depth rather than to cover a broad body of knowledge superficially.

Clearly, there is considerable interest in critical thinking these days. And that interest has grown. Consider, for example, newspaper articles that refer to "critical thinking" as a key theme or in passing. As Figure 1-1 illustrates, there has been a sharp increase in the number of such articles, from 2001 to 2015. The number of articles more than doubled from 2001 (583 articles) to 2005 (1,234 articles) and doubled again from 2005 to 2010 (2,535 articles). From 2010 to 2015, the number of articles referring to critical thinking nearly doubled again (from 2,535 to 4,394). In fact, newspaper coverage of critical thinking increased at a more rapid rate (an astonishing 654 percent)

FIGURE 1-1   Newspaper articles referring to critical thinking, 2001–2015

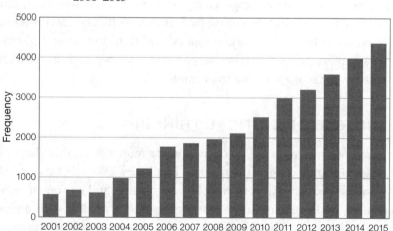

Source: Lexis-Nexis search of newspapers, with press releases and duplicates removed.

than coverage of other hot topics during the same period, such as partisanship, yoga, and rap music (see Figure 1-2). Apparently, critical thinking is a pretty exciting topic!

THREE DEFICITS

Critical thinking is of special interest in the United States today because of growing concern over three big deficits in our society: the college-readiness deficit, the career-readiness deficit, and the civic-readiness deficit.

College Readiness. Because high school graduation rates have climbed in recent years, to 82 percent, one is tempted to conclude that US students are better prepared for college than they used to be.[3] But these statistics are misleading. Although high school graduation rates have increased somewhat, for a variety of reasons, college enrollment

FIGURE 1-2   Trends in newspaper coverage: critical thinking versus other hot topics, 2001–2015

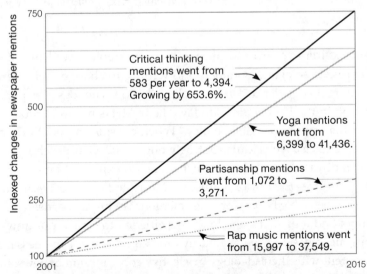

Source: Lexis-Nexis search of newspapers, with press releases and duplicates removed.

rates dropped from 69 percent to 66 percent between 2008 and 2013.[4] The most sobering statistics are these: according to National Assessment of Educational Progress (NAEP), fewer than 40 percent of US high school seniors are ready for college work.[5] Not surprisingly, many students enroll in college and then drop out because they can't handle the work. Saddled with debt, they have little to show for all the money they spent.[6] What exactly is missing in these students? It could be grit. It could be money. It could be knowledge. Or it could be critical-thinking skills. Whatever the precise combination of reasons, most of our young people are not on track to receive a college degree, despite a good deal of rhetoric and some public policies aimed at promoting that goal.

Career Readiness. Numerous studies report a growing gap between the skills employers say they require and the skills workers possess. Thousands of jobs go unfilled because employers cannot find workers with the right set of skills.[7] A recent survey found that 33 percent of small business owners had unfilled jobs because they couldn't find workers who were qualified for the job.[8] Employers routinely cite critical-thinking skills as a key requirement for a job, and they also cite the absence of critical-thinking skills as a worrisome problem.

Civic Readiness. In an ideal democracy, the public is well informed, attentive to relevant evidence, and willing to change their views based on that evidence. Unfortunately, that does not describe public opinion in the United States today. The public is not well informed on either politics or public policy.[9] When considering political and policy choices, Americans routinely engage in what psychologists call "motivated reasoning," which means seeking out information that reinforces their prior opinions.[10] Motivated or biased reasoning has received a big boost from the emergence of highly partisan news outlets and a growing tendency for citizens to screen out unwelcome messages and rely primarily or even exclusively on messages consistent with their ideology.[11] Selective consumption of news and opinion locks us into rigid positions, exacerbates polarization, and makes compromise highly unlikely.

To sum up, most of our young people are not prepared for college, not prepared for work, and not prepared for citizenship. Although critical thinking may not be the magic elixir to cure all of these ailments, it is arguably a way to make progress on all of these fronts.

DEFINITIONS

What exactly is critical thinking? Critical thinking has been defined in many different ways by many different people and by many different organizations. The best starting point for understanding what it means is John Dewey, the great philosopher and education reformer who taught at Columbia University for twenty-five years. Dewey was long interested in how we think and how we might be taught to think better. For Dewey, the key concept was "reflective thinking," which he defined as "active, persistent, and careful consideration of a belief or a supposed form of knowledge in the light of the grounds which support it and the further conclusions to which it tends."[12]

If we parse this definition, what exactly was Dewey trying to say? First, critical thinking (or reflective thinking) is an intense mental activity, not a casual one. It requires alertness, patience, and a commitment to accuracy and precision. It is not for the feckless or the faint of heart. Second, critical thinking focuses on a belief or a set of beliefs or something that is thought to be true. In effect, we reappraise something that we believe or that others believe. We probe for weaknesses, lapses of logic, flimsy claims. The aim is to subject a belief to a withering stress test, to see whether it can survive a tough cross-examination. Third, critical thinking asks two big questions about the belief being considered: what reasoning supports it, and what implications does it have if it is true? The first of these questions requires strong logic, strong evidence, or both. The second requires one to draw inferences about the consequences of this belief for how we should think, how we should live, or what we should decide to do, individually or collectively.

I will offer my own definition in the next chapter. It will not depart radically from Dewey's definition, though it will place a stronger emphasis on open-mindedness and objectivity. To me, that is important because it is so often missing in mass media rants on highly inflammatory topics, which increasingly have become most of the topics that constitute our public discourse today. It is also not clear to me that intellectual activity must begin with a particular belief to qualify as reflective thinking or critical thinking. Why not a question as a starting point? Why not a pair of competing beliefs as a starting point? Perhaps Dewey would have regarded these as "friendly amendments." I like to think so because there is so much to admire in his way of thinking.

Other definitions, in contrast, differ more strikingly from Dewey's. For example, Richard Paul calls critical thinking "thinking about thinking."[13] This definition has the advantage of simplicity, but it implies that critical thinking is some sort of epistemological enterprise of particular interest to philosophers, logicians, psychologists, and neuroscientists. In fact, critical thinking often has more practical motivations and more practical consequences and broader appeal than this definition suggests. The US Department of Labor offers a rather different definition. On its O*NET website, it defines critical thinking as "using logic and reasoning to identify the strengths and weaknesses of alternative solutions, conclusions or approaches to problems."[14] If it is practicality we seek, this definition is admirably practical. On the other hand, it blurs the distinction between critical thinking and practical problem solving. As I shall argue in the next chapter, these two concepts often overlap but are not identical.

Other terms are sometimes used, in lieu of critical thinking. For example, some foundations prefer to talk about "deeper learning," and some academics like to talk about "higher-order thinking." Charlotte Danielson, author of the widely used Framework for Teaching, refers to "student intellectual engagement."[15] According to Danielson, one can promote that by asking students to explain their thinking and to formulate logical arguments buttressed by evidence. Or one can encourage students to question the thinking of others. Each of these terms has its merits. But the phrase "critical thinking" is more familiar, more widespread, and more easily understood. Jacqueline King of the Smarter Balanced Assessment Corporation, which produces tests that are consistent with the Common Core, puts it this way: "We use the term critical thinking quite a bit. We use other terms with educators. But parents and legislators understand critical thinking. So we use the term critical thinking publicly."[16]

Critical thinking bears a striking resemblance to the higher echelons of Benjamin Bloom's famous taxonomy of thinking, with knowledge at the base of the pyramid and evaluation at the top. According to Bloom, higher-order thinking includes analysis, synthesis, and evaluation. Of these, evaluation, which Bloom defined as justifying a stand or decision, probably comes closest to critical thinking. To justify a position or a preference, one needs evidence and clear norms or values. Critical thinking involves both.[17] In a nutshell, critical thinking is a credible, nuanced evaluation.

A final perspective on critical thinking comes from those who assert that it is only meaningful (or most meaningful) when embedded in a substantive discussion from a particular discipline (history, English, math, science) or a particular subject.[18] The College Board implicitly embraces this approach in outlining its expectations for various Advanced Placement exams. In discussing the AP History Exam, for example, the College Board specifies four historical thinking skills, including chronological reasoning, comparison and contextualization, crafting historical arguments from historical evidence, and historical interpretation and synthesis. Each of these skills also involves certain subskills. From a pedagogical point of view, there is much to be said for learning critical thinking while immersing oneself in a particular subject or discipline. But that should not discourage us from defining critical thinking broadly enough to encompass intense efforts to validate or invalidate beliefs in diverse subjects or fields (or that transcend diverse subjects or fields).

FIVE MYTHS

Given the absence of a clear consensus on what critical thinking actually is, it is perhaps not surprising that some myths about critical thinking have circulated widely. In this book, I will be challenging five such myths:

MYTH 1 *Critical thinking implies criticism and disapproval.*
Critical thinking may lead to a negative appraisal of someone else's ideas or someone else's preferred policies, but critical thinking at its best implies self-criticism, which should lead to a more

open-minded appraisal of other people's ideas. In some instances, critical thinking requires you to shed your beliefs and embrace someone else's. Also, critical thinking requires a close review of relevant evidence. If that review supports someone else's theory or preferred beliefs, then a true critical thinker will go where the data led him or her. Critical thinking may begin with deconstruction but culminate in reconstruction. Madison's critique of the Articles of Confederation was brilliant, but so too was his blueprint for a new republic. Criticism may be the starting point, but not the end point, of critical inquiry.

MYTH 2 *Critical thinking is a narrowly focused activity with limited utility.* Critical thinking is often associated with high school English teachers, who ask students to deconstruct a text, or high school history teachers, who ask students to analyze a document from the early days of the republic. It is also associated with college professors who invite their students to critically interpret Chaucer or Proust or Frederick Douglass or Elizabeth Cady Stanton. But critical thinking is and should be multidisciplinary. It is also the province of natural scientists, social scientists, engineers, mathematicians, lawyers, physicians, and journalists. And it is more than just reinterpreting classic texts, admirable though that is. A lot of critical thinkers work for Google and for Microsoft. A lot of critical thinkers work for Pixar Studios and Disney. Critical thinking is a form of logical reasoning with wide applicability.

MYTH 3 *Critical thinking only facilitates school-based learning on school subjects.* Numerous studies show that most employers deeply value critical thinking and regard it as one of the essential skills most lacking in recent high school graduates or even college graduates. To employers, critical thinking involves the capacity to solve problems, including complex problems, and the capacity to adapt to new situations quickly and intelligently. Many other studies confirm the value of extracurricular activities, which can enhance students' hard skills and soft skills simultaneously. Critical-thinking skills are indispensable to debate teams, school newspapers, and STEM-related clubs. They are even relevant to sports. It was hockey star Wayne Gretzky who explained his extraordinary success by saying, "I skate to where the puck is going to be, not where it has been."[19] That is a splendid example of critical thinking!

MYTH 4   *Critical thinking is a solitary activity.*   Critical thinking is often learned best when it is combined with small group instruction, one-on-one instruction, or project-based learning. Small group instruction and one-on-one instruction permit useful give-and-take between the teacher and the individual student. Small group instruction and project-based learning provide valuable opportunities for students to learn from one another. Rodin's *The Thinker* is one model for critical thinking. Project Apollo, which put a man on the moon, is another. When members of a group think critically, they challenge one another's ideas, vigorously but respectfully. Group thinking exercises help prepare students to be future workers and future citizens.

MYTH 5   *Teachers would rather not be teaching critical-thinking skills.*   It is certainly true that teachers seldom welcome a new set of top-down reforms. But some reforms are easier to embrace than others. Kellan McNulty, a teacher at the Kipp King Collegiate High School in San Francisco, puts it this way: "I think the hardest thing for teachers in adopting a critical-thinking model is that it requires them to kinda step back and let the students do all the work."[20] Well, maybe not all the work. But the basic insight is a good one. Teachers and students both seem to thrive when critical-thinking skills are taught. It is liberating for both. In the classrooms I observed, teachers who promote critical thinking and their students who practice it seem to experience a sharp adrenalin surge. It is exciting to watch. There is undoubtedly a difference between teachers who promote critical thinking on their own initiative and teachers who are coaxed into doing so. But even in the latter case, initial skepticism often gives way to full-throated enthusiasm.

GROWING SUPPORT

Despite some confusion about what critical thinking is and how it manifests itself, critical thinking enjoys widespread public support.

Critical thinking received a big boost in 1983 when a commission led by US Secretary of Education Terrel Bell issued the sobering report, *A Nation at Risk*. That report, which bluntly assessed the education crisis facing the United States, argued that "many 17-year-olds do not possess the 'higher order' intellectual skills we should expect of them" in the "information age" that has reshaped the world's economy. The Commission went on to note that "nearly 40 percent (of 17-year-olds) cannot draw inferences from written material; only one-fifth can write a persuasive essay; and only one-third can solve a mathematics problem requiring several steps."[21] *A Nation at Risk* raised public awareness of widespread educational deficiencies in the United States and identified critical thinking as a potential antidote.

The most vivid example of contemporary support for critical thinking is the surprisingly quick agreement by forty-five states and the District of Columbia to adopt Common Core Standards to guide instruction in public school classrooms across the United States. Although enthusiasm for the Common Core has diminished and three states have actually abandoned it, forty-two states remain committed to it, and others embrace many of its central ideas, while eschewing the name. According to most interpretations of the Common Core Standards, a key ingredient is a strong emphasis on critical thinking. Certainly, that is true of mass media coverage of the Common Core. To assess that, I analyzed Common Core coverage in dozens of newspapers from 2011 through 2015, using Lexis-Nexis. The content analysis revealed that "critical thinking" was cited more often than any other phrase in trying to explain what the Common Core is all about (see Figure 1-3).

Admittedly, critical thinking is seldom defined, with precision or at all, in public utterances on the subject. Still, it does appear that employers, politicians, and educators agree, roughly, that students need to develop higher-order thinking skills to succeed at work, in college, and in life. Business groups, such as the US Chamber of Commerce, have stoutly supported the Common Core Standards, with its strong emphasis on critical thinking.[22] Governors and chief state school officers have been particularly vocal in support of the Common Core, though a handful of governors reversed course in the wake of

FIGURE 1-3   Newspaper links of Common Core to key concepts,
2011–2015

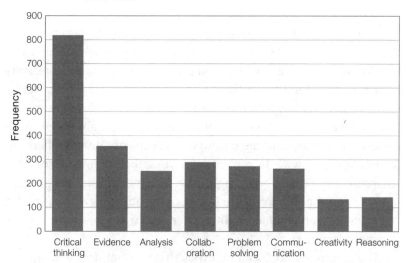

Source: Lexis-Nexis search of words within twenty-five words of *Common Core* in newspaper articles, with press releases and duplicates removed.

erroneous criticisms that the Common Core "federalized" educational standards.[23]

Even the teacher unions have embraced the Common Core, so long as it is viewed as a "guide" and not a "straitjacket."[24] As American Federation of Teachers President Randi Weingarten put it in 2013: "It is no secret that the AFT is a big supporter of the Common Core State Standards. We believe these standards have the ability to transfer the DNA of teaching and learning to ensure that ALL children, regardless of where they live, have the critical thinking, problems solving and teamwork skills and experience they need to succeed in their careers, at college and in life."[25] One year later, AFT members reaffirmed their support for the Common Core in a formal vote, while at the same time expressing serious reservations about the implementation of the Common Core.[26] The National Education Association's position on the Common Core is roughly the same. In the words of NEA President Dennis Van Roekel, "My greatest fear for the students of America is that we may lose the promise of the Common Core Standards because we screwed up the implementation."[27]

The implementation of the Common Core—and especially the implementation of new tests that measure students' ability to meet Common Core educational standards—has been challenging for teachers and has led to some erosion of teacher support for the Common Core. Polls that explicitly link the Common Core to demands for greater public school accountability have even found that most teachers now oppose the Common Core. However, polls that simply ask about the Common Core, without linking it to accountability, find that teachers are evenly divided, with 44 percent supporting the Common Core standards and 43 percent opposing them.[28] The modal teacher's position seems to be that the Common Core's philosophy is great but that it needs to be implemented with greater sensitivity and with greater teacher discretion.

The Common Core Standards, though important, are not unique in promoting critical-thinking skills. Recent trends in STEM education, such as the integration of STEM subjects and utilization of project-based learning in the classroom, also promote the same goal. By integrating math and science or science and engineering classes, students can apply insights from one discipline to another. Such transfers, from one subject to another, lie at the heart of critical thinking. Special projects, especially those that involve designing artifacts, such as small robots, can be especially instructive because the consequences of failure are plainly evident (e.g., the robot won't move on command). Also, they are fun, and they yield tangible products that can be a source of pride and accomplishment.[29]

Teach for America, which now trains approximately five thousand teachers per year (from a pool of approximately forty-eight thousand applicants), has also promoted critical-thinking skills.[30] In describing the kinds of college graduates they seek to recruit, TFA lists several criteria, including the following: "Excellent critical thinking skills, including the ability to accurately link cause and effect and to generate relevant solutions to problems."[31] The highly successful charter school program known as the Knowledge Is Power Program, or KIPP, has also stressed critical thinking in its curriculum, especially through the use of the Socratic method.[32]

Critical thinking is increasingly important to Advanced Placement and International Baccalaureate coursework in high school. In February 2011 the College Board announced that it would radically restructure AP biology and US history exams, placing greater emphasis on bigger concepts and analytical thinking. As the *New York Times* reported, "The new approach is important because critical thinking skills are considered essential for advanced college courses and jobs in today's information-based economy."[33] The College Board has also revamped its tests to place greater emphasis on words that matter (as opposed to vocabulary for vocabulary's sake) and to put greater emphasis on a close reading of the text .

IB courses are also closely identified with critical thinking. As one IB brochure puts it, "Life in the 21st century in an interconnected, globalized world, requires critical-thinking skills and a sense of international-mindedness, something that International Baccalaureate (IB) Diploma Programme students learn to know and understand."[34]

In an age of partisanship and conflict, such a strong consensus in support of any educational goal is striking and somewhat surprising. Perhaps the consensus will evaporate once implementation problems arise, as with the No Child Left Behind Act, which enjoyed broad political support at the time of its enactment, only to become toxic to members of both political parties a few years later. Or perhaps advocates will discover that the consensus applies to the abstract concept of critical thinking but not to specific operational versions of that concept. For example, does critical thinking include the willingness to consider alternative points of view? Does this extend to raising questions about the wisdom of our Founding Fathers? Does it extend to raising questions about the wisdom of US policies throughout the world? If so, some folks may support it, whereas others may demur. As this occurs, the thread that currently binds disparate groups may quickly unravel.

On the other hand, it is also possible that we have embarked on a new educational journey, in which critical thinking, problem solving, and intellectual flexibility enjoy a privileged position in K–12 classrooms. If so, it is important to understand what is happening, why it is happening, how to teach critical thinking, when to teach critical thinking, how to assess critical thinking, what problems may arise, and how these problems might be overcome. Also, we need to explicitly consider trade-offs. If we emphasize critical thinking, does this mean, inevitably, that we are not emphasizing something else? If so, what?

CROSS-NATIONAL COMPARISONS

Oddly enough, critical thinking may be our comparative advantage in the United States. Other countries seem to recognize the virtues of critical thinking, but they have found it easier to talk the talk than to walk the walk. In China, our leading economic competitor, the Chinese Service Center for Scholarly Exchange launched a program ostensibly devoted to critical thinking. But when an American visited an "Introduction to Critical Thinking" class in Fujian Province, she found a pedagogy that was in fact a grotesque parody of critical thinking. For example, the program focused on social and economic problems in the United States. When a young man proposed to discuss a problem in China, his instructor ruled this out of bounds: "Since our textbook focuses on America, let's stick with American examples."[35] The final assignment of the course asked the students to make an argument that either (a) everyone should be forced to exercise, or (b) TV should be abolished. No one seemed aware of the obvious fact that this assignment stymied critical thinking by effectively limiting students to two extreme points of view. In this domain, the United States, for all its faults, is light years ahead of China.

In China, students outdistance us on standardized tests, but the educational system continues to be dominated by an emphasis on rote learning and memorization, with very few opportunities for critical thinking. This emphasis on passive learning, sometimes referred to as the "feed the duck" model (feed the duck . . . until it is full), dates back to Confucianism, which stressed students learning from a wise master rather than students learning how to find the truth themselves, as in a Socratic approach. It also reflects the views of Ivan Kairov, a prominent education expert and public official in the former Soviet Union, who wrote a book on pedagogy that strongly influenced Chinese thinking about education under Chairman Mao.[36]

Lieu Jinghai, the principal of a middle school in Shanghai, puts it this way: "Why don't Chinese students dare to think? Because we insist on telling them everything. We're not getting our kids to go and find things out for themselves."[37] Saga Ringmar, who attended high school in Shanghai for two years, is even more caustic: "The ideal Shanghainese student is like a sea sponge blindly absorbing any and all information, and spewing it all out during the tests."[38] One reason for the absence of critical thinking in China is that certain topics and certain points of view are taboo politically. An even more basic barrier is the Gaokao, the national university entrance exam taken by as many as ten million students per year. Lucia Pierce, an educational consultant in Shanghai, puts it this way: "As long as the Gaokao scores are what get you, a student, into college . . . parents and principals and teachers can't afford to really experiment with a kind of learning that encourages independent thinking, and perhaps, learning from mistakes."[39]

In India, too, questions have been raised about the educational system's weak support for critical thinking. Raju Narisetti, a product of India's public schools, who went on to become the managing editor of the *Washington Post*, put it bluntly: "I never found education in India to be about allowing you to become a critical thinker."[40] The *Times of India* argued that three skills need more attention in India: critical thinking, communications, and teamwork. Of these, they asserted, critical thinking is probably the most important.[41]

THREE GOALS OF CRITICAL THINKING

What kind of critical thinking should we be emphasizing? The kind of critical thinking that prepares young people for college? The kind of critical thinking that prepares young people for a career? The kind of critical thinking that prepares young people for citizenship? To the extent that this involves different pedagogical strategies and exercises, we need to think critically about the mix of skills and habits of mind that we want students to learn in our classrooms, from pre-K through grade 12.

In this book, I will argue that critical thinking in K–12 schools takes somewhat different forms, depending on whether our goal is college readiness, career readiness, or civic readiness. In each of these settings, it is vital to be able to connect big ideas to evidence, to distinguish between good and bad evidence, and to draw appropriate inferences from evidence. In each of these settings, it is important to be skeptical. In each of these settings, it is important to be self-critical. But there are also subtle differences of emphasis across these venues (see Table 1-1).

If our goal is college readiness, then textual analysis is likely to receive prime attention. To succeed in college, students need to be able to decipher a text (whether fiction or nonfiction), to recognize its key elements, to understand its point of view, and to be able to offer a plausible counternarrative. Other skills that matter in college are self-expression, logical reasoning, and the ability to make evidence-based arguments. David Coleman, the President of the College Board, summed it up well when he said that we want students to be able to "read like a detective, write like an investigative reporter."[42]

Career readiness requires a somewhat different skill set. To flourish at work, you need to be able to solve problems, perform relevant tasks, and promote your organization's mission. Related skills that matter at work are priority setting, adaptability, and "satisficing," which Herbert Simon defined as choosing the first satisfactory option that presents itself rather than searching endlessly for the perfect solution.[43] To put it simply, at work, you must learn to calculate, then recalculate. Make some reasonable decisions and make them quickly . . . but be ready to reconsider and try something else.

Civic readiness calls for many things but especially good judgment. A citizen must be able to make good decisions about when

TABLE 1-1   Three goals of critical thinking

	COLLEGE READINESS	CAREER READINESS	CIVIC READINESS
Unit of Analysis	Individual	Team	Community
Key Skill	Textual Analysis	Problem Solving	Wisdom
Other Skills	Self-Expression, Logical Reasoning, and Evidence-Based Arguments	Priority Setting, Adaptability, and Satisficing	Tolerance, Deliberation, and Compromise
Slogan	"Read like a detective, write like an investigative reporter."	Calculate, then recalculate.	Reconcile competing values and interests.

to participate, how to participate, and for what cause. Activists and politicians, who engage in civic life regularly, perhaps even daily, must have the same abilities and more. Related skills include tolerance, a capacity for reasoned deliberation, and the willingness and ability to compromise. In a nutshell, civic readiness requires you to reconcile competing values and interests.

In chapter 2, I will shine a brighter light on critical thinking by defining it with greater precision and by citing many concrete examples. I will also define and discuss two cognate concepts of special importance: creative thinking and problem solving. Finally, I will argue that blended thinking, which combines two or more of these concepts, is an especially attractive addition to our intellectual arsenal. When critical thinking occurs, it elevates our debate. When critical thinking combines with creative thinking and problem solving, it can transform our understanding and our practices in profound and enduring ways.

2

Critical Thinking, Creative Thinking, and Problem Solving

TO UNDERSTAND or explain critical thinking, we need to distinguish it from other useful forms of thinking, such as creative thinking and problem solving. In this chapter, I define each of these terms and cite multiple examples from the worlds of literature, science, medicine, music, art, and public policy. I also discuss the virtues of blended thinking, which combines two or more of these categories. When critical thinking, creative thinking, and problem solving are all employed in pursuit of the same goal, the results can be truly wonderful.

CRITICAL THINKING DEFINED

Critical thinking is an *open-minded* inquiry that seeks out *relevant evidence* to *analyze a* question or a proposition. It may begin with a hypothesis (deductive reasoning), or it may lead to a hypothesis (inductive reasoning). It may apply abstract ideas to concrete problems or relate one set of abstract ideas to another set of abstract ideas or connect concrete cases from one domain to concrete cases from another domain. It may be used to guide verbal reasoning or the construction of mathematical equations or artistic expression or something else.

In short, it takes many different forms, but it is important to stress its key features.

Critical thinking is an open-minded inquiry. Unlike motivated reasoning, which often screens out unwelcome ideas and information inconsistent with prior convictions, critical thinking tests the limits of prior convictions.[1] In an election campaign, for example, critical thinking means taking a fresh look at your preferred candidate after some credible allegations against him or her come to light. In contrast, motivated reasoning means working backward from your preferences and concluding incorrectly that the allegations must not have been true after all. Critical thinking is rooted in intellectual humility and reflects considerable tolerance for and appreciation of alternative points of view. Critical thinking rejects bias in favor of the truth, even if the truth may prove embarrassing or disappointing.

At its best, critical thinking challenges fundamental assumptions held by others, by society at large, and by the thinker himself or herself. When the critical thinker ponders a question, nothing should be sacred and everything should be on the table. No organization, person, or idea should be immune from criticism, including the critical thinker and his or her own preferred notions. Not every question requires a wholesale reassessment of fundamental premises. You shouldn't shoot a squirrel with an elephant gun. Nevertheless, open-mindedness means being open to recognizing both minor and major flaws in personal and societal assumptions.

Critical thinking is empirical. It seeks out information that can shed light on a subject. That information may consist of cases, events, propositions, findings, or experiences. Information gathering may be systematic or informal, wide ranging or narrowly focused. But it must be relevant. The purpose of the information gathering is not simply to be better informed but rather to be better informed about a particular phenomenon that is worth analyzing.

At the heart of critical thinking is analysis, which means a purposive, rigorous inquiry. It implies a specific goal. It also implies a degree of intensity or seriousness of purpose. And it implies a self-conscious strategy or methodology aimed at moving forward. Analysis typically involves a series of steps, though the precise sequence may depend on the phenomenon being investigated.

My definition of critical thinking does not differ radically from what Dewey called reflective thinking, though I include open-mindedness as an explicit requirement, and I define open-mindedness to include radical reassessments of one's own views and other people's views. Compared to Dewey, I also entertain more starting points as legitimate ways to embark on a critical-thinking exercise (a belief, a question, a hypothesis).

CREATIVE THINKING DEFINED

Important though it is, critical thinking is not all-encompassing, nor is it the only form of higher-order thinking. Creative thinking is also a skill to be cherished and cultivated. Creative thinking may be defined as the *production* of a *new* idea or a new product through inspiration, concentrated thought, or both. Like critical thinking, it also manifests itself in many different ways—in the brilliant architecture of Frank Lloyd Wright, in scientific discoveries that win a Nobel Prize, in the clever jokes of stand-up comedians.

Despite these variations, creative thinking has some common denominators. It yields not just credible propositions but new ideas, products, services, or strategies. Novelty is more of a spectrum than a dichotomy. The invention of a new idiom, like bebop in jazz, is more novel than an appealing riff within an existing idiom. The invention of a hybrid automobile, like the Prius, is more novel than adding a sunroof or a GPS to a more conventional car. Always, though, creativity involves the creation of something new.

Creativity is often less abstract than critical thinking. It may yield a new idea (quantum physics, for example) or a new product (a robot that can wash dishes) or a new service (Facebook). It may yield a new law (the Affordable Care Act) or a new organization (Mothers Against Drunk Driving) or a new type of organization (microcredit institutions in poor rural areas). In some respects, the products of creative thinking are more tangible than the products of critical thinking.

And yet the creative-thinking process is also, arguably, more mysterious and more intuitive than the critical-thinking process. Although it may involve intense concentration and rational thought, it frequently emerges from inspiration, a sudden burst of insight, a mood that seeks expression.

PROBLEM SOLVING DEFINED

A third type of thinking is problem solving—a *focused* attempt to *solve* a *problem* of public or private importance. Much of what we know about problem solving comes from personal experience because we try to solve problems all the time—how to get to work despite icy conditions, how to stretch the family budget during difficult times, how to lose weight. These examples illustrate practical problem solving. In the public domain, we also can find plenty of examples of practical problem-solving efforts, as we confront such huge issues as international terrorism, global warming, and the legacy of racial discrimination. Less familiar is the domain of theoretical problem solving, as when a mathematician tries to solve a complex problem.

As the definition implies, problem solving typically has a relatively narrow focus. Its goal is not to understand how the world works but to solve a particular problem. If one's intent is problem solving, other considerations get squeezed out. For example, a critical thinker might be more interested in understanding the dynamics of dysfunctional families than in drafting a piece of legislation to solve the problems associated with them. In contrast, the problem solver will be eager for a solution, even if the contributing causes remain opaque.

Some problems are really difficult to solve. Realistically, problem solving sometimes results in the mitigation of a problem, not its elimination. A new highway may reduce traffic congestion at a key choke point but not eliminate it altogether. A new dam may eliminate threats from flooding but not eliminate flooding altogether. A new telecommuting strategy may reduce fuel consumption and strengthen families but not eliminate pollution or work–family tensions. And, of course, some problem solving is simply unsuccessful, as in failed attempts to lose weight or quit smoking.

Other problems are relatively easy to solve—so easy in fact that we may be able to rely on what Daniel Kahneman calls System 1 thinking to resolve them.[2] Unlike System 2 thinking, which involves intense, concentrated effort, System 1 thinking is intuitive, experiential, and almost effortless. It applies to many routine decisions we make during the day—getting from point A (a familiar location) to point B (also a familiar location), taking a shower, taking out the trash, and so on. To put it differently, System 1 thinking involves problem solving without critical thinking.

It is tempting to think of problem solving in the grand sense as public policies aimed at bettering the lot of mankind. And indeed much problem solving fits that description. But private individuals and private companies face many vexing problems that ache to be solved. A company that experiences shrinking revenues in the wake of globalization must adapt or perish. A nonprofit charity that cannot serve all those in need must develop an algorithm for deciding who gets served first. An individual who struggles at home, at school, or at work must develop coping mechanisms for performing better. These mundane considerations remind us that problem solving is ubiquitous and that we engage in it all the time.

HOW DO CRITICAL THINKING AND PROBLEM SOLVING DIFFER?

Critical thinking and problem solving are related concepts. They overlap, quite a bit, in theory and in practice. Still, since both are important to this book, it might be useful to draw some distinctions to guide the reader in classifying a given piece of thinking. Imagine some young children at the beach who decide it would be nice to build a sand castle. From a problem-solving perspective, they must envision a sand castle in their heads, figure out how to build one, and arrange for some rough division of labor. All of this is pretty manageable, though it may take awhile. But perhaps some of the children have critical-thinking skills. They notice that the tide is coming in, so they position themselves further away from the advancing water line. They start scooping sand with their hands but realize that this could take all day, so they scavenge for shells or plastic shovels to speed things along. They notice that if they put some water in the sand, it is more likely to stay packed together and not collapse. These are simple examples of how critical thinking can advance a project to completion and make it better.

Let's take a more complicated problem, like bullying at school. From a problem-solving perspective, the key is to investigate allegations that bullying is widespread, identify situations in which it occurs, and come up with solutions like monitoring, supervision, and counseling. What happens when critical thinkers take a crack at this problem? Perhaps they ask whether bullying or something else—a lack of empathy, for example—is the root problem. If a dearth of empathy is the underlying problem, why do certain individuals lack empathy for their classmates? Critical thinkers may gather evidence on perpetrators and victims in an effort to pin down the circumstances when bullying occurs. This could yield a profile of bullies and their targets. With this information in hand, students can determine whether bullying follows a singular pattern or takes different forms. If the former is correct, then one solution may suffice. If the latter is correct, then different solutions may be needed to deal with different types of bullying. Whatever happens as the project unfolds, critical thinking can transform a routine assignment into a rich investigation into human nature.

Obviously, the concepts of critical thinking and problem solving bleed into one another, just like gardening and brush removal, banking and finance, sports and exercise. But they differ enough from one another that we should not use the terms interchangeably.

BLENDED THINKING: PRIMARY COLORS AND THEIR PERMUTATIONS

Although critical thinking, creative thinking, and problem solving can be defined, and they do differ from one another, they are not mutually exclusive categories of thought. In fact, they often occur in combination, and that is a good thing, not simply because it expands the number of possibilities, but because each of these combinations is better suited for some tasks than any one form of thinking in isolation.

To appreciate this, it is useful to compare critical thinking, creative thinking, and problem solving to the primary colors (red, yellow, blue; see Figure 2-1). When you combine a primary color with another primary color, you produce another equally interesting color: red + blue = purple; red + yellow = orange; blue + yellow = green. And

FIGURE 2-1   Blended Thinking: any combination of thinking types

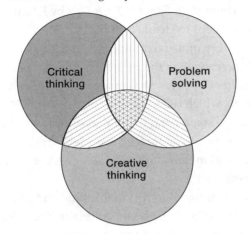

when you combine all three, you get brown. As any artist will tell you, these colors are not interchangeable! Depending on what image you are trying to produce, some colors are more appropriate than others. The same is true of tasks that require different forms of thinking.

CRITICAL THINKING AND CREATIVE THINKING

The late philosopher John Rawls combined critical thinking and creative thinking when he wrote his classic book, *A Theory of Justice.*[3] The book is a striking example of rigorous logic (critical thinking) in an effort to spell out some enduring principles of justice. A creative idea known as "the original position" enabled Rawls to formulate principles of justice that satisfied the criterion of procedural fairness. Imagine, Rawls said, a situation in which you do not know whether you are rich or poor, male or female, young or old, brilliant or dimwitted. That is the original position. If, in the original position, you choose some principles that will apply to you and to everyone else, those principles can be said to exemplify justice as fairness. This conceit enabled Rawls to develop an elegant theory that has triggered considerable interest and won many supporters over the years.

Some of the most creative mysteries ever written depart from conventional norms by portraying a murderer or an accomplice not as evil but as someone consumed by a personal loss or deep empathy for another human being. *The Secret in Their Eyes* by Eduardo Sacheri is a chilling story that flips the usual formulas upside down and explores the feelings of a very unusual murderer.[4] *The Devotion of Suspect X* by Keigo Higashino considers the lengths to which a person will go to help someone after that person has made a tragic mistake.[5] In addition to artful plotting, which reflects a good deal of critical thinking, both authors challenge some fundamental assumptions about criminal motives. This creative twist forces the reader to reflect long and hard on who deserves sympathy and who deserves condemnation when one crime begets another.

If individuals can combine critical thinking and creative thinking, so too can organizations. A good example is Pixar Studios, which under John Lasseter's leadership has produced some delightful and spectacularly successful films (*Toy Story, WALL-E, Up, Inside Out,* and many others). If there is a formula, of sorts, it is that each film combines imaginative storytelling (toys that come to life, a love-smitten robot) with technically sophisticated animation (e.g., new rigging, animation, shading, and rendering techniques in *Up*).[6] Roughly speaking, the artists provide the creativity, while the technicians provide the critical thinking so that whimsical ideas come to life.

In his book on creativity, Jonah Lehrer describes how Steve Jobs, the founder of Pixar Studios, went to great lengths to ensure that the cartoonists and the geeks hired by Pixar would not simply work for the same company but would interact with one another, in a meaningful way.[7] To ensure that the artists and the technicians actually ran into each other, Jobs insisted on one building rather than separate buildings for different types of specialists. He then added the coup de grace: he located restrooms in spots that would require artists and technicians to use the same facilities! Thanks to this simple arrangement, serendipitous conversations now ensure frequent informal communications across specialties. In all probability, some critical thinking, based on evidence from years of experience, led Jobs to conclude that technicians and artists work best when they work together. It was a stroke of creative genius to see that something as prosaic as shared lavatories could bring them together.

CRITICAL THINKING AND PROBLEM SOLVING

When combined, critical thinking and problem solving yield both rigor and practicality. Data-rich problem solving has become a staple in the field of public policy analysis. It is also widely used in the business community—market surveys (before unveiling a new product), feasibility studies (before choosing a new plant location)—and in the military—for example, strategic planning and simulations.

During World War II, a mathematician, Abraham Wald, was asked to analyze damage to returning airplanes to determine where Great Britain should add extra armor. The British Air Ministry had decided to focus on the plane's extremities, rather than the main wing and tail spars or the engine or the core fuselage, because that's where a disproportionate share of the bullet holes were located. Wald said the experts had gotten this exactly wrong. In fact, damage to the engine and the core fuselage was probably so fatal that these airplanes crashed and never returned. He said: don't put the armor where the bullet holes are . . . but where they aren't! This is a splendid illustration of critical thinking plus problem solving.[8] Like British Air Ministry officials, Wald was committed to solving the problem of Allied airplanes being shot down by enemy fire. Unlike Air Ministry officials, Wald, a critical thinker, figured out that returning airplanes constituted a skewed sample of all airplanes. This led him to draw radically different inferences from bullet hole locations.

In recent decades, medical science has led the way in harnessing critical thinking to practical problem solving. Careful research, published in the *New England Journal of Medicine*, the *Journal of the American Medical Association*, and elsewhere, has provided physicians with valuable evidence to guide them in making life-or-death decisions involving individual patients. The well-established practice of holding weekly morbidity and mortality (M&M) conferences to review difficult surgical cases has enabled many major medical centers to improve their practices and reduce error rates into the future.[9] Also, increasingly, organizational report cards have helped to guide consumers as they choose a hospital for coronary artery bypass grafting (CABG) surgery or a nursing home for long-term care.[10]

Medical research has also helped inform public officials charged with the task of making health policy. To cite one notable example, research documenting the connection between cigarette use and lung cancer paved the way for numerous public policies, at the federal and state levels, aimed at discouraging cigarette consumption, especially by young people.[11] These tobacco control policies, spurred by a high-profile Surgeon General's Report in 1964, have led to approximately eight million fewer premature deaths, from 1964 to 2012.[12] Affected individuals, on average, lived nineteen years longer. Researchers have rightly referred to tobacco control efforts as "the most dramatic and successful public health campaign in modern history."[13]

The Obama administration supported "evidence based medicine" as a technique for encouraging smarter, more efficient choices of health-care options by patients, in consultation with their physicians. Although the Affordable Care Act took only modest steps in this direction, it is clear that the Obama administration saw this as an excellent technique for "bending the cost curve" and preventing health-care costs from gobbling up an even greater share of our nation's GDP (currently 17 percent).[14]

More broadly, the Obama administration was exceptionally active in promoting the integration of critical thinking and problem solving at the federal level. In multiple policy domains (early childhood education, home visiting programs, employment and training programs), the administration encouraged "evidence based policymaking." It did so by insisting that federal agencies demonstrate a strong preference for program strategies that have proven to be effective, based on rigorous empirical research.[15]

In the third sector, think tanks like the Brookings Institution are excellent examples of organizations that explicitly and affirmatively embrace a strong connection between critical thinking and problem solving. They do so by recruiting academics (to tackle real-world problems) and former public officials (to engage in more reflection than would be possible if they were still in office). As at Pixar Studios, these individuals rub elbows on a daily basis. In fact, they routinely appear on panels together and sometimes coauthor papers or books.

In practice, some think tanks exhibit a greater spirit of open inquiry than others. Think tanks closely associated with the right (the Cato Institute, the Heritage Foundation) or the left (the Progressive Policy Institute, the Center for American Progress) serve a useful purpose, as informed advocates for a certain point of view, but there are limits to their willingness to move beyond shared ideological assumptions. In contrast, the Brookings Institution has tried, especially in recent years, to be more receptive to diverse points of view, as exemplified by its hiring practices (prominent Democrats and Republicans can be found throughout Brookings' centers and divisions).

CREATIVE THINKING AND PROBLEM SOLVING

A new solution to an old problem can be a wonderful thing. And it may not require much data analysis to get the idea off the ground. Consider, for example, Teach for America. The problem was a perceived decline in teacher quality, as women pursued new job opportunities outside the teaching profession (medicine, law, commerce, higher education, and so on). One manifestation of the problem was that nearly half of all teachers came from the bottom third of their class.[16] The solution, as conceived by Princeton graduate Wendy Kopp, was to create a new teacher corps consisting of outstanding students from outstanding universities.[17] Unlike education school graduates, these individuals would not have benefited from extensive training in the art of teaching. But they would know their subjects (math, English, science) extremely well. A summer preparatory course would, in principle, give them the teaching skills they needed.

Since its inception in 1990, Teach for America has generated new excitement about teaching as a vocation and has propelled more than thirty-two thousand outstanding college graduates into our nation's classrooms as teachers.[18] A careful evaluation of TFA by Mathematica Policy Research Inc. found that TFA teachers produced a bigger gain in student math scores than a control group of teachers—with an effect size of 0.15 of a standard deviation or the equivalent of one month of instruction.[19] No effects on reading were discerned. A later Mathematica study found that TFA teachers produced bigger math gains than other teachers as a whole, teachers who were novices or experienced, and teachers certified through traditional means or through alternative certification.[20] One legitimate criticism of TFA is that many of its recruits quit teaching after their two-year stint. However, many of those who stop teaching accept other important jobs in the education field, where they bring a valuable former teacher's perspective to education publishing, education advocacy, education policy making, and related fields.

Another example of a new solution to an old problem is kidney transplant exchanges. Although kidney transplants have saved many lives in recent years, a common situation is one in which a willing donor is a poor match for the friend or loved one he or she would like to help. This predicament led researchers at Johns Hopkins University to propose swapping arrangements in which Donor A would give a kidney to Recipient X (a friend of Donor B), while Donor B would give a kidney to Recipient Y (a friend of Donor A). Over time, these swaps have become even more complicated, producing longer chains that resulted in more lives being saved.[21] Recently, the United Network for Organ Sharing (UNOS) decided to adopt a national pilot program to implement this idea on a broader scale.[22]

Some creative ideas solve two problems simultaneously. A few years ago, Luis von Ahn, then a computer science professor at Carnegie Mellon University, told a colleague that he believed he could get large numbers of people to translate newspaper articles (and other online documents) from one language into another for free. His colleague was dubious. But sure enough, von Ahn created a free foreign language instruction program on the Internet, which does exactly that, and more. The program, called Duolingo, is totally voluntary and totally free. A volunteer starts to learn a foreign language by responding to a series of questions and prompts that gradually build up his or her expertise in that foreign language. Along the way, the volunteer is asked to translate short articles or to try to improve on other people's renderings of the same articles. As this occurs, in an iterative process, the translations get better and better. Before long, the translations are good enough to be disseminated to the general public. Clearly, this is a win-win arrangement. Individuals learn a foreign language, at their own pace, and for free. At the same time,

Duolingo acquires good translations of previously untranslated documents that can be sold to interested parties (like CNN), with revenues improving the range of services offered by Duolingo. These translations appear to be superior to those developed by Google, which relies on machines to scan text.[23] It turns out that real human beings with limited foreign language skills can capture idioms far better than a computer.

THE FULL PACKAGE OF SKILLS

Occasionally, the full package of skills is on display—critical thinking, creative thinking, and also problem solving. When this occurs, marvelous developments are possible. Perhaps the most striking example, at least to Americans, is the genesis of the US Constitution. In 1786, the Union was in danger of falling apart. State governments, under new state constitutions, were too strong. The national government, under the Articles of Confederation, was too weak. Many of our nation's political leaders thought that the solution was to revise the Articles of Confederation. But James Madison, of Virginia, reached a radically different conclusion.

Madison, a voracious reader, closeted himself from September 1786 to the spring of 1787. During that period, he read numerous history books about different forms of government throughout the world, both ancient and modern, and reflected on lessons to be drawn.[24] He devoted special attention to the challenges faced by loose confederations. Over the course of several months, Madison thought critically about the fundamental problem to be solved—the tension between centrifugal and centripetal forces in politics. The question boiled down to this: how to cure America's current ailment (a weak national government, overweening state governments) without creating a worse monstrosity (a national Leviathan that trod roughshod over the states)? The conventional wisdom at the time was that a strong national government and strong state governments could not coexist. Inevitably, it was thought, one would extinguish the other.

Madison came to think otherwise. Based on his readings and reflections, he concluded that the solution to America's predicament was not a loose union of states but rather thirteen republics within a single republican government, each retaining sovereignty and some independence.

This brilliant new idea, which came to be known as federalism, remains a key linchpin of our system of government to this day. In effect, it posited that the ultimate source of authority for both state governments and the federal government was the people, whom Madison described as "the fountain of all power."[25] From this vantage point, the creation of a strong federal government was not an attack on state sovereignty because the states were not truly sovereign in the first place.

Madison also promoted the concept of an "extended Republic" that encompassed an enormous expanse of territory. Previous political theorists had concluded that this notion was infeasible and unrealistic, that it would eventually degenerate into despotism. Madison, however, argued that a geographically large and socially heterogeneous society was actually better able to cure "the mischiefs of faction" than a smaller, more homogeneous one. He reasoned that diverse factions would clash and check one another, thus preventing any one faction from dominating the rest. In effect, this would create a political system that would function well even if its citizens were not altogether virtuous.[26]

These new ideas, arrived at through a focused inquiry and a shrewd assessment of a massive amount of evidence, became the cornerstones of the Constitution adopted by our Founding Fathers in 1787. The political transformation that took place was both remarkable and profound. In the words of Gordon Wood, "the erection of a national government represented a political revolution as great as the revolution of a decade earlier, when the British monarchy had been overthrown and new state governments formed."[27] To recap, Madison confronted a serious problem: the union was falling apart. He thought critically about the problem, examining evidence from contemporary and ancient governments. His creative solution was "federalism" combined with an "extended Republic." In Madison's own words, he sought to create "a system without a precedent ancient or modern, a system founded on popular rights, and so combining a federal form with the forms of individual Republics, as may enable each to supply the defects of the other and obtain the advantages of both."[28] That political system has endured for well over two hundred years.

Scientific paradigm shifts also illustrate the exciting possibilities that arise when critical thinking, creative thinking, and problem solving converge. As discussed in Thomas Kuhn's brilliant book on the structure of scientific revolutions (itself a splendid example of critical thinking, creative thinking, and problem solving), a scientific paradigm shift represents an abrupt departure from "normal science."[29] As Kuhn sees it, normal science typically involves problem solving (or puzzle solving, as he puts it), plus the analysis of evidence (or critical thinking). It does not, however, involve a new way of thinking. The reason is that scientists, like most human beings, typically feel most comfortable working within a well-established and widely accepted theoretical framework.

A scientific paradigm shift arises when an unexpected anomaly causes the investigator to rethink the prevailing theory under which he or she has labored. The discovery of oxygen, the production of X-rays, and the discovery of the Leyden jar all illustrate this pattern. Less commonly, a new theoretical framework emerges from a brilliant thinker (Copernicus, Newton, Einstein) and displaces the prevailing framework, triggering a series of empirical investigations.[30]

Although Kuhn wrote about scientific paradigm shifts, by which he meant paradigm shifts in the natural sciences, it is possible to observe paradigm shifts in other areas. The French Revolution, the American Revolution, and the Russian Revolution are good examples of political paradigm shifts. Recent changes in social norms, such as the rise of female employment, the decline of the nuclear family, and greater use of contraceptives are good examples of cultural paradigm shifts. Many of these paradigm shifts have proven controversial, and not all of them are good. But if we were to take a closer look at each of them, we would probably see a familiar mix of critical thinking, creative thinking, and practical problem solving.

CONCLUSION

Now that we understand critical thinking better and how it differs from some other forms of thinking, we need to ask some basic questions: When does critical thinking originate? Where does it originate? How does it develop? What can teachers do to help students to master it? To answer these questions, if only partially, we next turn to an exotic and exciting field—neuroscience—to learn how the brain works and how critical-thinking skills develop over time.

3

Critical Thinking and the Brain

TO TRULY APPRECIATE critical thinking, we need to have a rough understanding of the marvelous organ that produces it—the human brain! In this chapter, I identify executive functioning as a key precursor to critical thinking and discuss how the brain develops over time. I highlight the extraordinary potential of young children to learn (e.g., executive-functioning skills), subject to important limitations (e.g., poverty and toxic stress). I conclude by discussing opportunities for teachers to teach critical thinking.

FLUID REASONING

Psychologists do not routinely use the phrase "critical thinking." Instead, they typically talk about "fluid reasoning" or "executive functioning." Fluid reasoning is the capacity to think logically and solve problems in novel situations, independent of acquired knowledge.[1] This sounds a lot like critical thinking, though there are some subtle differences. For example, notice that fluid reasoning is a *capacity* to think a certain way rather than the actual *act* of thinking. Also, notice that the textbook definition of fluid reasoning stresses problem solving in novel situations, which could be construed as problem solving or even creative thinking or an amalgam of all three rather than critical thinking per se. So the concepts are similar but not identical.

One way to think about fluid reasoning is that it is a precursor to critical thinking. Fluid reasoning is the most general of cognitive abilities.[2] It includes both deductive and inductive logical reasoning.[3] It can be measured by multiple-choice nonverbal tests such as the Raven's progressive matrices test, in which the subject is asked to identify the missing item in a logical progression.[4] Even though it is fundamental, fluid reasoning can be improved through effective teaching and other interventions.

EXECUTIVE FUNCTIONING

Another key psychological concept is executive functioning, sometimes described as the mental processes required to concentrate and think.[5] As Judy Willis puts it, "Executive functions can be thought of as the skills that would make a corporate executive successful."[6] The ability to plan and complete a task is a good example, though there are many more. Executive functioning involves three key components: working memory, inhibitory control, and cognitive flexibility.[7]

Working memory is like an online work bench—it is the information that is readily available to us as we approach a task. It is limited in capacity but highly accessible. The larger the working memory, the better. Working memory should not be confused with short-term memory. As Adele Diamond explains, working memory involves holding information in mind and manipulating it, while short-term memory is just holding information in mind.[8] Working memory is a good predictor of positive academic outcomes, such as early mathematics achievement.[9]

Inhibitory control is vital because it enables us to suppress certain impulses and concentrate on a narrow band of tasks. As Walter Mischel showed in his famous "marshmallow" experiment, a preschooler's ability to say no to a marshmallow immediately in order to receive a second marshmallow in a few minutes predicts his or her attentiveness as an adolescent—as measured by parental reports—and his or her ability to succeed academically—as measured by SAT scores.[10] In short, these early skills translate into big gains a decade or more later.

Flexibility is also important because it enables us to shift from one task to another, to adapt. In an elementary school classroom, it means shifting from reading to math or from schoolwork to recess. It will eventually mean shifting from one way of thinking to another way of thinking, from one set of conceptual lenses to another, from a nationalist perspective to a global perspective, from speaking English to speaking Spanish. Flexibility, like working memory, is a good predictor of positive academic outcomes.[11]

Executive-functioning skills begin to develop shortly after birth. There is a window of opportunity for them to grow dramatically between ages three and five (see Figure 3-1).[12] Executive-functioning skills improve over time, especially if they are given a friendly push. But they manifest themselves in different ways at different points in our lives. Take inhibitory control, for example. As preschoolers, we are very rule-oriented, but we can discard a rule when necessary. As teenagers, we are torn between self-indulgence and self-control. As adults, we are more consistent in regulating our impulses in pursuit of more distant goals. Similar developmental differences apply to working memory and cognitive flexibility (see Table 3-1). Preschoolers

FIGURE 3-1   The growth of executive-functioning skills ages 0–85

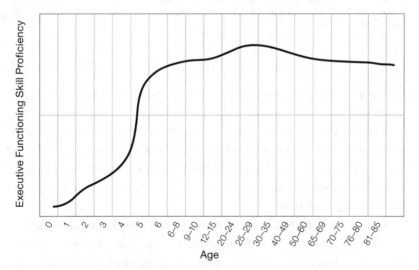

Source: Center on the Developing Child at Harvard University, "Building the Brain's 'Air Traffic Control' System" (working paper 11, Cambridge, MA, 2011, 5), http://developingchild.harvard.edu/wp-content/uploads/2011/05/How-Early-Experiences-Shape-the-Development-of-Executive-Function.pdf.

TABLE 3-1   Executive-functioning skills at different ages

WORKING MEMORY	INHIBITORY CONTROL	COGNITIVE FLEXIBILITY
Adults: Can remember multiple tasks, rules, and strategies that may vary by situation	Adults: Consistent self-control; appropriate situational responses (e.g., resists saying something socially inappropriate, resists "tit for tat" response)	Adults: Able to revise actions and plans in response to changing circumstances
Teenagers: Develop ability to search varying locations, remember where something was found, then explore other locations	Teenagers: Continue to develop self-control, such as flexibly switching between a central focus (such as riding a bike or driving) and peripheral stimuli that may or may not need attention (road signs and pedestrians versus billboards)	Teenagers: Continued improvement in accuracy when switching focus and adapting to changing rules
Preschoolers: Can hold in mind two rules at a time; understand that appearance and reality may differ	Preschoolers: Can discard a rule when necessary; can delay eating a treat	Preschoolers: Can shift actions according to changing rules (e.g., take shoes off at home, leave shoes on at school)

Source: Adapted from Center on the Developing Child, "Building the Brain's 'Air Traffic Control' System" (working paper 11, Harvard University, Cambridge, MA, 2011, 9), http://developingchild .harvard.edu/wp-content/uploads/2011/05/How-Early-Experiences-shape-the -Development-of-Executive-Function.pdf.

can work with two rules at a time; teenagers can retrieve information from multiple sources; adults can remember multiple tasks, rules, and strategies. Preschoolers can change their behavior in response to changing rules; teenagers can switch focus with growing speed and accuracy; adults can rethink their behavior as circumstances change. Together, these changes signify growing improvements in executive functioning over time.

Fluid reasoning and executive functioning are distinguishable but overlapping concepts. Fluid reasoning is more general, more abstract. It is sometimes described as the root of intelligence.[13] Executive functioning is more specific, more concrete. It is sometimes regarded as the key to success.[14] Studies show a close connection between the two concepts. For example, Scott Decker, Scott Hill, and Ray Dean found strong correlations between widely used measures of executive functioning (like the Wisconsin Card Sorting Test) and widely used measures of fluid reasoning (like Woodcock and Johnson's Verbal Analogies Test).[15] Another study found a strong correlation between fluid reasoning and one aspect of executive functioning: working memory.[16]

Where does critical thinking fit into all of this? Like fluid reasoning, critical thinking often involves transferring knowledge and ideas to new situations. Like executive functioning, critical thinking requires memory, inhibitory control, and flexibility. But critical thinking involves more than that. If it's rush hour and I decide to take a detour to work, I rely on my working memory to remind me of the time and its implications for travel. I suppress or inhibit the urge to follow my usual route to work, and I choose from a short menu of alternative routes. I demonstrate flexibility as I deviate from my normal route. I have made a sound, sensible decision, but it hardly qualifies as critical thinking. The reason is that the evidence I need to make this decision has been handed to me on a silver platter. I do not need to sift and winnow to distinguish between good and bad evidence (or good and bad routes). I have done this many times before, and the search for an alternative route is almost effortless. The level of uncertainty and the risk of failure are both quite low.

Now imagine that you're driving a rental car on mountainous terrain in northern Italy. You have a GPS, but it's not terribly reliable. You have a map, but the towns are unfamiliar. You have directions from a hotel clerk, but his English wasn't very good. Twilight is descending, your child is screaming in the back seat, and you encounter a traffic jam. You must consider your options carefully. You need to acquire some new evidence (e.g., by asking for help at a nearby town) or carefully weigh the evidence you already possess (which source of directions is truly the best) or introduce a new option into the mix (checking in at a nearby hotel and starting fresh the next morning). That is a more daunting assignment, and if you're up to the challenge, you've probably engaged in some critical thinking. In short, critical thinking is different from routine thinking, though it builds upon it.

THE DEVELOPING BRAIN

Children begin to reason very early in life, after developing basic perceptual, attentional, and motor skills. Cells in one part of the brain become connected to cells in other parts of the brain, through synapses, which become stronger through more frequent use. Myelination, dendrite growth and differentiation, synaptic pruning, stronger links between the left and right brain and between different brain regions, and generally thicker connections—all create a more powerful brain.[17] These changes have important implications for learning. As Sylvia Bunge and Samantha Wright explain, "Both cortical pruning within prefrontal and parietal regions and increased neuronal connectivity within and between these and other regions are likely to underlie improvements in cognitive control and fluid reasoning during development."[18] As David Dobbs puts it: "As we move through adolescence the brain undergoes extensive remodeling, resembling a network and wiring upgrade."[19]

Studies show that children, adolescents, and adults use different parts of the brain when performing certain basic tasks, such as retrieving information from working memory. Children rely especially on the ventromedial prefrontal cortex and the caudate nucleus and anterior insula, while adults rely more on the dorsolateral prefrontal cortex (DLPFC) and the parietal regions.[20] Adolescents, whose hormones are raging but whose PFC is not fully mature, differ from both children and adults.[21]

The immaturity of the teenage brain has been recognized not just by neuroscientists and developmental psychologists but also by the U.S. Supreme Court. In *Roper v. Simmons*, the Supreme Court considered whether or not a teenager convicted of a serious crime, such as premeditated murder, could be sentenced to death. After reviewing the facts of the case and a good deal of scientific evidence on the teenage brain, the Court concluded that the death penalty violated the Eighth Amendment's prohibition against "cruel and unusual punishment" because young people are more likely to exhibit a "lack of maturity and an underdeveloped sense of responsibility" than adults.[22] This ruling was consistent with a brief submitted by the

American Psychiatric Association and the National Association of Social Workers and with an abundance of brain research by neuroscientists and psychologists.[23]

The young adult brain is, relative to both younger and older individuals, quite marvelous. Studies show that fluid-reasoning skills peak during young adulthood and decline thereafter.[24] In contrast, domain-specific knowledge tend to get better over time, well into a person's fifties. Thus, younger adults seem better able to engage in novel reasoning, whereas older adults seem better able to marshal useful information gained from years of experience. Thus, it is perhaps appropriate that PhD students write dissertations, while established faculty advise them. PhD students in their twenties are often brimming with new ideas, while senior faculty members have an abundance of knowledge in their chosen field. Often, this is a winning combination.

WHEN DOES CRITICAL THINKING BEGIN?

It is widely agreed that fluid-reasoning and executive-functioning skills begin to emerge very early in life. But what about critical thinking? Much depends on how strictly one defines critical thinking. By way of analogy, consider more familiar skills, such as reading, writing, and mathematical problem solving. Some psychologists, when assessing the embryonic skills of four-year-olds and five-year-olds, refer to their performance on standardized tests as prereading, prewriting, and premath skills. Similarly, one might label early fluid-reasoning and executive-functioning skills as evidence of emerging critical-thinking skills.

However one resolves these semantic issues, the good news is that young children are capable of learning a lot, and very quickly. In fact, younger learners actually have some surprising advantages over older learners. For example, research shows that younger learners are more adept than older ones at learning unusual abstract causal principles from evidence because they are less encumbered by experience and more open to new ideas. Psychologist Allison Gopnik puts it succinctly: "Adults may sometimes be better at the tried and true, while children are more likely to discover the weird and wonderful."[25] The reason for this may be that as we get older, we both know more and explore less.

In thinking about certain causal relationships, young children are actually better learners than adults. A key distinction is between disjunctive and conjunctive relationships. A disjunctive relationship is one in which one or more activities independently cause a certain outcome. For example, either a burglar or a gust of wind can trigger a burglar alarm. A conjunctive relationship is one in which two or more activities must occur together to cause the outcome. For example, a microwave will function only if it is plugged in *and* if the start button is pressed. In a fascinating experiment, using objects that they called "blickets," Christopher Lucas and his colleagues found that young children (ages four and five) are actually better at recognizing conjunctive relationships than adults.[26] They speculate that this is because children are relatively unencumbered by real-world experiences that seem to privilege disjunctive relationships. They also speculate that children are more capable of Bayesian reasoning, in which they recalibrate expectations quickly based on new evidence. Note that the ability to process new evidence is one of the hallmarks of critical thinking. So, at least in this respect, young children are better critical thinkers than adults!

Neither brain research studies nor observations by developmental psychologists support the proposition that the development of critical-thinking skills is a smooth, linear process. As Deanna Kuhn has argued, critical thinking rises and falls over time and changes its form with some regularity.[27] During the early years, which Kuhn calls the "realist" years, children can get by without critical thinking. This gives way to an "absolutist" stage in which critical thinking is a valuable tool for comparing assertions with reality and determining whether they are true or false. Next comes what Kuhn calls a "multiplist" stage in which critical thinking becomes irrelevant because everyone has his or her own truth. Finally, in the "evaluative" stage, critical thinking is valued as a vehicle that promotes sound assertions and enhances understanding. This developmental framework may not accurately describe all children. Some children may never "graduate" from the absolutist stage; others may find value relativism appealing enough to embrace it for many years. The lesson to be extracted from this framework is not that it works as an iron law for all of us as we grow older but rather that we may embrace critical thinking with different degrees of enthusiasm over time.

WHERE DOES CRITICAL THINKING TAKE PLACE?

Critical thinking takes place in the brain, but where exactly does it take place? The short answer is the prefrontal cortex (or the PFC), in the frontal lobe (see Figure 3-2). As Daniel Krawczyk notes, "The PFC is in an advantageous position to contribute to reasoning through integrating relational information, as PFC subregions are densely interconnected and it has reciprocal connections with multiple other brain areas."[28] As noted earlier, the PFC is the primary home to the brain's executive-functioning skills.

In fact, however, critical thinking draws upon several regions of the brain, including the frontal lobe, the parietal lobe, and the temporal lobe.[29] In some situations, even the occipital lobe may be involved, if visual imagery is transmitted. Many regions of the brain are engaged during reasoning, including the frontal cortex, the parietal cortex, and the striatum.[30] For spatial reasoning, in mathematics,

FIGURE 3-2 Lobes of the brain

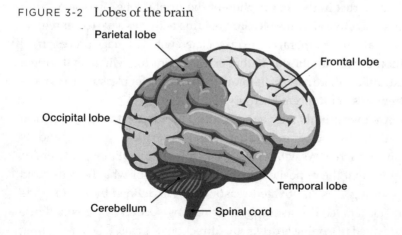

Image credit: iStock.com/IconicBestiary

the parietal cortex is particularly important. When puzzling over certain mathematical problems, students use their parietal cortex in conjunction with their prefrontal cortex.[31] The hippocampus and the motor cortex also play important roles in cognition.[32] For example, studies show that the hippocampus is activated when people imagine future scenarios.[33]

Admittedly, it is not very instructive to say that critical thinking is everywhere, or almost everywhere. What we really want to know is whether critical thinking is somewhere in particular and whether its physical location differs from that of other mental activities. If so, this might confirm the supposition that critical thinking is neurologically different from other forms of thinking. It might even offer some clues as to how teachers might pursue particular pedagogical tasks.

Reading is an interesting case in point. Although reading is commonly, and appropriately, associated with the prefrontal cortex in particular, recent studies show that reading involves different parts of the brain, depending on the type of reading involved. Natalie Phillips, an expert on Jane Austen, has shown that a close reading of a literary text (as a graduate student might read it) and casual reading of the same text involve different parts of the brain. Close reading activates diverse regions of the brain, including the somatosensory cortex in the parietal lobe (which helps us situate ourselves spatially) and the motor cortex in the rear portion of the frontal lobe (associated with physical activity), while pleasure reading activates a narrower region, especially the temporal cortex, associated with language processing.[34] Another way to put this is that critical thinking, when analyzing a text, utilizes more parts of the brain than reading for pleasure. It is a more strenuous, multifaceted activity.

Another useful study has advanced our understanding of critical thinking by focusing simultaneously on critical thinking and its opposite. Drew Westen, a psychology professor at Emory University, argues that the opposite of critical thinking—or what he calls "cold reasoning"—is "motivated reasoning." As defined by Ziva Kunda and others, cold reasoning is driven by "accuracy" goals, while motivated reasoning is driven by "directional" goals.[35] Cold reasoning sheds biases, linked to emotional needs, while motivated reasoning embraces them. Cold reasoning—or critical thinking—is an open-minded search for the truth, whereas motivated reasoning seeks to confirm established presuppositions.

In a study of thirty men, Drew Westen and colleagues presented subjects with an initial statement on their preferred presidential candidate, followed by a contradictory statement.[36] As a basis of comparison, the same individuals then received an initial statement on a neutral figure, followed by a contradictory statement. Motivated reasoning, which occurred when the preferred candidate's integrity was challenged, activated the lateral and medial orbital PFC, the anterior cingulate cortex (ACC), insula, and posterior cingulate and contiguous precuneus and parietal cortex. These parts of the brain are typically associated with emotion regulation. The presumption, therefore, is that emotions are aroused when one's preferred presidential candidate is caught in a contradiction. In contrast, cold reasoning has been shown to activate the DLPFC in particular.

The ACC, which played a prominent role in the Westen study, also proved important in a study of cognitive dissonance—the familiar phenomenon of people changing their attitudes to fit their behavior, when the two conflict. In a study of fifty-three California college students, Vincent Van Veen and colleagues induced conflict in the treatment group, but not the control group.[37] Participants in the treatment group (who experienced cognitive dissonance) changed their attitudes more than participants in the control group following counter-attitudinal behavior, and their dorsal ACC was more likely to be activated. Once again, it appears that the ACC plays a role in reconciling conflicting dispositions (either divergent attitudes or conflict between attitudes and behavior).

POVERTY AND THE BRAIN

It is widely understood that children from low-income families are more likely to struggle in school, at work, and in life than children from middle-class or wealthy families. As Greg Duncan and colleagues have noted, poverty has negative effects on IQ and encourages internalizing and externalizing behaviors that may impair learning and later success.[38] Poor children complete fewer years of schooling, earn less money, work fewer hours, receive more in food stamps, and have poorer health than children with higher family incomes.[39] Also, studies show that children from lower socioeconomic status (SES) backgrounds perform worse on executive-functioning tests.[40] In short, we know that poverty negatively affects children, and we are learning more about how it does so.

Thanks to recent research, it now appears that poverty affects the very structure of the brain. One set of studies has focused on brain volume. The surface area of the PFC is one indicator of intellectual ability because of the PFC's central role in memory, language processing, and executive functioning. Surface area depends on the number of cells in the cortex. In general, the larger the surface area of the cortex, the stronger the child's cognitive skills.

In a recent study of 1,099 children, ages three through twenty, Kimberly Noble and her colleagues found a positive relationship between family income and the size of the cortical surface area, after controlling for other demographic variables.[41] The relationship was nonlinear, which is to say that the effects were more pronounced in the lower income categories, less pronounced in the upper income categories. Noble and colleagues could not determine whether middle-class children had larger brain volumes because they received more intellectual stimulation from their parents; because they were less likely to be exposed to air pollution, lead poisoning, and other adverse environmental conditions; or because they received more nutritious meals than children from more disadvantaged backgrounds and neighborhoods. They were also unable to rule out genetic effects.[42] For example, poor children might have inherited smaller brain sizes from their parents. But differences were clear and substantial. Some differences in cortical thickness were also found, with children from higher-income families having thicker cortexes.

Another recent study found a strong relationship between child poverty and the strength of connections between the hippocampus and the amygdala and other parts of the brain. In this study, Washington University researchers found that poor children have weaker connections between the hippocampus and the amygdala and other parts of the brain (the superior frontal cortex, the lingual gyrus, the posterior cingulate, and the putamen) than children from higher-income families.[43] Furthermore, these differences, unlike some others (e.g., the volume of gray matter or white matter), are extremely difficult to change once they emerge. Connections between different parts of the brain are vitally important because, as Marvin Minsky has put it, the mind is best viewed as a community of agents.[44] In isolation, a given part of the brain can accomplish very little. In contrast, when different parts of the brain act in concert, the brain can accomplish wonderful things.

Poverty is not the only source of problems for the brain development of young children. More broadly, toxic stress makes it difficult for young children to learn. A child who experiences multiple risk factors—poverty, a single-parent family, homelessness, exposure to violence—will have great difficulty developing the key fluid-reasoning skills that are so important throughout life. For such children, the development of circuits in the PFC may be inhibited by problems in more primitive parts of the brain, including the amygdala and the hippocampus. If a child lives in fear—of a parent, a neighbor, or a peer—then the amygdala will overreact to external stimuli. Jack Shonkoff and colleagues explain: "Toxic stress can have an adverse impact on brain architecture. In the extreme, such as in cases of severe, chronic abuse, especially during early, sensitive periods of brain development, the regions of the brain involved in fear, anxiety and impulsive responses may overproduce neural connections while those regions dedicated to reasoning, planning, and behavioral control may produce fewer neural connections."[45] In short, the child's ability to learn valuable executive-functioning skills depends on the absence of threats to the child's safety and self-esteem. Some of these threats, unfortunately, come from the child's actual caregivers. Educators must be aware of these threats and should try to remediate those missing skills, as the basis for higher learning down the road.

CRITICAL THINKING AS A TEACHABLE ABILITY

Although some scholars have characterized fluid reasoning as a relatively stable characteristic of an individual, as opposed to something that can be taught, recent laboratory research has challenged that assumption.[46] In a study of twenty-eight low-income children, ages seven to nine, in Oakland, California, Allyson Mackey and associates exposed one group to after-school games (computerized and noncomputerized) that were intended to develop fluid-reasoning skills (e.g., the ability to engage in matrix reasoning by identifying a symbol that logically belongs with another set of symbols), while the other group of children was exposed to games that were intended to develop speed training (e.g., more rapid responses to game instructions). After eight weeks of training (two days per week, one hour per day), the FR group exhibited more facile matrix reasoning. The authors concluded: "FR is modifiable by environmental influences, contrary to claims that it is a relatively fixed ability." Although the authors did not generate brain images in this particular study, they speculated that the FR group made progress through myelination and dendritic branching.[47]

It also appears that certain components of executive functioning can be taught. Take, for example, self-regulation skills. Teachers who respond to their students warmly, with sensitivity and humor, *and* who create a well-ordered, well-organized classroom environment are better able to instill self-control in their students.[48] The key seems to be a combination of positive reinforcement and classroom management—two qualities that are not always associated with the same teacher.

There is, however, an important point buried here, and that is that the benefits of learning and practicing executive-functioning skills tend to be relatively specific. As psychologist Adele Diamond has noted, "Training working memory improves working memory, yes, but it doesn't improve inventory skills, data processing, or reasoning."[49] The research on executive functioning indicates that executive-functioning skills can be taught and can be taught early. However, most executive-functioning training programs, though useful, yield narrow transfer opportunities rather than broad ones.[50]

Some recent studies have shown that learning to play a musical instrument enhances executive functioning. In one study, musically trained children performed better on measures of verbal fluency and processing speed; they also demonstrated greater activation in the supplementary motor area (SMA) and the right ventrolateral prefrontal cortex (VLPFC) while performing executive-functioning tasks.[51] This research helps to explain why children with musical proficiency do better on reading and math tests.[52]

Among the executive training programs that have been validated through empirical research are computerized training, traditional martial arts (e.g., taekwondo), and two specific curricula (Tools of the Mind and the Montessori method).[53] Why do these programs work, whereas many others do not? Diamond believes that the more successful programs have several characteristics: they reduce stress; they cultivate joy and self-confidence; they take an active, hands-on approach to learning; and they engage children in teaching one another. Note that some executive-functioning skill-building programs feature physical activity as a key component. This reinforces a broader finding that regular strenuous physical exercise facilitates learning. When combined with character development as a goal, physical exercise can be especially efficacious.

Another strategy for improving critical thinking—and learning generally—is what is sometimes called "whole brain teaching." This approach, in the hands of a skilled teacher, helps to activate different parts of the child's brain (the PFC, the hippocampus, even the motor cortex) in pursuit of deeper learning. At the Francis Scott Key Elementary School, in Philadelphia, for example, third-grade teacher Jasselle Cirino uses relatively simple methods to engage different parts of the brain. By getting students to teach one another after she has taught them something, she gets them to develop both listening and speaking skills. By encouraging students to gesture frequently, Cirino engages their motor cortex. Is this a good teaching strategy? According to Columbia University neuroscientist Daphna Shohamy, more physical activity is not necessarily better. However, to the extent that whole brain teaching promotes the element of surprise, that is a good thing. Shohamy explains: "If I give you a $20 bill, now, all of a sudden, you will sort of have a burst of activity in your dopamine neurons. They fire. But if I do that regularly, like every five minutes, I give you $20, your dopamine neurons will stop firing."[54] In short, something novel captures students' attention and helps them learn.

LESSONS FOR TEACHERS

Neuroscientists, who have drawn our collective attention to the specific locations of specific brain functions and activities, are also among those who warn laypersons who think about the brain to focus less on the *where* and more on the *how*. If teachers were physical therapists, confronting a patient with a bad back, they might recommend a series of exercises aimed at strengthening the extensors, flexors, and oblique muscles in or near the back. But the brain is different. For one thing, many of the brain's more formidable activities involve connections between different parts of the brain. This makes it difficult to say, for example, that if one wants to improve critical thinking, one should exercise the PFC or the temporal lobe, because often they work in tandem when one engages in critical thinking. Furthermore, although it is useful to know which parts of the brain light up when one engages in fluid reasoning or executive functioning or critical thinking, it is even more useful to know how to promote critical thinking, in light of what we know about the brain and how it works.

With this in mind, I would offer teachers several lessons that are supported by recent brain research. First, some brain activities are especially useful for a wide variety of cognitive tasks. One of these is drawing analogies, which can help students transfer insights from one setting to another. Analogical reasoning has been justifiably celebrated as a higher-order skill, but some analogies are better than others. In general, semantically distant analogical reasoning is regarded as more demanding and more valuable than semantically near analogical reasoning. Researchers have found that a certain region of the frontopolar cortex is "recruited more strongly" when subjects think about more distant cross-domain analogies than when they think about less distant within-domain analogies.[55] Teachers may want to encourage such analogies in the classroom. For example, a comparison of housing vouchers to school vouchers may be more challenging (but also more fruitful) than a comparison of school vouchers to charter schools. Interestingly enough, an explicit cue is sometimes enough to induce distant analogical reasoning. For example, Adam Green and colleagues found that when they encouraged subjects to think creatively, they were more likely to conjure up (focus on) more semantically distant analogies.[56]

Second, teachers can obtain useful feedback from neuroscientists and neuroscientific monitoring devices aimed at illuminating the functioning of the brain. For example, researchers at the University of Washington found that certain test questions used by math teachers were more difficult than others. No surprise there. What was surprising was that they were difficult not because the math problems were harder but because the question wording was more confusing. The areas of the brain that lit up for these questions were not those normally associated with mathematical reasoning but rather those commonly associated with language processing.[57] This is almost certainly not what the teachers who administered the tests intended. With that valuable knowledge, teachers can revisit test questions, focusing on making them more intelligible.

Third, teachers who seek to promote creativity (and not just critical thinking) should be aware of the fact that creativity often involves suppressing some parts of the brain so that another part of the brain can take over. Herbie Hancock, the great jazz pianist, describes what happens: "Improvisation—truly being in the moment—means exploring what you don't know. It means going into that dark room where you don't recognize things. It means operating on the recall part of your brain, a sort of muscle memory, and allowing your gut to take precedence over your brain. This is something I still work on every day: learning to get out of my own way. It's not easy, but the times when you can do that are truly magical."[58]

Charles Limb, a neuroscientist at Johns Hopkins University, has conducted research that confirms Hancock's insight. Limb invited six jazz musicians to visit his lab for four short musical performances and four brain scans. After some initial tests using a C major scale, he asked each musician to play an original blues tune that each had been asked to memorize. Then he asked each musician to improvise over the same chords. He studied their brain waves, using fMRI. Lo and behold, the musicians were using different parts of their brain! When switching from memorization to improvisation, the jazz musicians deactivated their dorsolateral PFC (the site of working memory), while activating their medial prefrontal cortex (the site of analogic reasoning).[59] This is a great reminder for teachers—and for students—that creative thinking requires you to suppress some of the things you know and some well-worn habits in order to release new ideas. In a sense this is an executive-functioning skill, as when someone who has learned to group multiple objects by color suppresses that command and proceeds to group the same objects by shape.

Can this skill be taught? The answer is yes. Certainly, jazz improvisation can be taught, though it is an open question whether that skill is best acquired *after* learning how to sight read or *in lieu of* learning how to sight read. Foreign languages may offer a clue here. If you've learned to speak one foreign language, you may have an advantage in learning another because you understand the need to think systematically about cases, declensions, and subject-verb agreement. But if you've learned Italian and you now want to learn Spanish, you may have to suppress your Italian skills to learn Spanish because the languages are so similar.

Fourth, teachers should always recognize that individual students use their brains differently, even when approaching similar tasks. The most obvious example of this, from brain research, comes from research on the thinking of liberals and conservatives. Studies show that liberals and conservatives differ neurologically. Liberals have more gray matter volume in the ACC, whereas conservatives have greater volume in the right amygdala.[60] This is important to know! Depending on your goals and your philosophy as a teacher, you might want to encourage liberals to use their amygdala more, conservatives to use their ACC more, for the sake of more mutual understanding. If you want to reach a conservative, you might appeal to his or her amygdala. To reach a liberal, you might appeal to his or her ACC. And you might take advantage of the fact that moderates can bridge the gap between rational and emotional appeals.

CONCLUSION

Now that we understand the brain better, it is time to turn to the heart of the book—an in-depth examination of critical thinking in pursuit of three different goals: college readiness, career readiness, and civic readiness. In the next chapter, I discuss the critical-thinking skills that are thought to prepare students for college. I argue that we have made considerable progress in promoting this goal but that much more remains to be done. One reason for this is that we have defined critical thinking too narrowly. Another reason is that we have not extended critical thinking as much to students with limited resources as to students with ample resources. We need to add a critical-thinking gap to the list of gaps that should concern us as a society.

Learning to Inquire: College Readiness

CRITICAL THINKING is vital to college readiness, given the strong emphasis that colleges and universities place on critical thinking and analytical reasoning. K–12 educators place a high priority on college readiness, and many of them promote critical thinking, often operationalized as sophisticated textual analysis. In this chapter, I highlight some successes in preparing students to succeed in college, such as higher enrollments in AP courses and the implementation of Common Core reforms that emphasize critical thinking. But problems persist, such as our deteriorating position in international test comparisons and our inability to narrow the achievement gap between high-SES and low-SES students. What factors help explain these persistent problems? And how might critical-thinking instruction enable us to improve college readiness for children as a whole and for low-SES students in particular?

EVIDENCE OF PROGRESS

In some respects, our nation's public schools and our nation's teachers have done and are doing a respectable job of preparing students for college. Although there have been surges and declines, and substantial disparities in access by race and social class, approximately 48 percent of young adults ages eighteen to twenty-four are enrolled in or have been enrolled in a two-year or four-year college.[1] Also, most students who enroll in a four-year college receive a degree within a reasonable period of time. Specifically, 59 percent of first-time, full-time students who enroll in a four-year college or university complete their degree requirements within six years.[2] The situation for community colleges is less impressive: 40 percent of those who enroll in a two-year college receive a degree, there or elsewhere, within six years.[3]

A growing percentage of our nation's high school students take AP classes (approximately one-third of all students), and a growing percentage of AP exam takers actually pass their exam.[4] Moreover, the AP exams themselves have been transformed for the better. For example, the AP History test now places greater emphasis on critical thinking and evidence, less emphasis on isolated facts and dates, as recommended by professional historians.[5] The AP Biology test has been redesigned to devote more attention to hands-on experiments and analytical thinking.[6] More students also seem to be enrolling in International Baccalaureate courses, though at the moment the number of high schools offering AP courses far exceeds the number offering IB courses.[7] IB courses, like AP courses, stress critical-thinking skills.

Approximately forty-two states are implementing the Common Core, with its strong emphasis on critical thinking, the use of evidence to draw reasonable inferences, and other intellectual activities that tend to be vital to college success. Although teacher support for the Common Core varies, many teachers have embraced its central tenets, and many report positive changes in their pedagogy and in their students' learning. Instead of writing personal narratives, memoirs, and small works of fiction, elementary school students are being required to write informative and persuasive essays.[8] Instead of thinking of mathematics as "a list of disconnected tricks or mnemonics," students are invited to think of it as "an elegant subject in which powerful knowledge results from reasoning with a smaller number of principles, such as place value and properties of operations."[9] Students are being exposed to more nonfiction across the curriculum, in English language arts classes and elsewhere; and students are coming to understand math more deeply and more intuitively and to invent their own solutions to mathematical conundrums.[10] In subject after subject, students are being asked to articulate key claims, the evidence that supports them, and the reasoning behind whatever conclusions they reach.[11] A recent survey of English and math teachers in grades 4–8 found that three-quarters of English teachers and 82 percent of math teachers have altered their instructional materials because of the Common Core.[12] Eighty-six percent of all ELA teachers report more writing assignments that require the use of evidence, and 85 percent report more nonfiction in reading assignments. Eighty-one percent of math teachers report greater emphasis on conceptual understanding, and 78 percent have placed greater emphasis on the application of skills/knowledge in response to the Common Core.

Critical thinking has now been codified in K–12 tests, through assessments developed by two consortia (Smarter Balanced and PARCC) currently being used by twenty-one states.[13] These assessments are explicitly aimed at measuring critical thinking, among other skills. Jacqueline King of Smarter Balanced explains: "Critical thinking is a big part of our work. We have tried to create a test environment that asks students to analyze a problem and to look at evidence and to bring to bear an array of knowledge and skills they have acquired . . . as opposed to just regurgitating information."[14] For example, after reading an essay on the merits of a longer school day, students might be asked to cite evidence for and against such a reform.

This growing emphasis on critical thinking deserves applause, if college readiness is our goal, because most colleges emphasize critical-thinking skills. Critical thinking is of vital importance to success in college, whether the college in question is a community college, a small private college, or a large state university. According to a recent survey of colleges and universities, 85 percent have a common set of intended learning goals or learning outcomes that apply to all undergraduate students. Critical-thinking and analytical-reasoning skills are stressed by 98 percent of the schools reporting common learning goals (see Table 4-1).[15] As Dan Berrett has noted, learning goals for writing, critical thinking, analytical reasoning, and quantitative reasoning skills are "almost universal" among colleges and universities.[16]

Critical thinking often surfaces in college writing assignments, where students are required to formulate arguments, develop themes, weigh evidence, and reach conclusions. In these courses, critical

TABLE 4-1   Proportion of colleges and universities with learning
outcomes for all students that address specific
intellectual skills

	2008	2015
Writing Skills	99	99
Critical Thinking and Analytic Reasoning Skills	95	98
Quantitative Reasoning Skills	91	94
Oral Communication Skills	88	82
Intercultural Skills And Abilities	79	79
Information Literacy Skills	76	76
Ethical Reasoning Skills	75	75

Source: Hart Research Associates, "Trends in Learning Outcomes Assessment," Association
of American Colleges and Universities, February 17, 2016.

thinking takes a verbal form, encompassing logical reasoning and
incisive analysis. We see this, or hope to see it, in English literature
classes, political science classes, economics classes, history classes,
sociology classes, philosophy classes, and many others.

The websites of professional associations confirm this emphasis
on critical thinking in college classrooms. For example, the American
Political Science Association website proclaims: "As a political science
major, you will hone the writing, communication, analytical, and data
skills that are fundamental to a liberal arts education. This kind of
education will prepare you to think critically and independently, help
you appreciate differing points of view, and broaden your knowledge
of current affairs."[17] According to Marissa Kelly and Brian Klunk,
critical thinking is one of the most frequently mentioned learning
outcomes in undergraduate political science programs, a close second
to writing.[18] Similarly, the American Historical Association website
says: "Why study history? The answer is because we virtually must,
to gain access to the laboratory of human experience. When we study
it reasonably well, and so acquire some usable habits of mind . . . we
emerge with relevant skills and an enhanced capacity for informed
citizenship, critical thinking, and simple awareness."[19]

PROBLEMS

Despite these positive signs, much more remains to be done. In a competitive global economy, it may not be enough for us to do a bit better than we did in the past. In a postindustrial, information-based, technologically sophisticated society, it may not be enough to convey knowledge without the capacity to transfer knowledge to new settings, quickly and efficiently. In a stratified society with persistent and even widening inequalities, it may not be enough for us to do a good job for only some of our students. Indeed, there are plenty of storm clouds on the horizon.

First, when it comes to college completion, we are doing somewhat better in absolute terms but worse in relative terms. As recently as the 1980s, the United States was the undisputed world leader in the percentage of citizens who completed a college degree. Unfortunately, while many other nations have experienced a sharp upswing in college completion rates among young people, the US percentage remains essentially the same as it was a generation ago.[20] The United States now ranks sixteenth in the share of young adults (ages twenty-five to thirty-four) who hold a two-year or four-year college degree.[21] The situation appears somewhat better if we focus instead on the percentage of all adults (ages twenty-five to sixty-four) who hold a college degree.[22] But that is more a reflection of our past progress than of our future trajectory. The statistics on young adults suggest that the United States is falling behind other nations in this vital area.

Second, a substantial number of students who enroll in college are ill-equipped for college. A whopping 68 percent of community college students and a disappointing 40 percent of public, four-year-college students take at least one remedial course in college.[23] A recent international test, administered by the Program for International Student Assessment (PISA), which measured problem-solving skills, found that US fifteen-year-olds ranked roughly in the middle of the pack, compared to students in other Organisation for Economic Co-operation and Development (OECD) countries.[24] Perhaps this will change for the better, as the Common Core becomes deeply embedded in K–12 lesson plans and in students' intellectual repertoires. But we still have a long way to go.

Third, a disproportionate share of low-income students and students of color are not ready for college, and they struggle once enrolled in college. The dream of college readiness is widely shared, but that dream is much more likely to be realized if you are white and middle class.[25] For students in the highest family household income quartile, 71 percent have a college degree; in contrast, for students in the lowest family household income quartile, only 10 percent have a college degree.[26] Racial disparities are also sharp. Whereas 43.9 percent of whites and 59.4 percent of Asians have a college degree (two-year or four-year), only 27.6 percent of blacks, 23.4 percent of Native Americans, and 19.8 percent of Hispanics have one.[27]

EXPLANATIONS

What is going on that might explain these disappointing developments?

First, students do not get enough exposure to writing in K–12 schools. Writing is vitally important if students are to develop their critical-thinking skills. A good deal of research shows that the abilities to write well, speak well, and read well are closely interconnected.[28] Well-designed writing instruction can promote all three. But that is not what we have in most US schools. In fact, 61 percent of high school teachers say they never ask their students to write a paper more than five pages long.[29] The situation is even more alarming in some school districts. For example, a ninth-grade English teacher in San Benito, Texas, discovered that none of her students had written an essay longer than one page![30] First-year undergraduates report that the most frequently assigned high school writing tasks required them to offer and defend opinions, with a secondary emphasis on summarizing and synthesizing information.[31] Students were rarely asked to criticize an argument, define a problem and propose a solution, adapt their writing to their audience's needs, or revise their writing based on teacher feedback. It is not surprising that only a fourth of our eighth graders and twelfth graders are designated as "proficient" or "advanced" in writing on the NAEP tests.[32]

Part of the problem is that writing may not flourish in an age of social media. Text messages and tweets substitute short, punchy, flippant, and often trivial messages for more extended arguments with a logical progression of ideas, artful transitions between paragraphs, and big themes. This presents a big challenge to educators. In many ways, the writing habits children acquire through social media inhibit the development of more formidable writing skills. Somehow teachers must figure out how to get students to connect multiple ideas and supportive evidence in a coherent, compelling way.

Another part of the problem is the rise of standardized testing, which gobbles up a growing amount of classroom time. Eighth graders now devote 2.3 percent of their time to taking standardized tests, and several other grades are not far behind.[33] Additional time is devoted to test preparation. This leaves less time for writing assignments and for other assignments as well. Ironically, one threat to critical thinking time in the classroom is a proliferation of tests now linked to standards that seek to promote critical thinking!

Second, students do not engage in enough big projects that require planning, reflection, and coordination. A multipronged, carefully designed strategy is usually needed: a small group learning experience will go nowhere if the task is not clearly defined and gripping or if the students' responses are prematurely straitjacketed; an authentic experience can be valuable but does not in itself guarantee learning. Making small group projects work requires at least three steps: developing norms of cooperation, developing appropriate tasks, and developing strategies for discussion that support deeper learning. If small group experiences are to work, students must have opportunities to share insights, to resolve differences, to explain their thinking, to observe others' strategies, and to listen to the explanations of others.[34]

A small but growing body of research attests to the power of project-based learning. A North Carolina study of fourth and fifth graders in a gifted students program in the Midwest found significant differences between treatment group and control group children on a critical-thinking test after the treatment group children participated in a project-based learning activity for nine weeks. Their mission was to define and find solutions related to housing shortages in several countries.[35] A UK study of thirteen- to sixteen-year-olds found that students exposed to a project-based learning curriculum over three years did better than students in traditional curriculum classrooms on a national exam: specifically, conceptual problem solving in math.[36]

Brigid Barron and Linda Darling-Hammond summarize the scholarly consensus in support of team projects in the classroom: "There are significant learning benefits for students when they are asked to work together on learning activities as compared to approaches where students work on their own."[37]

Third, students do not get sufficient hands-on exposure to science or to the scientific method. In California, for example, 40 percent of elementary teachers reported spending no more than one hour per week teaching science.[38] A key reason for this skewing of classroom time is probably the extraordinary emphasis No Child Left Behind placed on fourth-grade test results in reading and math. One consequence of inattention to science, especially in the early grades, is that many students lose interest in science and never recapture it. As Tony Murphy has noted, by the time students reach grade 4, about a third of children have lost interest in science. By grade 8, almost 50 percent have lost interest or concluded that it is irrelevant to their future plans. In Murphy's words: "At this point in the K–12 system, the STEM pipeline has narrowed to half. That means millions of students have tuned out or lack the confidence to believe they can do science."[39]

Fourth, students get so many neatly packaged questions and so many formulaic answers that they don't always get the chance to discover the truth for themselves. Take math. For years, students learned formulas and when to apply them without really figuring out what the formulas mean or why they make sense. The Common Core has attempted to change that. But problems remain. For example, math exercises designed to be answerable often have the unintended consequence of protecting students from grappling with a difficult problem. Deborah L. Ball, the Dean of the School of Education at the University of Michigan, illustrated how to overcome this when she taught fractions to elementary school students.[40] Instead of simply showing students a rectangle with three equal segments, she showed them a rectangle with three parts: the first was one-fourth of the rectangle; the second was one-fourth of the rectangle; and the third was one-half of the rectangle. Then she asked students to estimate each fraction. It took a full twenty-two minutes, but one student eventually figured it out: "The parts have to be equal to identify a fraction," he exclaimed.

This discovery helped the other students understand fractions, deeply and enduringly. The key is to give students an unusual problem and to give them plenty of time to grapple with it. Unfortunately, many students seldom have that opportunity.

Each of these explanations for educational deficits suggests its own remedy. Our schools need to emphasize writing more, encouraging thematic development and helping students connect evidence to ideas. Our schools need to assign more big projects, which promote teamwork and inspire creativity. Our schools need to expose students to the scientific method, and not just in science classes. Our schools need to assign more applied math problems, with practical applications. These strategies are not revolutionary, are already underway in many schools, and are well within our reach (see Table 4-2 for specific examples).

Two other problems are more vexing and will require more sustained systemic interventions if underlying conditions are to change: our growing reliance on electronic means of communication and the stubborn persistence of educational inequalities by race and social class.

TABLE 4-2   Ways to improve college readiness

REMEDY	RATIONALE	COGNITIVE SKILLS	EXAMPLE
More emphasis on writing	Writing requires that you express yourself coherently.	Thematic development; connecting evidence to ideas	Write two short essays on marriage from two different points of view.
More big projects	We learn by testing the limits of our abilities.	Priority setting; teamwork; creativity	Replicate the Ellis Island experience.
More exposure to the scientific method	The scientific method is useful even in the humanities.	Hypothesis formation; hypothesis testing; pattern recognition	Design an experiment to reduce bullying at school.
More applied math	We learn by grappling with authentic mathematical problems.	Problem solving; mastering mathematical logic	Build a robot based on mathematical calculations.

ELECTRONIC CONNECTIONS, MENTAL DISCONNECTIONS

It is well known that young people today are more connected to electronic communication technologies than the rest of us were a generation or two ago. It seems hard to believe, but 87 percent of all teenagers (ages thirteen to seventeen) have access to a mobile phone, and 93 percent have access to a computer.[41] Teenagers routinely communicate with one another—and less often with adults—via Snapchat, Instagram, and e-mail. Teenagers spend a considerable amount of time viewing YouTube, and they idolize YouTubers. Teenagers, especially boys, spend a considerable amount of time playing video games, and not just games with educational value like Minecraft.[42]

Some of these developments may actually facilitate learning, inside and outside of the classroom. For example, 75 percent of teachers assert that the Internet and search engines have mostly had a positive impact on students' research skills.[43] To the extent that Internet access makes it easy to find relevant evidence, and to the extent that students make a deliberate effort to find credible evidence, that facilitates critical thinking. Also, some studies show that laptops in the classroom can serve constructive educational purposes.[44] On the other hand, 90 percent of teachers believe that digital technologies are creating an easily distracted generation with short attention spans.[45] Also, a good deal of research indicates that television viewing and video games can be harmful to young people. Because of the rapid pacing of television programming, viewers have few opportunities to reflect on what they see and hear on TV. Because television viewing is a relatively passive activity, it does not encourage proactive or interactive behavior. Because visual images, whether on TV or a video game, leave little to the imagination, the imagination suffers. As Sandra Calvert and Patti Valkenburg note, the literature generally shows a negative relationship between media use, especially "lean-back" media such as TV, and creativity.[46]

A related problem is that these activities divert students from reading for pleasure, which has declined dramatically in recent years. The percentage of thirteen-year-olds who read for fun almost every day has gone from 35 percent (1984) to 27 percent (2012), and the percentage who never/hardly ever read for fun has gone from 8 percent (1984) to 22 percent (2012). Similar changes have occurred for seventeen-year-olds.[47] Even J. K. Rowling, whose magical Harry Potter books introduced a generation of children to the joys of reading, found that video images have broader appeal than the printed word. Whereas 31 percent of Americans have read a Harry Potter book, 61 percent have seen a Harry Potter movie.[48]

As Patricia Greenfield points out, reading enhances thinking and engages the imagination in a way that exposure to visual media does not. By using more visual media, students can process information more quickly and acquire multitasking skills. However, most visual media are "real-time" media that do not allow time for "reflection, inductive analysis, critical thinking, mindful thought, and imagination." Reading is the key to developing these skills. If we really care about critical thinking, we need to encourage students to read, as opposed to using visual media. Otherwise, reflection and critical thinking will diminish. In Greenfield's words, "the developing human mind still needs a balanced media diet."[49]

The challenge for teachers is twofold. First, they must be able to communicate with a generation that is now accustomed to ingesting information in formats that have all the trappings of entertainment—arresting visual images, fast pacing, easy interaction, a clear and compelling story line. This means actually using some of the media that young people use or mimicking these media in classroom presentations or classroom assignments. Second, they must also try to wean young people away from these technologies so they can devote more time to reading, reflection, and critical thinking. Declaring a cell phone holiday—or a computer holiday—for a day or a weekend—might be one way to do this, although it could be hard to enforce. Admonitions on the drawbacks of multitasking are also vitally important. And, of course, parents should be monitoring media use and setting boundaries on a regular basis. According to a Kaiser Foundation survey, 28 percent of students in grades 7–12 use another medium most of the time when reading, and 30 percent do so some of the time.[50] Not only are routine multitaskers not reading enough, but they are not concentrating enough on reading when they actually sit down with a book.

SOCIAL STRATIFICATION AND
THE ACHIEVEMENT GAP

Public schools remain highly stratified, with disadvantaged students receiving a lower quality education than their middle-class counterparts. This gap is apparent as early as preschool. For example, a study of pre-K quality in eleven states found large and significant classroom quality gaps between disadvantaged children and middle-class children and between children of color and white children.[51] For the widely respected CLASS measure of instructional support and emotional support, black–white gaps were especially large. And these gaps widen afterward. Roland Fryer and Steven Levitt found that the black–white achievement gap grew by approximately .1 of a SD per year after kindergarten.[52] By grade 3, black students were far behind their white counterparts.

Social class gaps—and racial gaps—are also evident in high school. For example, fewer high-poverty schools offer AP courses to their students. High-poverty schools also offer fewer team sports to their students.[53] This is unfortunate because studies show that sports team participation builds "social capital," which can be extremely valuable for success later in life.[54] Another challenge is disparities in access to guidance counselors. Black and Hispanic students are less likely to have counselors and less likely to have well-trained counselors, even though they could benefit greatly from good advice about college options that they are less likely to receive at home.[55]

A key reason for SES gaps in school quality is disparities in financial resources. Over the past decade, differences in government spending between the poorest and the wealthiest communities, already substantial in many states, have grown. States now spend 16 percent less in their poorest schools, as opposed to 11 percent less a decade ago. In Pennsylvania, where spending gaps are especially striking, students in poor and wealthy school districts have vastly different experiences. At Martin Luther King High in Philadelphia, textbooks are not available for every student, and teachers often have to buy basic supplies, such as paper, themselves. At Lower Merion High, in a suburban community just ten miles away, each student has a school-provided laptop, a swimming pool is available, and an arts wing offers specialized courses in photography, ceramics, studio art, and jewelry making.[56]

The more fundamental problem is that disadvantaged students are less likely to be exposed to effective teachers than middle-class students, which reinforces preexisting disparities. A study of North Carolina high schools, which measured teacher effectiveness by using value-added modeling, found that students in the bottom decile are taught by teachers who are, on average, at the forty-first percentile of the value-added distribution, whereas students in the top decile are taught by teachers who are, on average, at the fifty-seventh percentile of that distribution.[57] A study of Florida and North Carolina elementary schools found that teachers in high-poverty schools are worse, based on their value-added measures, especially in North Carolina and especially in reading (less so in Florida, less so in math). The biggest difference, according to the researchers, is at the low end of the teaching pool. As the authors put it: "The best teachers in high-poverty schools are on par with the best teachers in lower-poverty schools but the least effective teachers in high-poverty schools are much less effective than their counterparts in lower-poverty schools."[58]

It is important not to exaggerate these differences or their implications. One cannot be sure that teachers who are less effective in boosting standardized test scores are less likely to teach critical-thinking skills or to teach them well. For this reason, it would be useful to know whether disadvantaged students are more likely to be taught by teachers employing "didactic" teaching styles (emphasizing basic skills), as opposed to "constructivist" teaching styles (where critical thinking is more likely to flourish). One study did find support for this hypothesis, but it was conducted some years ago.[59] Another study, focusing on tenth-grade science instruction, found a more complicated pattern—blacks and Hispanics were more likely to be exposed to didactic classroom instruction, but so too were high-SES students.[60] A third study, of 314 kindergarten and first-grade classrooms in three states, reached more definitive conclusions: low-income students and minority students were considerably more likely to receive didactic instruction and considerably less likely to receive constructivist instruction.[61] Rachel Valentino's preschool study provides additional support for the notion that disadvantaged children and children of color are more likely to receive didactic instruction.[62]

WHEN TO START AND HOW TO START

Critical thinking evolves from fluid-reasoning and executive-functioning skills, which emerge early in life and serve as an anchor for later learning. Thus, a good strategy for early childhood educators to shape young children's thinking is probably to cultivate a good working memory, a capacity for self-regulation, and flexibility or the capacity to switch nimbly from one task to another.

The best starting point for thinking about young children as learners is that we should not underestimate them. Tony Murphy, a professor at St. Catherine's University in Minnesota, puts it this way: "Children at birth are natural scientists, engineers, and prob-lem-solvers. They consider the world around them and try to make sense of it the best way they know how: touching, tasting, building, dismantling, creating, discovering, and exploring. For kids, this isn't education. It's fun!"[63]

It is also important to dispel the myth that young children should be playing and not learning. In fact, the two go hand in hand. As Doug Clements and Julie Sarama have noted, "When children 'play,' they are often doing much more than that. Preschoolers can learn to invent solutions to solve simple arithmetic problems, and almost all of them engage in substantial amounts of pre-mathematical activity in their free play . . . Through higher-level play, children explore pat-terns, shapes, and spatial relations; compare magnitudes; and count objects . . . It is high-quality education that can help all children utilize their inherent skills in order to truly mathematize."[64] In fact, studies show that almost nine out of ten children engage in at least one math activity during a play episode.[65]

Preschool is a great place to introduce rudimentary math and sci-ence concepts. For example, the Hopkins School District in Minnesota recently added some early STEM instruction in its preschools.[66] By purchasing wooden ramps and colorful plastic balls, they were able to set the stage for playful experiments in which students tried to get the balls to move faster. Eventually, the students figured out that elevating the ramps produced the desired result. Not every student will make the connection between velocity and slope, but this early lesson is likely to leave a lasting impression on many, making it easier for K–12 teachers to elaborate on these concepts later.

Kindergarten and first grade also provide great opportunities for hands-on STEM education. Much can be accomplished, for example, with sand tables, marbles, rulers, boxes, and cups.[67] After giving children a chance to play with these items, a teacher might ask, "How fast can you make the marbles roll?" Eventually, children are likely to discover that marbles move more quickly on a ruler. They may also discover that marbles move even more quickly if the ruler is propped up on a cup. From these experiences, students can continue to learn about velocity.

As astonishing as it may seem, young children are capable of understanding and articulating rudimentary scientific theories. A good example is "vitalist" biology—the theory that underlies thinking about life, death, and health. At ages four to seven, children can understand this theory, which says that air, food, and water are sources of vital energy or vital substance, that must be obtained from the outside world for the body to function properly.[68] A child who notices that a statue is visible but immobile while a recently deceased relative is now invisible has begun to grasp the essence of that theory and may soon be able to articulate the difference between animate and inanimate objects.

One great way to engage children of all ages is by asking open-ended questions that encourage students to think critically. Becka Wright, who teaches art history at the Falk Laboratory School in Pittsburgh, knows how to ask rapid-fire questions that get to the heart of the matter. A visit to her first-grade classroom made it clear that even first graders can think critically about great works of art (see "Deconstructing Banksy," pp. 90–91).

For older students, a good conceptual framework, especially one with broad applicability, can be a great way to generate excitement and encourage understanding. A good example is de Bono's hats, which Katie Nichter's students "wear" in order to grasp and master different thinking styles. When I visited her seventh-grade English class at

Swanson Middle School in Arlington, Virginia, I found students who approached the question of censorship very differently as they donned white, yellow, and red hats (see "Color Me Dark Green," pp 91–93).

THE ART OF ASKING GOOD QUESTIONS

Choosing the right questions to ask is one of the hardest but most important parts of teaching. To illustrate this, consider an English literature class. Unfortunately, most questions teachers pose in such classes ask students to identify basic elements of the text, such as grammar, plot, characters, and climax. An alternative approach is to ask questions that have no right answer but that provoke serious thought. In discussing *Charlotte's Web,* a teacher could ask a student a simple factual question: what does Templeton the rat do to help Wilbur the pig? Alternatively, the teacher could ask: Is Templeton the rat a good friend?[69] The latter question has no right answer, but it does lend itself to a range of interesting answers. Studies by researchers at the University of Pittsburgh find that such questions improve students' critical-thinking skills. English language learners seem to benefit especially from more open and in-depth class conversations.[70] The precise pedagogical strategy seems to matter. Although many strategies are successful in getting students to talk more, only a few are successful in improving their critical-thinking skills.[71]

The ability to ask good questions is one of the most important manifestations of critical-thinking skills and is therefore very important for students as well. One clever research project asked fifth-grade students and college students to perform a task neither had confronted before: to develop a plan for protecting bald eagles from extinction. The initial results were surprising and disappointing: the recovery plans of the fifth graders and the college students were not radically different, which raised questions about how much learning had taken place in middle school and high school. But then researchers took a closer look at the questions each group of students was asking. The fifth graders asked these questions: What do eagles like to eat? What size are they? What kinds of trees do they live in? In contrast, the college students asked these questions: What kinds of ecosystems support eagles? What kinds of experts are needed to carry out recovery plans? Do other animals need to be recovered in order to recover eagles? Researchers reached two positive conclusions: first, the college students had acquired some valuable insights from their middle school and high school biology classes; and second, the college students were able to transfer these insights to a new situation, asking questions that were much more sophisticated and much more likely to lead to a good recovery plan.[72] In a nutshell, they had acquired some critical-thinking skills.

SCHOOLS OF EDUCATION

Whether teachers actually ask good questions and promote critical thinking in the classroom depends in part on what schools of education choose to do. Training can help, and we need to harness professional development more explicitly to the teaching of critical-thinking skills, but what teachers learn in college is vitally important. Because 56 percent of K–12 teachers have a master's degree or higher, graduate instruction is also really important.[73]

Conversations with several education school administrators suggest the following tentative conclusions about graduate programs in education:

First, aspiring teachers encounter the concept of critical thinking in courses that focus on methods of inquiry. In these courses, preservice teachers learn that how to ask a question is very important. They also learn that they should give their students the opportunity to struggle with a question and confer with fellow classmates before receiving an authoritative answer from their teacher.

Second, aspiring teachers are unlikely to take an actual course in critical thinking.[74] Although such courses exist in some colleges, especially elite colleges like Harvard or Columbia, they are typically aimed more at PhD students than at master's students. At George Mason University's School of Education, for example, it is hard to identify a course in critical thinking per se. On the other hand, plenty of courses, including required courses, place a strong emphasis on inquiry as the key to successful learning.[75]

Third, at most schools of education, the teaching of critical thinking, when discussed at all, is discussed in the context of a specific discipline or field like science or math or social studies. In this setting, future teachers can learn how to ask probing questions in science if that is their specialty. Or they can learn how to encourage the use of good sources for evidence in social studies if that is their specialty. As they improve their craft, it is essential for teachers to be able to think like students, to understand their misconceptions, whether the subject is math or science or social studies. In a study of middle school students who took physical science courses, Philip Sadler and Gerhard Sonnert found that students performed better on science tests if their teacher genuinely understood science concepts, but also that they performed better if their teacher had a good awareness of common student misconceptions.[76] In other words, when trying to teach difficult scientific concepts, teachers should understand wrong answers as they seek to guide students to right answers. It helps to know how struggling students think if you want them to think better.

BEYOND THE CLASSROOM

Many schools offer additional after-hours opportunities for students to become better thinkers. One such opportunity, aimed at promoting "creative problem-solving skills," is called the Odyssey of the Mind. Established in 1978, the OM program arranges a series of local and regional competitions that culminate in an annual national championship.[77] Students join a team of peers in their age bracket and work on a project together, under the guidance of a coach. Although assigned problems vary, they generally fall into five categories: (a) design a vehicle that moves; (b) produce a classical performance (e.g., art or drama); (c) produce a technical performance (usually involving a device that executes certain tasks); (d) produce a contemporary performance (e.g., one laced with humor); or (e) build a structure entirely out of balsa wood and glue. OM encourages collaborative problem solving that can be fun and that yields a product or experience that can generate considerable pride. Although the emphasis is on creativity and problem solving, critical thinking may be an important by-product of the group's craft.

Anne Kitchens, who took two teams to the state championships when she worked for the Johnson City School District in eastern

Tennessee, recalls that OM competitions required creativity and improvisation, among other skills. Her students conjured up an eight-minute skit, "O Moonshine," loosely modeled after Shakespeare's "A Midsummer Night's Dream," as required by OM. They zigzagged back and forth from the twenty-first century to the sixteenth century and used props to good advantage. "One girl stuck raisins in her teeth, to look real hillbilly," she recalls. "One guy made hair out of a mop, to look like a woman." Together, the students composed songs with funny lyrics. At the regional competition, one shy boy was overcome by stage fright. "I found him in the corner crying," Kitchens recalls. "I said, 'You get up there! These kids are counting on you.'" He did, and his team won at the regional level and went on to place third at the state competition in Nashville. The young man with stage fright is now a professional musician and actor in New York City. Odyssey of the Mind helped him make that journey.[78]

Field trips can be another valuable way to engage students, especially disadvantaged students who may prefer sights and sounds and smells (a museum, a play, a forest, a farm) to a classroom lecture. A recent study by Jay Greene and his colleagues found that elementary, middle school, and high school students improved their critical-thinking skills after spending a day at the Crystal Bridges Museum of American Art in Bentonville, Arkansas.[79] Students randomly assigned to the treatment group were more engaged in observing, interpreting, evaluating, associating, problem finding, comparing, and flexible thinking than students randomly assigned to the control group. Critical-thinking gains were especially striking among students from high-poverty and rural schools, who might otherwise not have had such an experience. This interesting research is a useful reminder that we pay a price when we forgo field trips because they are logistically challenging or because they cost money or because they cut into classroom time. Unfortunately, that is exactly what has been happening at many public schools.[80]

TEMPLATES

A number of schools and school systems have embarked on strategies that emphasize critical thinking and some of the pedagogical approaches outlined in the preceding sections. These programs have demonstrated that a strong emphasis on critical thinking, combined with project-based learning, team projects, and high-stakes oral presentations, can yield impressive results.

One example is Envision Education, a cluster of three high schools that educate disadvantaged children in Oakland, California. Founded by Bob Lenz in 2001, Envision Education schools emphasize deeper learning, which includes critical thinking, problem solving, effective communication, and teamwork.[81] One of the hallmarks of Envision Education is a strong emphasis on project-based learning. Beginning in grade 9, students work on at least one big project a year, sharing the excitement and satisfaction of focusing on a substantial undertaking that requires sustained attention and some ingenuity. Another hallmark of Envision Education is a requirement for a forty-five-minute portfolio defense in order to graduate. Each student, alone, must make a compelling oral presentation that satisfies a panel of judges that he or she is ready to graduate. These defenses are usually fraught with tension because students know that there is no guarantee that they will pass. As Lenz puts it, "Whichever way it turns out, it's a tear jerker either way."[82] Based on some of the usual indicators, Envision Education is succeeding. Approximately 75 percent of its high school graduates are accepted into a four-year college, and approximately 55 percent of its high school graduates actually enroll at a four-year college.[83]

Education researchers have found that literacy coaching can improve students' critical-thinking skills by improving classroom discussions or by strengthening the scaffolding that teachers provide. One strategy that has proven successful is Questioning the Author, which seeks to engage students deeply in the process of making meaning from text and which encourages students to question the author's position as an expert. Basically, students are encouraged to think of authors as fallible. Teachers guide students through a text, assisting them in the construction of meaning through the use of questions that focus their attention on the meaning of an author's words.[84] Either fiction or nonfiction can be the focal point. A study of several alternative approaches found that Questioning the Author was especially effective at improving students' critical-thinking skills.[85] Another study found that Questioning the Author strengthened students' reading achievement ability, including critical-thinking skills, by improving the quality of classroom discussions.[86]

Team teaching can be a great way to stimulate critical thinking because it exposes students to two different, complementary points of view and forces them to look at the same question through the lenses of two disciplines. Many schools have found that a winning combination is English literature and social studies. I encountered an excellent example of this in a visit to a tenth-grade Cultural Literacy class at Pittsburgh's City Charter High School (see "Understanding the 1920s," pp. 93–94).

Another useful template that kills two birds with one stone (the scientific-knowledge bird and the critical-thinking bird) is a project-based learning curriculum with a science focus. A good example is a biology curriculum (Bio I) used in several Illinois middle schools and studied carefully by two researchers.[87] The focus of this ten- to twelve-week curriculum was on how to redesign school lunch choices and physical exercise choices to meet our bodies' needs. Students measured the energy in food, learning about chemical changes and the properties of matter in the process. Students learned where in our bodies energy stores are used and how to use a one-way valve to collect a fellow student's expired air while engaging in a given physical activity. After determining the number of calories used by the body's working cells, students calculated the number of calories consumed by particular school lunch foods. By comparing the two (calories ingested versus calories burned away through exercise), they were able to make recommendations for striking a better balance between the two, thus improving overall student health.

Through a pretest, posttest study at nine Illinois middle schools, researchers found that participation in the project-based biology curriculum substantially improved student knowledge of important scientific processes. They also discovered a positive relationship between teacher content knowledge and student achievement and between teacher pedagogical awareness and student achievement. Unexpectedly, however, researchers found a small *negative* relationship between participation in the project-based curriculum and students' attitudes toward science and also students' plans to study science in college or to pursue a career in science. The researchers speculated that this could be because any disruption in traditional instructional techniques may be off-putting to students, at least initially. In other words, they learned more, but they enjoyed the experience less. On the positive side, researchers did find that teachers who used an inquiry-based approach in the classroom experienced not only higher student achievement but also more favorable student attitudes and plans.[88] Thus, the key to making this approach work may be to get teachers to use a specific pedagogical technique while implementing the curriculum.

It should be noted that the Bio I study specifically focused on students from three racial and ethnic minorities (blacks, Hispanics, and Native Americans) because these groups are strikingly underrepresented in the scientific and engineering professions.[89] It is heartening that these students were able to learn more from the project-based learning approach. It is, however, disheartening that these students were somewhat less likely to view science favorably and to see themselves as future scientists. Clearly, this strategy, though promising, needs some fine-tuning if it is to propel underrepresented racial and ethnic minorities into STEM occupations.

If a project-based curriculum like Bio I promotes the acquisition of scientific knowledge generally, does it also promote critical thinking? Researchers broke test items into three categories (low, medium, and high cognitive difficulty) and found positive effects on student knowledge in all three areas. They found that the correlation between teacher knowledge and student performance was especially high for test items characterized as high cognitive difficulty.[90] Examples include students applying course content in a context different from that in which they learned the idea or drawing new connections between concepts. In short, a project-based science curriculum can promote critical-thinking skills, especially if the teacher has mastered the relevant knowledge.

HARVESTING YOUTUBE

Another way to promote critical thinking is to take advantage of some amazing educational options through YouTube. The basic premise is

"If you can't beat 'em, join 'em." According to recent reports, 74 percent of teens aged fourteen to eighteen and a whopping 97 percent of high school seniors in the United States use YouTube. More teens use YouTube than Facebook or Twitter.[91] Teens are eager to discuss YouTube videos, and they are just as eager to learn from them. With scaffolding from teachers, the educational value of YouTube could grow exponentially.

Consider, for example, a marvelous YouTube video from the Axis of Awesome, three singer comedians from Sydney, Australia.[92] In an amusing video, they complain that they've never had a hit single because they've never written a "four-chord song." One member of the group (Benny) plays four simple chords on the keyboard (I—V—vi—IV) and then launches into brief snippets from dozens of well-known pop tunes, all of which use these same four chords (and not much more). I recognized a few of them—"Let It Be" (the Beatles), "Can You Feel the Love Tonight?" (Elton John). My daughter recognized many more.

A savvy music teacher could use this brilliant video to illustrate the architecture of popular music. Ask students to contribute their own examples of familiar four-chord songs. Ask students why pop musicians have gotten into such a creative rut. Ask students if there are other familiar chord progressions. A lesson that begins with this five-minute video could illuminate the "craft" of pop music composition with drama and humor and could spark students' intellectual curiosity and get them to look for other more imaginative chord progressions.

ALTERNATIVE PATHS TO COLLEGE READINESS

A stronger emphasis on critical thinking is by no means the only viable strategy for enhancing college readiness, generally or for disadvantaged students in particular. Other strategies have been tried with some success.

One strategy is to lengthen the school day, the school year, or both. Some studies show that this change can enhance educational achievement, though the evidence is far from overwhelming.[93] The KIPP charter schools, which educate approximately fifty thousand students per year, 86 percent of whom are low income, have long emphasized more classroom time as a key pillar of their program, and KIPP has generated substantial improvements in student test scores over time.[94] It is difficult to know how much of KIPP's success is due to a longer school day or a longer school year, as opposed to strong teaching, tough discipline, motivational tools, or other features of the KIPP approach. But it is certainly possible that more classroom hours will enhance college readiness.

A second strategy would be to shrink the size of our public schools, especially our high schools. Although this strategy, once embraced by the Gates Foundation, has been discredited and indeed abandoned by the Gates Foundation itself, the verdict may have been premature.[95] A recent MDRC study of New York City's Small High Schools found that these smaller schools generated impressive gains in educational achievement for disadvantaged students. Specifically, they raised high school graduation rates by 9.4 percent and boosted college enrollment rates by 8.4 percent.[96] As with KIPP, it is difficult to know whether these gains are due to smallness, close personal relationships between teachers and students, an emphasis on relevant instruction . . . or something else. But it is possible that smaller high schools, when combined with a strong curriculum, could improve college readiness, especially for disadvantaged students.

A third strategy would be to more aggressively promote extra-curricular activities, including extracurricular activities at school. Numerous studies show a strong relationship between extracurricular activities and good academic outcomes, including college enrollment rates. For example, Bonnie Barber and Jacqueline Eccles found that students who participated in sports or performing arts or an aca-demic club were more likely to get better grades as high school seniors and more likely to enroll in college.[97] Questions have, appropriately, been raised as to whether these relationships are causal. However, some studies control for early achievement and still find a signifi-cant relationship between extracurricular participation and academic success.[98] The key is to figure out which extracurricular activities and which extracurricular program characteristics are beneficial, for which groups, and how participation in these activities can be encouraged. Simply requiring participation is unlikely to work. On the other hand, reshaping these programs to make them both better and more appealing could entice more students to participate and benefit them more profoundly as well. Also, schools need to figure out better ways to inform parents, especially Hispanic parents who do not speak English, of the benefits that flow from extracurricular participation.[99]

A fourth strategy would be to establish more tutoring and mentoring programs for students, especially disadvantaged students, and especially in our middle schools and high schools. One model for this is the Diplomas Now program, which originated in Baltimore and is currently being implemented in fourteen school districts across the country. Under this program, near-peer mentors (ages seventeen to twenty-four) are available to disadvantaged students at selected schools from about 7:30 a.m. to about 7:30 p.m. They provide advice, support, and tutoring services throughout the day and throughout the school year. At Tulsa's Clinton Junior High School, for example, nine near-peers (ages eighteen to twenty-four, with salaries paid by United Way) work full time, focusing on attendance and literacy improvements as goals.[100] An MDRC evaluation of Diplomas Now is currently underway. Early indications are that implementation problems have arisen in several sites, including Tulsa.[101] However, as fidelity of implementation improves, this program could help disadvantaged students by connecting them to a relatively young role model who cares about them individually and who helps them navigate the often treacherous path to college readiness.

Modest improvements in more conventional counseling programs could also help. High school guidance counselors are pressed to the limit at many schools and especially at low-income schools. On average, a high school guidance counselor serves 347 students—a ratio that far exceeds recommended caseloads of 100 to 1 or 250 to 1.[102] Studies show that an additional high school counselor could increase a high school's four-year-college-going rate by about 10 percentage points.[103] It is essential that college counseling occurs early. Counselors should begin supporting students and their families in middle school so that students can take algebra and other gateway courses early enough to qualify for college prep courses.[104]

Note that not one of these alternative strategies zeros in on critical thinking as the key lever for systemic change. They are rooted in different premises, such as the idea that more time devoted to academic instruction is a good thing or that disadvantaged students need more mentoring and support. On the other hand, it is easy to imagine that any one of these strategies could be combined with a critical-thinking focus to sharpen and enhance program effects. An extended school day is the most obvious example. Why not extend the school day and devote that additional time to project-based learning or Socratic seminars that emphasize critical thinking? Why not make critical thinking the explicit goal of peer mentors who help struggling students get back on track? Why not integrate critical thinking into academic clubs that students are free to join? The approaches outlined here are structural reforms largely devoid of substantive content. Critical thinking is rich in content but adaptable to many different structural reforms. Together, these strategies could be a winning combination for K–12 students.

Some trade-offs are undoubtedly associated with some of these reforms. A longer school day would require a beefier school budget. If peer mentors focus on critical-thinking skills, they might have less time to devote to nagging personal problems that interfere with students' success. A science club that bills itself as a haven for critical thinkers may snag fewer recruits than one that focuses on robots or rockets. But some of these trade-offs are more apparent than real. Critical-thinking skills are applicable to socioemotional problems, and not just academic problems. Any effort to highlight transferability across domains should strengthen the case for mastering such skills. And advertisements for clubs need not make an either-or decision. An emphasis on critical thinking might appeal to parents, while an emphasis on robots or rockets might appeal to students. Whatever the promotional pitch, science clubs should be fostering critical thinking!

CONCLUSION

College readiness is already a key goal of the K–12 education establishment, including principals, teachers, and counselors. For high schools in particular, it is a tangible, measurable, and valued objective. High schools monitor and advertise their success in getting students to attend college. *U.S. News & World Report* and other entities celebrate high schools that have been relatively successful in getting their students to take AP courses, to pass AP courses, and to enroll in four-year colleges.[105]

Critical thinking is growing in importance as a way of improving college readiness. It is perhaps not front and center, as is student performance on standardized math and English language arts tests, which received a big boost from the No Child Left Behind Act and which continue to be important despite concerns about over-testing. But critical thinking is at least somewhere on the main stage, thanks to mass media coverage of the Common Core, AP, IB, and other developments.

Some nontrivial problems remain. First, critical thinking does not receive attention early enough. It gets a good deal more attention in high school than in elementary school or middle school, despite evidence that even preschoolers are capable of carrying out critical-thinking assignments if structured in developmentally appropriate ways.

Second, we have not been as creative and imaginative as we could be in designing critical-thinking projects and prods that could transform students from knowledge consumers to knowledge seekers and knowledge creators. For critical thinking to blossom in the classroom, students must become actively engaged in the search for meaning.

Third, there is probably a critical-thinking gap between high-SES and low-SES students, just as there is a gap in more conventional measures of academic achievements.[106] Some teachers may conclude, prematurely, that disadvantaged students are incapable of critical thinking.[107] Others may conclude that it is too time consuming to teach critical thinking or that the connection between critical thinking and standardized tests is too tenuous.

So, there is still much more to be done if the college readiness of US students is to improve. But at least college readiness has received a lot of attention. The same cannot be said of either career readiness or civic readiness. By focusing single-mindedly on college readiness as a goal, we have neglected both career readiness and civic readiness. This has led to a fundamental misallocation of resources—time, money, attention. College readiness is a great goal, and it would be premature to declare victory in this battle. But we also need to strike a better balance.

DECONSTRUCTING BANKSY

Art for first graders? If you're like me, you probably think crayons, paintbrushes, construction paper, and scissors. But what about art history? At the Falk Laboratory School, a Progressive K–8 school at the University of Pittsburgh, first graders routinely dissect works of art, looking for hidden meanings and deeper truths. On the day I visited, Becka Wright introduced twenty-one students to three works of art that explored violence, including Banksy's *The Flower Thrower*, which depicts a menacing masked man poised to hurl a bouquet of flowers at someone or something.

WRIGHT: What do you see?

STUDENT: He's getting ready to throw some flowers.

STUDENT: It looks like he's a gangster.

WRIGHT: How do you know?

STUDENT: He's wearing all black.

WRIGHT: I sometimes wear all black. Am I a gangster?

CHORUS of STUDENTS: NO!!!

WRIGHT: Is there something strange about this image?

STUDENT: It's kind of like he's gonna throw flowers. Maybe it's because his wife gave them to him and he's about to break up with her.

At this point, Wright intervenes, urging the students to adopt a different perspective. She does this by zooming in on the man . . . without the flowers in his hand.

WRIGHT: Pretend the flowers aren't there. Look at just the man. What would you *expect* him to be throwing?

STUDENT: A bomb.

STUDENT: A grenade.

STUDENT: I thought he might throw a weapon and thought he might hurt someone . . . but he didn't.

WRIGHT: Interesting! He had a change of heart. He threw flowers. What does it mean to give someone flowers?

STUDENT: You love someone.

STUDENT: Maybe he's saying , "If you find something good, you should do something with it."

WRIGHT: I'm going to retire!

Although Wright was tempted to focus on only *The Flower Thrower* in this lesson, she juxtaposed *The Flower Thrower* with two other interpretations of violence: *Disarm* (Pedro Reyes, 2013)—a provocative transformation of eight Mexican handguns into a piece of sculpture that also functions as a musical instrument; and *Girl with Balloon* (Banksy)—a piece of graffiti portraying a young girl who has just released—or perhaps lost—a heart-shaped balloon. After inviting the students to reflect on each of these works of art, Wright asked them to put them all together.

> WRIGHT: Ready for the bazillion-dollar question? Why did I curate these? What are the artists trying to tell us about people and how people treat each other and the world?
>
> STUDENT: Don't be violent towards each other.
>
> STUDENT: There's danger.
>
> WRIGHT: What can be done with dangerous stuff?
>
> STUDENT: You can make it into something beautiful.
>
> STUDENT: I think they're trying to tell us war isn't good.
>
> STUDENT: You should treat each other better.
>
> STUDENT: There's always a good side.

Throughout this class, hands were waving all the time. Wright intervened from time to time, repeating or rephrasing a student opinion, connecting observations, or introducing a new perspective. But mainly Wright let the students do the heavy lifting. After class, Wright explained what she was hoping to accomplish: "I use art history not just because I love it but because it's a universal way to get kids to think critically. My 'still waters run deep guys' just explode! For these kids, art history is a really accessible, fun way to do this."

COLOR ME DARK GREEN

Getting middle schoolers to engage in critical thinking is not a simple task. A self-absorbed preteen doesn't find it easy to imagine how another person might think. Wouldn't it be great if thinking like another person were as easy as, let's say, putting on a hat? Thanks to Edward de Bono, it is!

Katie Nichter, who teaches seventh-grade English at Swanson Middle School in Arlington County, Virginia, uses de Bono's hats to get students comfortable with critical thinking. Hats of different colors correspond to different ways of thinking, or what de Bono would call "parallel thinking." A red hat signifies feelings. A yellow hat person sees the up side or the sunny side of an idea, whereas a black hat person sees the dark side. A white hat means you're looking for new evidence or facts; a green hat means you're thinking creatively about a new solution to a problem. And a blue hat corresponds to metacognition, or thinking about thinking. De Bono's hats have been widely used in the business community as a tool for promoting organizational learning and continuous quality improvement.

"Think about the way you usually approach things," Nichter tells her students. "Do you have a go-to hat that you automatically go to when you're not thinking about it?" Hands shoot up. "Everyone wears a red hat, because everyone has an emotional instinct," one student volunteers. "But everyone also has their own dominant hat. Mine is green." Another student chimes in: "I think I'm kind of a green hat and a black hat. Like a dark green hat!"

This is the fourth day that the students have thought about wearing hats. Even so, these are stunning breakthroughs. The first student has grasped that we all think alike in certain ways, but that we are also different and that those differences are worth celebrating and exploring. The second student has transcended de Bono's categories and created a new hat—dark green. Another student riffs on the same theme. "I'm black but also a little white," she says. "Maybe I'm kind of gray!"

After other students weigh in, Nichter gives them a different assignment. Because they are discussing censorship this week, she asks them to read an op-ed extolling the virtues of an app that can excise profanities and other offensive words from a text. They read it out loud and pepper Nichter with questions. Then Nichter asks them to jot down phrases relevant to the censorship debate that correspond to each of five hats. She excludes blue because it is more daunting than the rest; she wears the metacognition hat.

The students take up each hat in turn. Red gets little attention, perhaps because its implications are so obvious. Yellow attracts interest. "It could be good for young kids to have things filtered out by an app," one girl asserts. Others echo that refrain. "But is the app just for young kids?" Nichter asks. "Parents feel safer with an app," one girl suggests. Next, it's black's turn. "If younger kids turn the settings off, they could pick up on all the curse words," one girl warns. Another student has a different worry: "Without the actual curse words, it's not as powerful; it doesn't carry as much weight."

Occasionally, the students forget which hat they're supposed to be wearing. If this happens, Nichter intervenes. During the black hat discussion, a student asks, "Would people who reject this app be stigmatized?" Nichter notes that this is probably a white hat question because you're looking for evidence. Soon, the students have a chance to wear the white hat. "How do authors feel about this app?" one girl asks. Another student responds: "I think they'd be a little upset because I wrote it this way and kind of created it to have a dramatic feeling." Nichter agrees: "It's like a lot of art. You wouldn't want to create something with your brain and heart, only to see it destroyed."

The class period ends abruptly, as students are just warming up to the prospect of wearing a green hat. Or maybe a dark green hat. Already, these students are on their way to becoming critical thinkers. Nichter sums up what they have accomplished: "It is definitely a challenge for them to see themselves switching gears in terms of how to approach something. It's hard to acknowledge that their initial perspective is not where other people are coming from." Hard, yes, but also important.

UNDERSTANDING THE 1920s

At Pittsburgh's City Charter High School on a wintry morning in February 2016, tenth graders are struggling to understand a quote from James Truslow Adams (*The Epic of America*, 1931) on the meaning of the American dream: not a dream of motor cars and high wages merely, but a dream of social order in which each man and each woman shall be able to attain to the fullest stature of which he or she is innately capable.

Thus begins a two-hour Cultural Literacy course, team-taught by English teacher Cristine Watson-Smith and social studies teacher Aleksandr Permyashkin. Some students are getting it. One student notes that poorly educated Americans may not come to experience the American dream. Another observes that we may need taxes to realize the American dream. A third student volunteers that Adams "created" the American dream. Watson-Smith gently corrects the student (Adams popularized the concept but didn't invent it) and moves on. With some promising ideas on the table, she gives the students fifteen minutes to write a short paragraph with some preliminary ideas.

Watson-Smith has already provided some scaffolding (Attention-Getter, Topic, and Thesis) and has offered a short paragraph of her own as a template. During a brief lull, Watson-Smith explains that the conceptual scaffolding might be viewed as "training wheels" and might get in the way at some point, but she is optimistic that her students won't need the training wheels for long. A key feature of City High is "looping," or multiyear teaching by the same teacher. Watson-Smith will have these students for four years in a row, so she can set a comfortable pace with many opportunities for students to stop, reflect, and spread their wings. Watson-Smith is enthusiastic about looping: "I can't imagine teaching at a regular school again."

At the end of the first hour, Watson-Smith passes the baton to Permyashkin, who has been present from the beginning, listening to Watson-Smith, fielding questions from students, and generally moving things along. Now, it is his turn. The focus of the second hour, Permyashkin announces, will be to find "contradictions" in the social, economic, and political developments of the 1920s. He asks students to explain what a contradiction is, and they come up with a serviceable definition. Then he asks how jazz illustrates the contradictions of the 1920s.

To structure the conversation, Permyashkin asks students to give him positive and negative examples of jazz's influence on society. On the positive side, students note that jazz gave people a way to express themselves, gave black musicians a start to their careers, and brought blacks and whites together to enjoy good music. On the negative side, students note that jazz exposed a pervasive racism in our culture because blacks and whites were separated in jazz clubs like the Cotton Club (with whites as patrons, blacks as performers and employees). They also note that jazz created or reinforced certain racist stereotypes (e.g., jungle music).

Later, Permyashkin notes that the search for contradictions is a recurring theme of the Cultural Literacy course. Early on, students considered Christopher Columbus as an explorer and a hero but also as a subjugator of Native Americans. They have also tried to understand how people whom we view as terrorists can see themselves as freedom fighters. "We want them to think critically, to build on that," Permyashkin explains. "They see the world from a very limited perspective. I challenge that a bit. Critical thinking comes in where they try to come to terms with their world view versus other people's world view." Watson-Smith agrees, emphasizing connections across disciplines and respectful dialogues on sensitive topics such as race in America: "They tie in things from literature with bigger social issues. We facilitate discussion, but they learn how to respectfully agree and disagree and support ideas with evidence."

Learning to Solve Problems: Career Readiness

DESPITE DESPERATE PLEAS from employers for workers who possess critical-thinking skills, such workers are in short supply. Part of the problem is that teachers are not focusing enough on career readiness. But another part of the problem is more subtle: when employers refer to critical thinking, they mean practical problem solving or blended thinking that includes both critical thinking and problem solving. When teachers refer to critical thinking, they often mean textual analysis, which for most employers is not enough. In this chapter, I document strong employer interest in critical-thinking skills and strong employer dissatisfaction with the skills job applicants possess. I also discuss changes in technology and the labor market that make critical thinking even more important. I then discuss in detail some skills that enhance employability: priority setting, applied math, inventory management, satisficing, adaptability, and teamwork. Several educational programs promote these skills, including Career Academies, P-Tech, Linked Learning initiatives, and apprenticeships, like those that have been enormously successful in Europe. The broader challenge is to make career readiness—and the critical-thinking skills that promote it—a higher priority for all students, and not simply those who have selected a vocational track.

CAREER READINESS DESERVES MORE ATTENTION

In contrast to college readiness, which remains the leading goal of K–12 education, career readiness—or employability—remains the forgotten stepchild of K–12 education. Given the well-known political clout of the business community, this is somewhat surprising.[1] In state after state, the business community has succeeded in securing tax breaks and other concessions to promote economic development. Yet, with few exceptions, the business community has largely failed to transform public education into a driving force to improve the skills of America's workforce.

As we shall see, it is not that the business community has been silent on these issues. But much of the momentum for reform has been channeled into vocational education, which regrettably has been viewed as a consolation prize for weak students rather than as one of the pillars of the educational system. Despite robust alternative models in western Europe, the United States has at best taken baby steps to strengthen career readiness in our public schools. As a result, our public schools devote far more attention to college readiness than to career readiness. As Carl Van Horn has noted, "Educators must recognize and act on the simple fact that the majority of high school graduates either do not attend college or do not obtain a degree. By embracing the college-for-all strategy, educators are doing a great disservice to the seven in ten young people who do not obtain a bachelor's degree."[2]

As we have seen, many teachers do promote critical thinking in the classroom. However, in many instances, critical thinking has been defined far too narrowly, with too much emphasis on textual analysis and not enough on practical problem solving. To put it another way, our schools do not do enough work in the fertile soil that lies between critical thinking and problem solving.

Debates over career readiness, when they occur, echo grand debates from over a century ago over the fundamental purposes of a public education. In 1893, a national commission headed by Charles Eliot, president of Harvard University, recommended that all high schools offer a relatively narrow curriculum that did not distinguish between college-bound and work-bound students. In contrast, a National Education Association report, issued in 1916 (and endorsed by psychologist Edward Thorndike), articulated several "cardinal principles," one of which was that high school students should be free to pursue their respective educational and career plans.[3]

These disputes, largely resolved in favor of a single highly structured academic curriculum and the goal of college readiness, reverberate today. In one camp, Achieve readily uses the phrase "college and career readiness," which strongly implies that the two have a great deal in common.[4] And indeed they do. For example, cognitive and noncognitive skills are both important, whether your immediate destination is college or the workplace. In contrast, the Association for Career and Technical Education (ACTE) prefers to distinguish between college readiness and career readiness. From their vantage point, career readiness encompasses core academic skills, *plus* employability skills (including critical thinking), *plus* technical job-specific skills related to a specific career pathway.[5] It should be evident by now that I agree with ACTE. College readiness and career readiness tug students in different directions, despite some overlap between the two. In practice, lumping the two together results in downgrading the value of career readiness and rendering students less employable than they otherwise could be. It also runs the risk of privileging a particular conception of critical thinking.

WHAT EMPLOYERS SAY

Employers have made it abundantly clear: they greatly value critical thinking in a potential employee, and they greatly regret that so many potential employees lack critical-thinking skills.

In a 2013 survey by the Association of American Colleges and Universities (AACU), 93 percent of employers said a demonstrated capacity to think critically, to communicate clearly, and to solve complex problems is more important than a job candidate's undergraduate major.[6] In a 2014 AACU survey, employers stressed the need for "cross-cutting skills" such as written and oral communication skills, teamwork skills, ethical decision-making skills, critical thinking, and the ability to apply knowledge in real-world settings.[7]

College students largely agree with employers on which skills are most important for success, though they disagree sharply on whether they possess these skills. For example, 66 percent of college students say they have good critical-thinking and analytic skills, whereas only 26 percent of employers agree that recent college graduates possess these skills. As the report concludes, "Students are notably more optimistic about their preparedness than employers are about the readiness of recent graduates in these areas."[8]

Studies that have interviewed employers and job experts in depth to investigate job skill deficits have reached remarkably similar conclusions. A 2010 *Wall Street Journal* survey of 479 college recruiters found that, when asked which skills new college graduates need to improve the most, more than half said some combination of critical thinking, problem-solving skills, and the ability to think independently.[9] A Conference Board study found that more than half of high school graduates were deficient in such skills as oral and written communication, critical thinking, and professionalism.[10] The Partnership for 21st Century Skills has stressed the need to develop twenty-first century skills such as the 4 Cs: critical thinking, communication, collaboration, and creativity.[11]

The National Research Council has summed up the job skills situation by calling for a massive increase in "transferable knowledge," which they define as "knowledge that can be transferred or applied in new situations."[12] In a sense, this is just another way of defining critical thinking: the capacity to take existing information, reconfigure it, apply it to a new problem or situation, and draw appropriate inferences. As David Perkins and Gavriel Salomon have noted, transfer of knowledge plays a key role in school and at work. Unfortunately, they point out, "very often transfer does not occur, especially 'far' transfer."[13] In principle, critical thinking can facilitate knowledge transfer, by identifying analogies that help us understand a novel situation.

WHAT EMPLOYERS MEAN

What exactly do employers mean when they say that they value critical-thinking skills? Clearly, they are not referring to communication skills . . . because they almost always mention such skills *in addition to* critical-thinking skills. In fact, communications skills have long been high on employers' list of priorities. Two decades ago, for example, Harry Holzer found that employers expected their employees to read paragraphs, talk with customers, and use computers on a daily basis.[14] In fact, this was true even in jobs that did not require a college education.

When they mention critical-thinking skills, perhaps employers mean problem-solving skills, which are of considerable value in the workplace. According to one recent study, about three-fourths of all workers say they solve problems at work on a daily or weekly basis.[15]

Clearly, employers do value the ability to recognize problems, the ability to anticipate problems, the ability to prioritize problems, the ability to gather evidence to solve problems, the ability to identify possible solutions to problems, and the ability to recognize that many solutions contain the germ of a new problem! Marie Artim, vice president of talent acquisition at Enterprise Rent-a-Car, puts it this way: "Our best employees are problem solvers and are able to weave everything they know together. They can think on their feet."[16]

So perhaps employers use the terms *critical thinking* and *problem solving* interchangeably. It is difficult to know for sure. When the Department of Labor asked employees in different occupations to rate the importance of specific abilities and skills, including critical thinking and complex problem solving, they rated critical thinking, on average, as being more important than complex problem solving.[17]

Let's apply a little critical thinking here. If you look closely at the DOL employee survey, the employees are not distinguishing between critical thinking and problem solving but rather between critical thinking and complex problem solving.[18] Presumably, a question about the importance of problem solving (the broader category) would have elicited more favorable responses than the narrower question about complex problem solving. Also, here is how the DOL defines critical thinking: "using logic and reasoning to identify the strengths and weaknesses of alternative solutions, conclusions, or approaches to problems."[19] So critical thinking, according to this definition, *encompasses* problem solving. In a nutshell, DOL is asking employees to compare critical thinking (broadly defined) to problem solving (narrowly defined). Not exactly a fair comparison!

In some jobs, critical thinking undoubtedly does matter and is not reducible to problem solving and actually resembles the kind of critical thinking that is valued by colleges and universities. Outstanding lawyers parse laws, regulations, and contracts with fiendish precision and an eye for subtle distinctions. Skilled physicians diagnose illnesses with brilliant flashes of insight, as in Dr. Gregory House's startling revelations in the television series of the same name. Scientists test hypotheses, objectively, with meticulous care and with close attention to internal and external validity. This is the kind of critical thinking that an Oxford don or an Ivy League professor would admire.

What goes on at most workplaces when critical thinking is on display? The Department of Labor has a wonderful website—O*NET—that dissects over one thousand jobs (or occupational titles) and specifies the skills and abilities required to succeed. These ratings are based on employer surveys, employee surveys, and judgments by a panel of occupational experts. For a wide range of jobs, from cyber security to contract specialist to auditor to economist to human resource specialist, critical-thinking skills are among those featured most prominently on the website.

Whatever critical thinking is, employers seem to be looking for it even more than before. In a recent analysis of job ads from several sources, consultants at Ernst & Young found that references to critical thinking in job postings doubled between 2009 and 2014.[20]

WHAT EMPLOYERS DO

Behavioral studies that use resume audits to gauge employers' revealed preferences have identified other variables that matter a great deal when employers are trying to decide which job applicants are interesting enough to warrant a call back for a job interview. These variables include race, age, gender, obesity and attractiveness, English-sounding names versus foreign-sounding names, and length of unemployment.[21] Clearly, employers favor individuals with certain demographic characteristics and discriminate against individuals with other demographic characteristics.

A few of these studies have included skills or skill-related attributes as predictor variables, but most have addressed these attributes only in passing if at all. A notable exception is a study that explicitly looked at math skills.[22] That study found that job applicants with higher math skills were more likely to receive a call back than others. Interestingly enough, this varied by type of occupation. For example, math skills clearly mattered a great deal for sales jobs but did not matter at all for customer service jobs. Another exception is Peter Hinrichs's study, which found that a teacher's GPA did not affect the likelihood of a call back from a school district seeking to hire a math teacher but that college selectivity did boost the likelihood for a call back, at least for public schools.[23]

In a study using data from the Department of Labor and from a Princeton employee survey, economists David Autor and Michael Handel have found that "abstract" job tasks (analyzing data, thinking creatively, interpreting information for others) yield a 20 percent wage premium in the marketplace.[24] In contrast, routine and manual job tasks yield a wage penalty of 10 percent and 19 percent, respectively. Thus, the market seems to value nonroutine thinking.

One of the best efforts to understand the changing economics of workplace skills comes, ironically, from two sociologists: Yujia Liu and David Grusky. In a splendid paper, they combine annual data from the Current Population Survey and the Department of Labor's O*NET survey (from multiple years) to generate estimates of rising demand for particular skills *and* rising wages for particular skills.[25] Their database is truly massive, with nearly four million observations. The skills they examine include different types of cognitive, creative, technical, and social skills.

Some of their findings are not terribly surprising. For example, they report increased demand for technical skills (think computers) and creative skills (ranging from artists to novelists to architects). They also find rising payoffs for managerial skills and technical skills. But the greatest payoff in recent years comes from "analytic" skills (see Figure 5-1). As they put it, "The most striking result from our model is that rewards are increasingly going to those who engage in critical thinking, problem solving, and deductive reasoning." In our zeal to understand the "computer revolution," they argue, we have neglected another equally important revolution, which they call the "analytic revolution."[26]

FIGURE 5-1   Wage payoff to cognitive skills over time

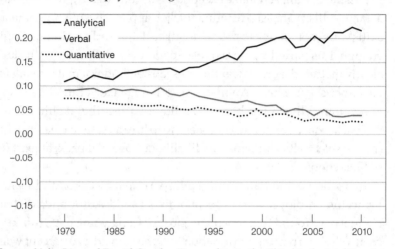

Source: Yulia Liu and David Grusky, "Inequality in the Third Industrial Revolution," *American Journal of Sociology* 118 (2013): 1358.

The implication of these findings is that critical-thinking skills are increasingly valued by employers, as manifested by their behavior, in the form of wage hikes for people employed in the occupations where critical thinking is most important. This evidence reinforces what employers have been saying all along, in survey after survey: they really do value critical thinking!

SCHOOLS

There is much that public schools can do to promote the kinds of skills and sensibilities that employers value.

First, schools must continue to stress basic communications and mathematics skills, but even earlier. Numerous studies show that high-quality pre-K programs enhance these skills in the short run, by improving prereading, prewriting, and premath skills at kindergarten entry.[27] A growing number of studies show that these same high-quality pre-K programs enhance academic achievement and other positive outcomes in the longer run.[28] In fact, several studies show that the long-term benefits of high-quality pre-K programs substantially exceed the short-term costs.[29] The moral of the story, from a neuroscience perspective, is that we need to lay the groundwork for good communications and mathematics skills before age five, while children's neurons and synapses are being formed. This is an excellent investment for us to make.

Second, teachers must do more to promote the kinds of "soft skills" that employers value. They include punctuality, responsibility, politeness, diligence, honesty, perseverance, and teamwork. A growing body of literature confirms the importance of soft skills.[30] And they can be taught in the classroom. For example, the Head Start REDI program has been shown to yield not just cognitive gains but also improvements in emotional understanding, social problem solving, and social behavior.[31] One way to teach perseverance may be by conveying the idea that intelligence is fluid, not fixed. As psychologist Carol Dweck has noted, students who think of intelligence as malleable tend to do better on standardized tests than students who think of intelligence as an inherited trait.[32] Presumably, the reason is that they work harder.

Third, schools should begin the all-important scaffolding process by integrating important critical-thinking and problem-solving skills valued by employers into the curriculum. If K–12 teachers are to take career readiness seriously, they need to be both more abstract and more practical. In terms of abstractions, they need to think abstractly about the kinds of intellectual activities that are expected in many workplaces and scaffold those activities in the classroom. In terms of practicalities, they need to use workplace examples so that work-bound students can make the connection between abstract classroom concepts and concrete workplace demands. In short, career readiness needs to be integrated into the mainstream school curriculum.

Table 5-1 provides a short list of concepts that K–12 teachers might emphasize in their lesson plans and how they might go about making them come alive: priority setting, applied mathematics, inventory management, satisficing, adaptability, and teamwork. Let's consider each of these in turn.

Priority Setting

Many first-hand accounts of the world of work confirm that employees must set priorities on a daily basis. They also have to revisit their

TABLE 5-1   Job skills that teachers should emphasize

SKILL	CAREERS	DEFINITION	PEDAGOGICAL EXAMPLES
Priority Setting	Universal	Ability to sequence tasks and requests	Big projects, job shadowing
Math Problem Solving	Engineering, construction, science	Ability to solve real-world problems with math	Manipulatives as learning tools; connections between math, art, and music
Inventory Management	Retail, manu-facturing, transportation	Ensuring that you have enough goods and supplies when you need them	Running a micro-business, monitoring art supplies
Satisficing	Management	Rational decision making, subject to time and information limits	Socratic seminars, simulations
Adaptability	Universal	Capacity to switch strategies and tactics quickly	Readings on cultural differences, foreign language classes
Teamwork	Universal	Cooperation and collaboration with coworkers and others	Complex science projects, simulations

priorities when new information comes to light. Consider, for example, the work of waitresses and waiters—a job most students can understand. A waitress in a busy restaurant often confronts multiple customers demanding her attention: someone who has just arrived and wishes to place an order; someone who has just begun to eat but who needs something else (a refill of a beverage, ketchup for French fries, etc.); someone who is causing a disturbance or a klutz who spills something; someone who has finished and who wishes to pay, and so on. As one waitress puts it, "You're never doing just a single task."[33] So, who comes first? Does it depend on the size of the dining party? On whether they seem agitated or at ease? On whether they are regulars or newcomers? On whether they are friends of the boss? On whether they are enjoying a romantic tryst? Ask students how to resolve these dilemmas and you will probably have a lively discussion. And the next time they visit a restaurant, they will be more observant. They may also acquire more empathy and respect for waitresses and waiters.

Alternatively, consider a nurse in a critical care unit. All the patients are seriously sick. They all require constant monitoring and attention. But some patient requests are more urgent than others. And some patient needs must be anticipated because the patient cannot verbalize them. Theresa Brown, a registered nurse who works at a Pittsburgh hospital, has written eloquently about these dilemmas in a book about critical care. In Brown's words, "I am pulled in multiple directions every day." A common strategy is to develop a "needs hierarchy" for patients, but often two or more patients rank really high on the needs hierarchy. This requires quick assessments of relative risk. Sometimes a patient's needs are more emotional or even spiritual than physical. For example, one of Brown's patients was diagnosed with cancer. He immediately requested a Bible. How do you compare that to a patient who needs to be fed or to have a dressing changed or to be taken elsewhere for an X-ray? Brown decided that the Bible was a really high priority. She set other tasks aside to find one, and quickly.[34] But was this the right decision? Again, this is a great opportunity for a class discussion. The next time students visit a hospital or think about a sick relative, the wheels will be clicking.

Priority setting is a particular type of executive-functioning skill, which builds upon the capacity for self-regulation that most children have begun to develop well before they enter school. As psychologists at Harvard University have noted, "Self-control enables us to set priorities and resist impulsive actions or responses."[35] The good news is that many students already have a running head start. For students suffering from toxic stress, on the other hand, learning how to set priorities will be harder.

Some teachers may say: "Well, my students set priorities all the time. They have to decide how much to study, how much to play, how much time to spend with friends, and how much time to spend at home. They must decide how much time to devote to long-term and short-term assignments. They must decide how much time to devote to English, math, geography, and Spanish." Fair enough. But will students make the connection between these choices and the world of work? Will students recognize that priority setting is about life and not just about school? As work examples proliferate in the classroom, students can acquire vital transferability skills. They can learn to make connections between something they already know and something they need to figure out. This is one of the greatest gifts a teacher can give to his or her students.

Applied Mathematics

Many companies expect their employees to be able to solve mathematical problems. Large firms hope that their workers can use statistics for process improvement, that they can prepare and understand graphs to highlight associations between inputs and outputs, that they can use mathematics to improve the efficiency of the production process.[36] Although many of these decisions are made by top executives, experts believe that intermediate-level employees are fully capable of contributing to these important discoveries and decisions.

What can schools and teachers do about this? They can help students make connections between mathematical formulas learned in class and practical challenges that arise in work settings.

One of the most important steps teachers can take is to shift instruction away from the familiar "I, We, You" pattern. A teacher who wants to show how to divide a three-digit number by a two-digit number normally proceeds as follows: "First, I'm going to show you how it's done" (I). "Second, let's see if we can divide 242 by 16 together" (We). "Third, now see if you can do this yourself: divide 336 by 12" (You). This time-honored mechanical approach gets students to the right answer but doesn't really strengthen their understanding of what's going on.

An alternative approach, suggested by Magdalene Lampert, who taught for years at the University of Michigan, is the "You, Y'all, We" approach.[37] First, students struggle with a problem on their own, which helps them realize what they don't know. Second, small groups of students share insights and misgivings with one another, which gives stronger students a chance to articulate what they know and weaker students a chance to ask questions in a nonthreatening setting. Third, the class as a whole wrestles with the problem, which gives everyone, including the teacher, a chance to weigh in. Studies of this approach have found that students learn math better this way.[38]

Inventory Management

A young friend of mine, who works as a chef, once described the toughest part of his job as inventory control. He and his boss need to decide, nearly every day, how much meat, vegetables, and fruit to purchase and what kinds. Because food is perishable, and because customers are increasingly sensitive to freshness, my friend and his boss need to get these decisions approximately right. If they don't, their bottom line or their customer satisfaction will suffer. Maybe both. Prosaic though it may be, inventory management is a central feature of many jobs.

A good example for classroom purposes is the Capital Bikeshare program, which serves the Washington, DC, metropolitan area.[39] For a modest fee, customers can pick up a bike at one location and then deposit it at another. For this system to work, there must be bikes to pick up at Station X (the point of origin) and empty racks at Station Y (the destination). Some of this is a function of rush-hour flows; some of it is a function of special events. For example, when the Washington Nationals play a baseball game, especially during the day, you need lots of bikes near Metro stations and lots of empty racks at Nationals Park, on South Capitol Street. You also need someone to develop an algorithm that guides these decisions, and you need someone to do Bayesian updating as new information rolls in. Is this a good system? How might it be improved? What kinds of calculations are needed? This could easily be the basis for a mathematics assignment or a discussion in an algebra class. The next time they go to a ball game, students will find themselves thinking in mathematical terms (and not just about batting averages!).

Some of the easiest examples to conjure up arise from actual school activities. Art classes frequently struggle with inventory management issues. Are there enough gum erasers and paintbrushes? An art teacher and a math teacher could easily team up for an ongoing exchange. Put a few students in charge of monitoring and managing art supplies. They could create histograms that capture declines in particular items over time. Based on pending assignments, they could anticipate when certain items need to be replenished. In the process, they will have acquired a valuable skill. And their classmates may learn something too.

Satisficing

Herbert Simon, who brought uncanny insights to the study of individual and organizational decision making, famously described the essence of decision making as "satisficing."[40] Most of the time, Simon argued, we do not try to optimize by seeking the best of all possible options. Instead, being realistic, we scan the environment to find an option that is reasonably satisfactory. Once we identify that option, we select it and move on. That is what Simon meant by satisficing. In effect, it is a way of coping with uncertainty in an environment characterized by limited time and scarce resources.

Satisficing is the norm in the overwhelming majority of jobs because we lack the time and the cognitive capacity to optimize. When a journalist needs a good source for a story, he or she must satisfice. The speaker of the house is not available, but perhaps another party leader or a former party leader or an aspiring party leader is. When a conference organizer needs a good speaker for a workshop or conference, he or she must satisfice. Stephen Colbert is not available, but maybe John Oliver is. Sanjay Gupta is not available, but maybe a local physician is.

Personnel decisions almost always involve satisficing. When a hardware store needs a new clerk, the owner must satisfice. When a school needs a new teacher, the principal must satisfice. Human resources experts sometimes refer, with tongue in cheek, to the search for a "purple squirrel"—an unrealistic effort to identify a job candidate whose mix of skills and attributes is perfect for the job.[41] If you become obsessed with the quest for a purple squirrel, a lot of very fine brown squirrels will slip through your fingers.

Extreme weather conditions also require satisficing. When snow and ice threaten to slow down a subway system, the manager must satisfice. Should snow removal crews be called to the scene? Should service be suspended or curtailed? The trick is to gather enough good data to make a decision as quickly as possible. When summer heat threatens power failures in a large metropolitan area, the utility executive must satisfice. Should brownouts be imposed? If so, when and for how long? These are not easy decisions, but better data can make them easier.

In each of these cases, the decision maker has to scan the environment for alternatives, with time constraints and cost constraints in mind, until a satisfactory alternative is found. Satisficing means abandoning the quest for perfection, but it does not mean abandoning the quest for excellence. By helping students strike a balance between high goals and realistic expectations, teachers can equip them with a valuable life skill.

Adaptability

Of all the skills that workers need, adaptability is surely one of the most important. Unlike the old days, when blue-collar workers faced routine, repetitive tasks at a steel mill or an auto assembly plant, today's medium-skill jobs require workers to perform nonroutine tasks that cannot be performed by computers.[42] For example, medical paraprofessional jobs, like radiology technician, phlebotomist, and nurse technician, require individuals who can combine routine (technical) and nonroutine (flexible) tasks. During the 1990s both high-skill (high-wage) and low-skill (low-wage) jobs increased, at the expense of medium-skill (medium-wage) jobs.[43] Since then, it appears that traditional medium-skill jobs (such as those in construction and manufacturing) have declined, but that new medium-skill jobs (e.g., health-care technicians, chefs, sales reps) have increased, albeit at a more modest pace.[44] A key challenge is to educate and train workers with these medium skills. Although much of that must be done by employers, K–12 teachers can develop adaptable habits of mind through simulations and through examples.

What does adaptability actually look like at work? One of my favorite examples comes from my piano tuner, Robin Olson, who had to adapt when he was asked to tune the piano for Barack Obama's first presidential inaugural, featuring Yo-Yo Ma on cello, Itzhak Perlman on violin, Anthony McGill on clarinet, and Gabriela Montero on piano. As the day approached, it became clear that the weather would be bitterly cold. Under such circumstances, a string could easily break mid-performance, which would be embarrassing, to say the least.

A week before Inauguration Day, organizers told Olson that he would need to "silence" the piano, because a recording would be used, while the musicians pretended to play on stage. A veteran tuner,

Olson knew that would be relatively easy. He could simply remove the hammers, which produce sound by striking the piano's strings. No hammers, no sound. But the promoters also wanted the keys to bounce up and down in response to Montero's touch, thus mimicking an actual performance.

Unfortunately, without hammers, keys are limp. So what to do? As he thought about the problem, Olson came up with an idea—to attach lead weights to every key. On the back of every key is something called a back-check—a wire and a pad. By attaching a weight to every back-check, Olson could simulate the phenomenon of having a hammer in place. Using masking tape, he was able to connect a weight to every key.

A brilliant solution! Though not a perfect one. After a dress rehearsal, Olson found that the masking tape fell off some of the keys. To rectify this problem, he placed fresh masking tape on the keys just before Montero's performance. To the naked eye, it looked as if she was actually playing the piano in real time.

Okay, you say, but how does a teacher give a student these skills? By definition, the ability to adapt requires you to handle a novel situation. Some people are great at improvising, whereas others are not.

One answer to this question is that, like any other skill, adaptation requires practice. So, my advice to teachers would be: place students outside their comfort zone and see how they react. Give them a different kind of assignment, let them flounder a bit, but let them also figure out a clever solution.

Teamwork

Almost every survey of employers cites the capacity for teamwork as a key criterion for being a good employee. Employers value this skill because so many important organizational decisions are group decisions that require coordination, cooperation, and give and take. Yet much of what students do in the classroom is solitary, and homework is almost always solitary.

Employers understand the importance of people working together to achieve a common goal. This means that it is vital not just to have critical thinkers but to have people who can think critically as a team. This is a different skill set. It means the ability to collaborate, to settle on assigned tasks, to specialize, to work under deadline pressure, to insist on moving forward when something is important, to defer when something is not, to use positive reinforcement and humor to defuse sensitive situations. Recent research confirms the growing importance of this particular soft skill. In a study using National Longitudinal Survey of Youth (NLSY) data and a rough measure of the capacity for teamwork (sociability), Deming found that the greatest growth in jobs and wages since 1980 has occurred in occupations requiring both cognitive skills and sociability.[45]

The ability to cooperate begins early and can have long-lasting effects. A recent study of children in four communities used a simple eight-item measure to capture children's social competence skills. That measure included, for example, children's ability to resolve peer problems, listen to others, share materials, and cooperate, as assessed by their teachers. Researchers found that these skills, which they called "social competence" skills, were excellent predictors of educational gains such as earning a high school diploma and attaining a college degree.[46] They also helped predict having a full-time job at age twenty-five, not committing a crime, and not abusing drugs. In short, the ability to cooperate with others at age five helps predict positive outcomes many years later.

Film classes are a great vehicle for encouraging teamwork because they require collaboration between actors, directors, and producers and because they can be lots of fun. Every summer the Education Theatre Company of Arlington, Virginia, holds a "Camp Comedy" that brings together school-aged children for many funny activities, including the production of a dozen or more short videos. In one of these videos, "Receptacles of Doom," folding chairs battled valiantly against homicidal waste baskets, in a titanic struggle enhanced by strong background music ("The Sorcerer's Apprentice") and wry commentary from the authors.[47] Together, the young crew demonstrated creativity, teamwork, and an impish sense of humor.

If teamwork is to be educational, of course, the teacher must structure, monitor, and evaluate teams with certain core principles in mind. It is not enough to split a class into teams and simply hope for the best. Also, if teamwork is to promote critical thinking, the project itself should be one that encourages students to seek relevant evidence with an open mind and to reflect not just on the assignment but also on the process. In appraising teams, teachers might consider what business scholars have learned about good and bad teams. For example, teams whose members talk and listen in equal measure perform better than other teams.[48] To put it differently, a team dominated by one individual is less likely to perform well. A savvy teacher will handle these interpersonal dynamics delicately and deftly. But it is important to draw lessons for students that will enhance their performance as team members in the future.

PUTTING IT ALL TOGETHER

Almost any course can be adapted to highlight some of these extremely practical skills that real employees need in the workplace. Anthony Cherry, who taught US history at George Washington Carver Middle School in Tulsa before accepting a new job at Booker T. Washington High School, came up with a brilliant technique for teaching work-related skills: he required his eighth-grade students to form mini-corporations, which sell history-related products to Cherry himself (they receive funny money that translates into letter grades). When I visited Cherry's class, I saw examples of priority setting, applied math, and teamwork (see "Are You Ready to Run Your Own Company?," pp. 122–123)

One of the striking features of Cherry's pedagogical choices is that he is not really sacrificing college readiness for career readiness. Corporate role playing enhances students' excitement about US history by getting them to focus, interact, and engage in the subject matter. At the same time, the content of US history makes the corporate exercise infinitely more substantive, more meaningful, and more rewarding. This is a great way to avoid trade-offs between advanced education and employability as classroom goals.

HIGH SCHOOL GUIDANCE COUNSELORS

High school guidance counselors seldom receive significant attention in discussions of career readiness, but they are part of the problem and could be part of the solution. High school guidance counselors

FIGURE 5-2   Time devoted by high school guidance counselors to career advising

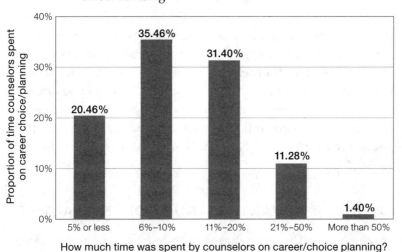

Proportion of time counselors spent on career choice/planning

- 35.46%
- 31.40%
- 20.46%
- 11.28%
- 1.40%

5% or less   6%–10%   11%–20%   21%–50%   More than 50%

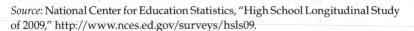

How much time was spent by counselors on career/choice planning?

Source: National Center for Education Statistics, "High School Longitudinal Study of 2009," http://www.nces.ed.gov/surveys/hsls09.

are expected to wear many hats—college advisor, career counselor, and even social worker. Traditionally, high school guidance counselors have devoted much more time to college advising than to career counseling. They also devote substantial time to relatively routine short-term decisions, like course scheduling.

The High School Longitudinal Study of 2009 includes detailed statistics on how high school guidance counselors spend their time. As Figure 5-2 indicates, 20 percent of counselors devote 5 percent or less of their time to career choice and planning, while 35 percent of counselors devote 6–10 percent of their time to career choice and planning. In short, most high school guidance counselors devote less than 10 percent of their time to career counseling. By way of comparison, 38 percent of high school guidance counselors devote 21–50 percent of their time to college readiness, selection, and application, whereas only 11 percent of counselors devote that much time to career choice and planning.[49]

Part of the problem is that counselors spend a good deal of their time on matters not explicitly related to either college advising or career counseling. As Patricia McDonough puts it: "We have ample evidence that in day-to-day practice, the overwhelming amount of effort of counselors revolves around the tasks of scheduling, testing, and discipline . . . with additional needs for counseling related to dropout, drugs, pregnancy, and suicide prevention, as well as sexuality and personal crisis counseling, yard duty, substitute teaching, etc." McDonough adds that "different constituencies would describe the primary job description (of the high school guidance counselor) as administrative, while others would say academic, and yet others would say therapeutic." Note that career advising is not even on the list.[50]

CAREER-RELEVANT INSTRUCTION IN PRACTICE

Although most US classrooms do not do much to promote career-relevant instruction, this approach has been tried in some jurisdictions. One of the more promising programs to date is CareerStart, which links the core academic curriculum to career information through the use of specific career examples. In one North Carolina school district, seven middle schools were randomly assigned to utilize this approach, while seven other middle schools were randomly assigned to retain the status quo. In the treatment schools, for all three grades (6, 7, and 8), teachers in four subject areas (English language arts, math, science, and social studies) received instructional packets with career examples, received professional development in how to teach this, and were told to do so. The instructional packets were developed with significant input from the school district's teachers themselves.

The results of this experiment were encouraging. At the end of seventh grade, and at the end of eighth grade, there were statistically significant differences between treatment group and control group children in math (though not reading). Overall, treatment group students experienced a sustained improvement of 33 percent over the average rate of growth in math test scores, for an effect size of .24.[51] This outcome is especially impressive because there was some contamination of the control group (e.g., some teachers and some students migrated from the treatment group to the control group while the study was underway). In other research, the authors shed light on what was going on: student engagement was higher in treatment group class-rooms (schools), which supports the idea that students learn better when what they are learning seems relevant to work or to life.[52]

Much more needs to be learned about this promising approach. Why did the program work for math but not for reading? Why did results appear at the end of seventh grade but not earlier? Can it work for other subjects also? Was the program's success due in part to the fact that the school district's own teachers helped to develop the instructional packets? Would the program work equally well if the packets were exported to another school district? How much professional development and school district support are needed for the program to make a difference? Also, what are the longer-term consequences of this early exposure to career-relevant instruction? Do students exposed to these occupational examples in middle school pursue more vocational coursework in high school and beyond? Do they make better choices when choosing a career? Do they earn more as adults?

WORK

In some ways, the best way to prepare for work is through work itself. This is one of the premises behind the Career Academies, small learning communities nested within high schools. They combine rigorous academic instruction on traditional subjects with vocational courses linked to a distinctive career theme, such as law, business, and digital media. They foster partnerships with employers and with postsecondary education institutions.[53] For example, the Ballard High School Academy of Finance, in Seattle, Washington, trains students for careers in finance and banking.[54] In Volusia County, Florida, Career Academies specializing in engineering partner with the Ford Motor Company. There are between six and seven thousand career academies in the United States, and the number seems to be growing.[55]

Career Academies have been quite successful in enhancing adult earnings.[56] On average, Career Academy graduates have earned $16,000 more than their peers over an eight-year period following their graduation, or 11 percent more than their peers. The earnings gain was even more substantial for young men of color—$30,000.

Enrollment in a Career Academy had no effect, positive or negative, on college enrollment rates. Thus, enrollment in a vocational education program does not preclude higher education as an option.

Anecdotally, students describe Career Academies in glowing terms and cite lots of valuable experiences: job shadowing opportunities, field trips, an emphasis on life skills, and teachers who really care.[57] More systematically, studies have found that students in Career Academies had "substantially more exposure to career development activities, including work experiences connected with school."[58] And a recent PhD dissertation found that Career Academy students generated more and better ideas when handling both academic and practical tasks.[59]

What is the magic that enables Career Academies to produce these results? David Stern believes it is the integration of instruction in traditional subjects with more practical education by members of a coordinated team; that is, they plan their lessons in advance with an eye toward making connections and helping students perceive connections.[60] Internships are also valuable and important. And school-based enterprises mimic the real world of corporations and nonprofit organizations—real customers, real clients, real consequences—although they do not use real money!

Not all Career Academies are stellar. According to James Kemple, who has studied these programs in depth, the workplace experience component is arguably the most important but also "the hardest part to replicate."[61] Ensuring fidelity to the Career Academies model is a growing challenge as these programs proliferate. Academies also differ in their ability to integrate students from different races and social classes. For example, at one northern California Career Academy, the Medical Academy was more successful in achieving such integration than the Graphics Academy.[62]

Other programs have sought to revive and reinvent vocational education. In California, the Linked Learning Initiative, a public-private partnership, supports "linked learning" initiatives in sixty-three school districts. In each instance, the school district establishes pathways between high school and one of California's fifteen major industries. In Long Beach, for example, one school focuses on architecture, construction, and engineering; another focuses on media and communications; and three others focus on other subjects. The goal is to combine rigorous academics with career-based classroom learning, workplace learning, and personalized support.[63]

Recent evaluations have reached positive conclusions about the Linked Learning initiative. At the end of five years, evaluators found that Linked Learning participants earned more credits, were more likely to be on track to complete coursework required for a four-year public college, and were more likely to stay in the school district instead of transferring or dropping out of high school. Student survey results were highly encouraging. For example, Linked Learning students were 10 percent more likely than other students to see connections between class and the real world, 15 percent more likely to have had a teacher explain how to apply material to the real world, and 20 percent more likely to have developed skills to collaborate in a group.[64]

In New York City, P-Tech has drawn favorable attention from President Obama and many others. Established in 2011, in Brooklyn, P-Tech offers students a technology-rich curriculum that leads to a high school diploma in four years and an associate degree two years later. Unlike most New York public schools, P-Tech is a partnership between the New York City Public Schools, IBM, the City University of New York, and the New York City College of Technology. In addition to traditional academic coursework, it offers business-centered courses in "workplace learning," which teach students vital networking, critical-thinking, and presentation skills.[65] Each student is paired with an IBM employee, who mentors that student over six years. IBM does not promise every P-Tech graduate a job, but it does promise to give P-Tech alumni a hiring preference. P-Tech's first class will graduate in 2017. At that time, we may have a better idea of whether the P-Tech formula actually works. Meanwhile, approximately forty schools have sprouted up throughout the United States, based on the P-Tech model.

Also in New York City, ninety-three high schools known as small schools of choice (SSCs) have become part of the education landscape available to disadvantaged students, thanks to former Mayor Michael Bloomberg and his appointee as school chancellor, Joel Klein. These schools, which have forged partnerships to varying degrees with community-based organizations and for-profit firms, boast higher high school graduation rates, improved English test scores on the state Regents Exam, and higher college enrollment rates.[66] What accounts for their success? The common denominator at these schools is a commitment to "rigor, relevance, and relationships," as specified in the original charter that created them. Rigor hints at critical thinking, relevance implies a career focus, and relationships suggest strong connections between students and their teachers. But how faithful are individual schools to these aspirational goals?

Urban Assembly Schools, a subset of the SSCs, seem to take rigor, relevance, and relationships seriously. For example, one of these schools, the Brooklyn-based School for Law and Justice, has partnerships with a local law firm and with government agencies that are part of the criminal justice system.[67] At Maker Academy, another Urban Assembly School, where students make digital and physical objects, there are partnerships with Intel, the Parsons School of Design, Control Group, and other companies.[68] It will be interesting to see whether students who graduate from the Urban Assembly Schools are more successful in landing good jobs and embarking on productive careers than those who do not. At the moment, that is an open question.

Other less comprehensive strategies may also be worthwhile. For example, Envision Education, which consists of three charter schools in Oakland, California, requires its high school students to participate in workplace learning activities one day a week for nine weeks.[69] Students have to find their own internships, though they do receive some help if needed. One requirement is unalterable: the student has to ask for the internship himself or herself. This requirement is considered to be good preparation for the real world. And indeed it is.

In Pittsburgh, City Charter High has gone even further by requiring every student to complete a thirteen-week internship before graduating *and* by specifying that the internship must be a daily, rather than a weekly, activity. When I visited City Charter High, I read many absorbing reports by students reflecting on the joys and frustrations of their internships. In addition to teaching students vital soft skills, City Charter High's internship requirement gets them to think critically about a presumptive career (see "Internships for All," pp. 124–126).

VOCATIONAL EDUCATION IN EUROPE

Of course, if we really want to promote vocational education—and critical thinking in the context of vocational education—we ought to take a closer look at some splendid examples in Europe. Unlike the United States, Europe has long placed a strong emphasis on vocational education, with explicit career-focused education options available to students in many European countries. In Germany, students who prefer an academic track and students who prefer to enter the work-force directly diverge at age ten. The former proceed to a Gymnasium, where they concentrate on traditional academic subjects and prepare for college, while the latter attend a Realschule, where they begin to learn a trade. More than half of all German students choose the vocational track.[70] In Switzerland, vocational education is even more widespread: an estimated 70 percent of all Swiss youths choose the vocational track, at age sixteen.[71]

The key to the European model is a strong apprenticeship system, which encompasses but also extends well beyond the construction and manufacturing trades. In Germany, students can specialize in tax accounting, hotel management, costume design, law enforcement, and air traffic control, among other occupations.[72] In Switzerland, students can specialize in banking, nursing, factory work, and many other occupations.[73] The costs of the apprenticeships are split between workers, who accept lower wages, and employers, who benefit from a large pool of highly trained workers who are available to work after a two- to four-year apprenticeship. While they work as apprentices, students usually earn about one-third of the wages of a trained, salaried worker.[74] But when their apprenticeship ends, they are paid a regular wage.

Cross-national comparisons suggest that countries that invest in vocational education enjoy substantial economic benefits. One comprehensive study found a strong relationship between the availability of career-tech in secondary school and secondary school attendance and graduation rates.[75] Also, a strong emphasis on vocational education does not seem to undermine academic achievement, as measured by PISA test scores. The reason may be that students continue to take academic courses while they work as apprentices. Also, students have the option of switching from a vocational track to a purely academic track if their interests shift over time.[76]

Although the apprenticeship model originated in Europe, signs indicate that it is beginning to spread to the United States. In Georgia, 143 out of 195 school systems are currently participating in an apprenticeship program serving nearly seven thousand students. Juniors and seniors who participate are paid for their work, and they also receive a postsecondary certificate or degree. According to one informal assessment, Georgia's apprentices have higher rates of graduation from high school than other comparable youth. In Wisconsin, two thousand five hundred students participate in the state apprenticeship program. Juniors and seniors who participate are paid for their work, and some also receive technical college academic credits. Apprenticeship areas include food and natural resources, architecture and construction, finance, health sciences, tourism, information technology, distribution and logistics, and manufacturing.[77]

CONCLUSION

A college degree is a beguiling goal for many young people, given the strong correlation between a bachelor's degree and economic success. [78] But only two-thirds of our high school graduates go on to college, and a fourth of all young people never even complete a high school degree. Also, one-third of those enrolled in a four-year college fail to complete a bachelor's degree within six years. As a result, only one-third of young people get a bachelor's degree.[79] What are we to do about the other two-thirds? And what are we to do about disadvantaged students, whose statistics are even grimmer?

Consider also the plight of those fortunate students who actually complete a bachelor's degree. A recent New York Federal Reserve report found that 44 percent of young BA holders under twenty-five are underemployed.[80] In short, even college graduates face uncertainties and disappointments when they apply for work.

If our young people, and especially disadvantaged youth, are to become more employable, we need to do a much better job of teaching them job-relevant skills in the classroom. Critical-thinking skills can be a great bridge between K–12 education and the labor market because they are valued in both sectors and because some of them (priority setting, adaptability, problem solving) are, in principle, transferable to more than one setting. On the other hand, they also manifest themselves in different ways, depending on whether the teacher's intent is college readiness or career readiness.

There are three basic strategies for enhancing career readiness. The first, which has already been tried with some success in the United States, is career and technical education through a "school within a school" that simultaneously promotes vocational education and academic instruction with a vocational flavor or emphasis. Career Academies and Linked Learning exemplify this approach, which has been shown to produce substantial improvements in employment and earnings. Yet these successful approaches have thus far been available only to a relatively small slice of American youth. The challenge here is to expand these valuable programs, to make them more widely available, and also to remove any social stigmas associated with attending such programs.

The second strategy, which has been tried in Europe, is an apprenticeship system that works through public-private partnerships between particular employers and particular schools. Apprenticeships help ensure a match between jobs and job seekers by training students to work not just within a given industry but literally for a specific firm. According to scholars who have studied these programs in depth, apprenticeships help account for the economic success of Germany, Switzerland, and other countries that have embraced this strategy wholeheartedly.[81] There are some mildly encouraging signs of growing interest in apprenticeships in the United States. In South Carolina, for example, Apprenticeship Carolina has signed up seven hundred companies and served over eleven thousand apprentices since it started in 2007.[82] Tax credits have helped, as has the presence in South Carolina of some big German manufacturing firms, such as BMW and Bosch. But South Carolina remains an isolated example. Much more needs to be done if we are to integrate the European apprenticeship model into the US system of education.

A third strategy, in some ways more radical than the first two, would be to make vocational education part of the mission and tool kit of every K–12 teacher in the United States. The truth is that *all* students need job-relevant skills, and *most* students are not getting such skills in school today. The primary and often exclusive goal of K–12 teachers and high school guidance counselors continues to be college readiness. Career readiness gets short shrift, if indeed it gets any shrift at all. What is required is not a wholesale transformation of the curriculum from academic instruction to vocational education but a more subtle shift in emphasis to include job-relevant skills, job-relevant situations, and job-relevant examples across schools, across grades, and across subjects. Such a shift could give *all* students the critical-thinking skills they need to succeed at work.

If more attention to career readiness is needed to improve our economy, more attention to civic readiness is needed to improve our polity, which, sadly, is in a state of disrepair. Although the need to produce better citizens was one of the original motivations for our system of publicly funded K–12 education in the United States, the goal of civic readiness has receded into the background. This is unfortunate because considerable evidence suggests that we are not well equipped to deliberate and reason together in a quest for common ground. It is also unfortunate because we are becoming increasingly polarized, along party lines and along ideological lines. As this occurs, deliberative democracy becomes an even more elusive goal.

ARE YOU READY TO RUN YOUR OWN COMPANY?

Anthony Cherry, who teaches US history to eighth graders at George Washington Carver Middle School in Tulsa, sits in front of the class with an American flag draped behind him. His twenty-four students have organized themselves into six independent corporations, each of which hopes to sell $3,000 worth of goods and services to Cherry before the fall semester ends in December 2015. Cherry calls this project "Society in Action."

According to the ground rules, each corporation employs a manager, a writing coordinator, a research specialist, and a visual design coordinator. Within the class, students perform other functions: IRS, contract management, time and materials management, media and technology management, recycling management, bursar, and class greeters, among others.

There are two catches. First, each product must be related to US history and specifically the era the class is studying (from the French and Indian War to Reconstruction). So, for example, a company can put on a musical performance, say a rap video, but the lyrics must concern a legitimate historical issue, or the song must have been popular in colonial America. To cite another example, one team of students baked cupcakes representing the thirteen original colonies and then configured them so that they mimicked Ben Franklin's Join or Die cartoon of a dismembered snake. Second, Cherry presides over an improvised market. In consultation with the students, he determines prices for everything sold. When too many goods of a certain sort are produced, he can declare a moratorium. "No more American flags, please!" he announces. "The market has been flooded with American flags!"

In a nutshell, what transpires in Cherry's classroom is parallel learning. As in a conventional history class, students learn about conflicts between colonialists and Tories, the origins of the Bill of Rights, and the mixed legacy of Thomas Jefferson with respect to human equality. But students also acquire valuable skills that will help them be good employees. They learn how to specialize (each company has a research coordinator, a writing coordinator, a visual design specialist, and a manager). They learn how to negotiate (the price of any good or service is negotiated and not fixed). And they learn how to function as members of a team. "It shows them how to work with people who are flaky, people who are type A, people who don't show up on time," Cherry explains. "The group is still responsible for producing products on deadline." Cherry wants to be sure that his mission is not misunderstood. "I'm not trying to be a corporate tool, but I'm trying to get them ready for occupational realities," he explains. "I try to promote problem solving."

Students appreciate the freedom Cherry gives them to choose their own products and services to sell. "He gives us free rein," one student says, "so long as it concerns the Constitution." "I love this class!" another student says. "It's very great! Other teachers give you a paper assignment. Here you get involved." Students say they also appreciate Cherry's high expectations. "We learned how to research better," one student explains. "He expects a lot of us when we turn our essay in."

INTERNSHIPS FOR ALL

The best preparation for work is work itself. At City High Charter School in Pittsburgh, every student must complete a trimester-long internship with an employer to receive a high school degree. Internship hours for one trimester (thirteen weeks) are Monday through Friday from 1:30 p.m. to 4 p.m. The school covers transportation costs if needed. The student receives a grade, based on attendance, feedback from the employer, and the student's own reflections in a daily log. Unless the student receives a grade of C or better, he or she does not graduate, though the student may subsequently earn a diploma by completing a new internship.

Support systems help ensure that this system works. At City High, the internship managers, Patti Kretschman and Keiha Peck, offer students internship opportunities that are roughly aligned with their career goals, their skills, and their temperament. Kretschman reports that she tries to strike a balance between the student's unvarnished goals and the realities of the job market or the student's own skill set: "We ask, 'What is your dream and why?' And we reverse engineer it." At the same time, Kretschman and Peck encourage their students to be realistic.

At the workplace, a mentor is designated. A City High internship manager visits the site to make sure that it is safe and appropriate. City High also requires that the mentor visit the school for an in-depth conversation before the internship begins. This visit helps ensure that everyone is on the same page. Considerable emphasis is placed on the kinds of soft skills that employers value, such as professionalism, responsibility, and punctuality. These skills are emphasized in the course work that leads up to the actual internship.

All this costs money, of course, and the cost of the transition office that runs the internship program is in the neighborhood of $400,000 a year. Years ago, the school's founders decided to forgo sports altogether and to offer relatively modest electives in the arts to pay for the transition office and a wellness office. As Principal Ron Sofo puts it, "Given the nature of the clients we're serving and the mission of our school (college and career readiness), we thought it was an investment worth making."

Students have learned a great deal from these internships—the etiquette of workplaces, the critical need for people skills, the challenges of coping with competing demands and competing points of view, and whether they are cut out for a particular career. Student reflections, submitted when the internship ends, attest to the importance of inventory management, adaptability, and teamwork. For example, students who interned at a restaurant and a small business learned how essential it was to have the right commodities available for customers when they want them. A student who interned for a construction claims and liability firm learned how to plan a schedule and then alter it in view of changing circumstances. A student who interned at a genetics lab learned how to conduct an experiment and then to redo it in light of new evidence. A student who interned for an educational team at the Carnegie Science Center learned to ask questions and get help from various staff members: "I think that is very important because working as a team is a huge part of being a teacher." A student who interned for a law firm also discovered the value of teamwork: "Nothing in the office was done alone . . . everyone helped each other get things done." This included proofreading each other's papers, helping meet deadlines, and sharing ideas or information.

A student who interned for a surgical procedure unit (SPU) at a local hospital learned the vital importance of setting priorities. "When you walk into a surgical center of any kind there is bound to be a million very important things happening all at the same time, so things can get pretty hectic." In her first week at the hospital, the student decided to make wheelchairs a priority. "Wheelchairs as it turns out are an essential part of the surgical process. Patients coming out of most surgeries are, by hospital regulation, not allowed to leave on foot, and most of the time simply cannot do so. The surgical process can be held up if even one wheelchair is missing . . . From that starting week it was clear to me that in order for things to run smoothly in the SPU wheelchairs had to be around all the time. So I made it my task to always keep a constant supply of wheelchairs. The nurses could not have been happier with that, as they could now spend their time treating patients and not running around the hospital searching for them." What a marvelous contribution and what a marvelous lesson for the future!

A recurring theme in student commentaries on their internship experiences was the value of customer service. A student who interned for a hair styling salon put it this way: "Being at the salon has taught me a lot of different things I didn't think about . . . Most importantly it has taught me how to keep my clients happy and put them first." A student who interned for a small business learned to familiarize herself with all products and their location: "The reason behind that is that customers will often time[s] ask for help finding either a specific item or they would request information on what exactly an item is." This same student picked up a few tips on how best to deal with "eccentric" customers.

Some students who began their internship with a specific career goal in mind came away even more excited and enthusiastic about that career. A student who interned at a genetics lab became even more committed to a career in medicine or women's health, and a student who hoped to become a lawyer deepened that resolve by interning for a law firm. Equally important, though, were epiphanies that led students to rethink their initial career choice. A student who saw herself as a future teacher and who interned at an elementary school reached a surprising conclusion: "I learned that I do not have the patience to work with young kids!" Other students fine-tuned their career goals, based on their internship experience. For example, a student who interned for a fashion design firm decided that she liked the design parts of the job but didn't like the technology parts. In each of these cases, the students learned something extremely valuable about the fit between their own interests and a specific career.

Learning to Deliberate: Civic Readiness

FOR A DEMOCRACY to function well, its citizens must be capable of reasoned argumentation, which benefits from a strong dose of critical thinking. In this chapter, I show how we fall far short of this ideal in our political knowledge, in the way we acquire information from the news media, and in the way we discuss politics and public policy with one another. I distinguish between two versions of democracy—participatory and deliberative—and show how critical thinking can promote the latter. Social studies courses have a vital role to play in using critical thinking to improve our civic discourse, but so too do other courses and assignments. I cite examples of programs and laws that may help move us toward a universe where citizens challenge others with good evidence and challenge themselves with probing questions that invite reconsideration.

THE CASE FOR GOOD CITIZENSHIP

We live in an age of partisanship, of polarization, of acrimony, of people talking past one another. Persuasion, negotiation, and compromise have taken a back seat. Our schools did not create this situation, but they can help restore a civic dialogue rooted in dispassionate reflection, rigorous analysis, and mutual respect. In a democracy, the role that schools play in developing good citizens is enormously important. As Horace Mann put it, "The qualification of voters is as important as the qualification of governors, and even comes first, in the natural order."[1] In fact, many state constitutions explicitly identify the need for good citizenship in a republic as a key rationale for requiring a system of free public education.[2] The Massachusetts Constitution, for example, begins its justification for a free public education by noting that "wisdom, and knowledge, as well as nature, diffused generally among the body of the people" are "necessary for the preservation of their rights and liberties." Similarly, the California Constitution says: "A general diffusion of knowledge and intelligence being essential to the preservation of the rights and of liberties of the people, the Legislature shall encourage by all suitable means the promotion of intellectual, scientific, moral, and agricultural improvements." The Constitution goes on to require the Legislature to provide for "a system of common schools."[3]

Ideally, we want citizens who know enough about politics and government that they can participate intelligently in the political process, including elections. But we need much more than that: citizens who can analyze arguments by competing politicians and judge their merits objectively, citizens who can distinguish between solid and flimsy evidence, citizens who can distinguish between truth and falsehood, and citizens who can make electoral choices consistent with some coherent vision of good public policy.

A 2003 Carnegie Corporation report summarized what good citizenship means.[4] Competent and responsible citizens, they stated:

a) Are informed and thoughtful; have a grasp and an appreciation of history and the fundamental processes of American democracy; have an understanding and awareness of public and community issues; and have the ability to obtain information, think critically, and enter into dialogue among others with different perspectives.

b) Participate in their communities through membership in or contributions to organizations working to address an array of cultural, social, political, and religious interests and beliefs.

c) Act politically by having the skills, knowledge, and commitment needed to accomplish public purposes, such as group problem solving, public speaking, petitioning and protesting, and voting.

 d) Have moral and civic virtues such as concern for the rights and welfare of others, social responsibility, tolerance and respect, and belief in the capacity to make a difference.

Building on the Carnegie Corporation report, David Campbell has argued that the elements of good citizenship include political knowledge, volunteerism, civic skills, and tolerance.[5] For our purposes, civic skills and tolerance are particularly important because they encompass reasoned argumentation (a manifestation of critical-thinking skills) and open-mindedness (a trait that promotes critical thinking).

CIVIC SKILLS AND CIVIC ENGAGEMENT

Before we attempt to gauge the extent of our civic skills, it is important to distinguish between civic skills and civic engagement. Sidney Verba and colleagues define civic skills as "the communications and organizational abilities that allow citizens to use time and money effectively in political life."[6] Critical thinking is one of the most important civic skills. Civic engagement, in contrast, refers to the extent to which citizens actually participate in politics, by voting, by volunteering for a worthy cause, by contributing time or money to a political campaign, or by speaking out on public issues. Critical thinking facilitates civic engagement and makes it less of a blunt instrument for expressing political opinions but is not literally a prerequisite for it.

A society characterized by high levels of civic skills can be called a "deliberative democracy."[7] In such a society, citizens possess critical-thinking skills that enable them to formulate good arguments and recognize bad arguments. They also possess communications skills that enable them to communicate their ideas; to challenge ideas advanced by others; and to persuade others by appeal to reason, shared values, and evidence.

A society characterized by high levels of civic engagement can be called a "participatory democracy."[8] In such a society, citizens care enough to vote, to affiliate with an advocacy group or a service organization, and to protest when dissatisfied with the status quo.

By most measures, the United States falls well short of being a full-fledged participatory democracy. This is especially evident when it comes to voting. Many Americans participate in politics minimally, if at all. Only 59 percent of the electorate voted in 2012, and only 42 percent voted in the 2010 mid-term elections.[9] The situation deteriorated even more dramatically in the 2014 mid-term elections, when only 36 percent of the electorate voted.[10] In 2016, only 60 percent of the electorate turned out to vote.[11] When we move beyond voting to other forms of participation (campaign contributions, volunteer work for candidates for office, participation in a rally or demonstration), those numbers are even less impressive.[12] The statistics for youth are especially depressing. Young people turn out to vote at lower rates than other citizens. In 2014, only 20 percent of voters aged eighteen to twenty-nine voted—the lowest turnout recorded in a federal election. Even in 2008, when youth turnout surged to near-record highs, young people turned out to vote far less frequently than other citizens.[13]

It is more difficult to assess whether the United States meets the standards of an authentic deliberative democracy. How do citizens make up their minds? Do they weigh evidence carefully? Do they seek out information and opinions that might challenge their beliefs and predispositions? Do they alter their views in response to new information?

Political scientists disagree on how to answer these questions. But a troublesome set of experiments by Charles Taber and Milton Lodge suggests that the average voter is a "motivated reasoner" whose biases can be overpowering.[14] When presented with information that challenges their prior convictions, most citizens find a way to dismiss inconvenient truths. Instead, they rationalize continued support for their preexisting views and opinions, which leads Lodge and Taber to call them "rationalizing voters." As Lodge and Taber put it: "Citizens are often partisan in their political information processing, motivated more by their desire to maintain prior beliefs and feelings than by their desire to make 'accurate' or otherwise optimal decisions."[15] The authors do not assert that citizens are consciously partisan or that accuracy goals are unimportant. Rather, they contend that a "competitive tension" between the drive for accuracy and the drive to promote established convictions characterizes human reasoning, with the latter triumphing most of the time.

Even though motivated reasoners are "critical" of certain arguments (those with which they disagree) as they strive to reach a conclusion, this is a far cry from critical thinking. Ideally, citizens should objectively weigh the evidence, give arguments and counterarguments their due, and accept the idea that they might be mistaken. Instead of trying to confirm their biases, they should subject diverse viewpoints, including their own, to withering scrutiny. Yet well-crafted experiments, by Lodge and Taber and others, suggest that that is not how the average American processes political information.[16]

A related problem, which is even easier to document, is that the average American does not possess a lot of accurate political information.

THE KNOWLEDGE GAP

As Michael Delli Carpini and Scott Keeter showed some years ago, the American public's knowledge of politics and public policy is shallow and partial. For example, only 35 percent of the public could correctly identify a right guaranteed by the First Amendment to the Constitution, only 20 percent could identify two, and only 9 percent could identify three. Conversely, many Americans see more rights in the Constitution than actually exist: 29 percent believe the Constitution guarantees a job, 42 percent believe the Constitution guarantees health care, and 75 percent believe the Constitution guarantees a high school education. More people know who said "What's up, Doc?" "Hi-yo, Silver," or "Come up and see me sometime!" than "Give me liberty or give me death!"[17] Nor has this political knowledge deficit improved over time, despite increases in the average educational attainment of the electorate over the past fifty years or so. In fact, the correlation between age and knowledge has grown steadily since 1948, attesting to a growing political knowledge gap between young and old.[18] The public was no more knowledgeable about politics in 2007 than they were in 1989, and they were no more knowledgeable in 1989 than they were in the 1940s and the 1950s.[19] A recent survey by the Annenberg School is equally depressing: only a third of respondents could name all three branches of government, and another third of respondents could not name a single one![20]

This lack of knowledge is worrisome because higher levels of information are highly correlated with more sophisticated forms of political reasoning.[21] Political knowledge is a good predictor of political tolerance, after controlling for education and other variables. More knowledgeable individuals have more stable and more internally consistent opinions. More knowledgeable individuals are also less susceptible to political propaganda and more receptive to relevant new information. Political knowledge is a necessary condition for civic readiness. It transforms critical thinking into a wonderful, purposive tool, when applied in a civic space.

REASONING AND ARGUMENTATION

A deliberative democracy requires citizens who possess political information, who can synthesize and assess that information, and who can judge public officials and public policies with that information in mind. Critical thinking makes all of this more likely. Critical thinkers are better able to acquire information that is credible and relevant. Critical thinkers are better able to distinguish between good and bad arguments. Critical thinkers are better able to discover cause-and-effect relationships. Critical thinkers are better able to formulate policy arguments that are credible, persuasive, and sustainable.

Acquiring political knowledge does not require critical thinking, though critical thinking might certainly be useful in determining which pieces of political information are worth knowing. Critical thinking does become indispensable when one shifts attention to the formation and refinement of policy arguments. Critical thinking is essential if policy arguments are to be credible, persuasive, and sustainable.

It would be nice to be able to report that the US Congress provides a good template for critical thinking in the context of a deliberative debate. Certainly, our Founding Fathers envisioned something along those lines.[22] In practice, though, the quality of congressional debate on important issues of the day is often mediocre. When Gary Mucciaroni and Paul Quirk investigated this issue, they found many logical lapses in Congressional rhetoric on the floor of the House and the Senate (especially the House). A recurring weakness was that members of Congress seldom directly rebutted an argument with a bona fide counterargument. Instead, they talked past one another. Overall, the two scholars found the quality of Congressional debate to be "somewhat disappointing."[23]

A better template for critical thinking and reasoned argumentation in a public forum can be found in some weekend-long exercises arranged by James Fishkin and his associates, aimed at creating conditions for citizens to reflect on and discuss public issues after being exposed to competing points of view in a setting where the explicit goal is to have a reasonable, open discussion of public issues. Fishkin and Luskin call this process "deliberative polling." In reviewing the evidence from deliberative polling exercises, Fishkin and Luskin note that participants gain information, that opinions often change, that vote intentions often change, and that changes in opinions and votes are related positively to information gains.[24] It sounds very much as if critical thinking has taken place.

Few public debates in the real world mimic the ideal conditions Fishkin and Luskin have created in their deliberative polling experiments. But they are useful reminders that ordinary citizens are capable of learning about politics, capable of disagreeing respectfully with one another, and capable of changing their minds on important issues of the day. Whether they live up to these ideals will depend on their knowledgeability, their education, their interests, their inclinations, and their experiences. It will also depend on their tolerance. Without tolerance and open-mindedness, reasoning and argumentation are more likely to resemble Lodge and Taber's motivated reasoning than Fishkin and Luskin's deliberative democracy.

TOLERANCE

According to David Campbell, tolerance is the most controversial of the elements of good citizenship (political knowledge, volunteerism, civic skills, and tolerance). Campbell recalls a debate with a former Republican member of Congress, who publicly questioned the wisdom of teaching tolerance in the classroom. He preferred knowledge of the Constitution as the cornerstone of the civics curriculum.[25] Of course, as Campbell pointed out, the First Amendment to the Constitution emphasizes the virtue of tolerance! Still, this is sometimes a hard sell.

The good news about tolerance is that the United States has more of it than many other countries. A recent survey of twenty-four countries in the Western hemisphere found that the United States ranked fifteenth for political system support but first in political tolerance. This ranking was determined by a question that asked whether political enemies should have basic political and civil rights, such as the right to vote and free speech.[26]

The bad news about tolerance is that certain changes in our society have made tolerance and open-mindedness more difficult to sustain. Of these changes, the foremost among them is the pronounced trend toward selective exposure to partisan mass media outlets.

SELECTIVE EXPOSURE TO CONTRARY OPINIONS

It is difficult to develop and sustain tolerance and open-mindedness if you are seldom exposed to alternative points of view. Unfortunately, changes in residential living patterns have exacerbated the physical and psychological distance between Americans with different points of view. With technological change and infrastructure improvements, it is now easier for citizens to live in a community other than the community in which they work. Increasingly, Americans have taken advantage of this disconnect to relocate to neighborhoods populated by citizens who look, think, and act like them.[27]

To make matters worse—much worse—a growing trend is for citizens to deliberately shut themselves off from viewpoints uncongenial to their own. As Natalie Stroud has argued, Americans increasingly engage in "partisan selective exposure"—choosing news outlets that are likely to vindicate what they already believe.[28] Thus, for example, conservatives listen to conservative talk radio and watch Fox news. Liberals read the *New York Times* and watch CNN or MSNBC. A report by the Pew Research Center reached a similar conclusion (see Figure 6-1).[29]

FIGURE 6-1   Mass media sources used by liberals and conservatives

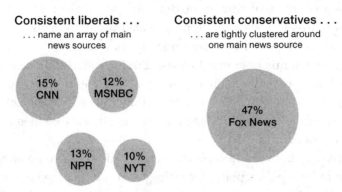

Source: Amy Mitchell et al. *"Political Polarization and Media Habits,"* (Washington, DC; Pew Research Journalism Project, October 21, 2014).

In contemporary America, partisan voters seek out like-minded media, which in turn contribute to even more partisan views. As Natalie Stroud and Alexander Curry put it, "The media both reflect and intensify partisan divides among members of the public."[30] Gary Jacobson agrees and contends that selective exposure has become "pervasive." It is perhaps not surprising, then, that voter partisanship has reached record highs. As Jacobson observes, "Partisan divisions among ordinary Americans, after steadily widening for several decades, reached new extremes during Barack Obama's presidency. The electorate that returned Obama to the White House in 2012 was more polarized along party lines than any in at least six decades."[31] A Pew Research Center report documented exceptionally high rates of party animosity in 2016, with 55 percent of Democrats saying the Republican party makes them "afraid" and 49 percent of Republicans saying the same about the Democratic party.[32]

THE RISE OF PARTISANSHIP

Extreme partisanship is a threat to reasoned argumentation because extreme liberals and extreme conservatives tend to lock themselves into unyielding positions and are not amenable to change through persuasion. The gap between liberals and conservatives is painfully obvious in the mainstream media. The gap between liberals and conservatives is also apparent in social media. On the positive side, according to a Pew research study, most users of social media "encounter a mix of political views." But the same study revealed a significant gap between liberals and conservatives in their exposure to diverse points of view.[33] Another study found that only 20 to 25 percent of the average individual's Facebook friends are members of a different political party.[34]

This gap between liberals and conservatives is also apparent in other public opinion polls. According to one fascinating Pew report, liberals and conservatives both believe that we should teach children to be tolerant, but liberals are much more likely to support this than conservatives.[35] Another survey found that conservatives are twice as likely to support book bans as liberals.[36] All of this suggests that conservatives will be much more likely to isolate themselves from persons with a different political point of view.

A key problem in twenty-first century America is that liberals talk mainly to liberals, and conservatives talk mainly to conservatives. Although most of us have some exposure to individuals with political views that differ substantially from our own (at work, for example), these encounters are typically less substantive and more superficial than conversations we have with relatives and close friends. As a result, our political conversations are usually with like-minded individuals, while our conversations with acquaintances—at work or elsewhere— are usually not political. As Diana Mutz has noted, this phenomenon makes participatory democracy more likely than deliberative democracy.[37] The reason is that conversations with fellow partisans can promote citizen activism, whereas conversations with a broader cross-section of citizens can promote reasoned deliberation. Educators need to reflect long and hard on these realities. If we wish to encourage deliberative democracy, a capacity for critical thinking is essential.

CIVIC ROLES FOR SCHOOLS

Can schools play a role in strengthening the ability of future citizens to think for themselves on important public policy questions and when choosing between candidates for elected office? Can schools help future citizens think critically about public affairs? Should schools go so far as to encourage dissent? Should they equip students with the skills and dispositions that facilitate the expression of dissenting opinions?

Plenty of evidence suggests that schools can make a positive difference in promoting civic readiness. Certainly, they can help students acquire political knowledge. Classroom discussions in history and civics classes can be enormously beneficial, in the short run and in the long run, as a technique for promoting civic knowledge, civic skills, and civic engagement. An analysis of NAEP civics scores in 2010 (grades 4, 8, and 12) found that students whose teachers discussed material in class on a regular basis scored much higher on civic knowledge.[38] An analysis of data from a Knight Foundation survey found that students who recall taking a class that mentions the First Amendment or the role of the media in society or that requires the use of the news media in assignments were more supportive of freedom of speech, as measured afterward. They were also more knowledgeable about the First Amendment.[39] A multinational comparison by Judith Torney reached similar conclusions.[40]

The mere presence of political knowledge, however, does not in itself confirm that critical thinking is taking place. In fact, we also need to know whether students feel comfortable with political conflict, where people with different interests and opinions pursue different policy goals. John Hibbing and Elizabeth Theiss-Morse have wryly observed that what we need are not "civics" courses but "barbarics" courses that simulate the rough-and-tumble world of politics where people get bruised, injured, and insulted.[41] In a clever nod to this idea, Campbell asks whether open-classrooms lead to an appreciation of conflict.[42] Using data from the 1999 IEA Civic Education Study, he defines open classrooms as ones in which students feel free to disagree with their teachers, make up their own minds, and express opinions not shared by other students.[43] In such classrooms, teachers respect student opinions, encourage students to express their views, and present several sides of an issue. With data from fourteen-year-olds in twenty-eight nations, Campbell found that students whose high school civics class more closely resembled the open classroom ideal have more political knowledge, appreciate conflict more, and are more likely to express the intent to vote.[44]

Schools should also promote reasoned argumentation. Socratic seminars, if conducted well, can encourage students to sharpen their own arguments, listen respectfully to their classmates' arguments, and engage in a robust debate. In this setting, students can learn how to criticize other people's ideas while at the same time critiquing their own. Studies confirm the value of structured debates in the classroom. In an experiment involving thirty-two at-risk eighth graders from two New York City middle schools, Deanna Kuhn and Wadiya Udell found that a forced dialogue between students with differing views on capital punishment resulted in two distinct improvements: their individual arguments became more sophisticated, and their assertions were more likely to include counterarguments and counters to counterarguments.[45] Although students in the control group also benefited from simply expressing their own views on capital punishment, students in the experimental group—forced to confront a fellow human being who harbored different views on that subject—benefited more. Another study, featuring a nonexperimental design, found that adolescents who took civics or social studies courses in which students expressed diverse points of view held more complex views on the merits of government regulation of risky behavior. In Constance Flanagan's words, "The school functions as a mini-polity, a space where, collectively, teachers and students and, by extension, families work out what it means to be a public in a democracy."[46] That, at any rate, is how schools *ought* to function.

Socratic seminars can be conducted badly. Deanna Kuhn of Columbia University, who has written extensively about how to promote reasoned argumentation, believes that rookie teachers sometimes make two mistakes when conducting a Socratic seminar. The first is having the teacher at the center of the seminar, with students as spokes of the wheel, interacting only with the teacher and not with one another. The second is for the teacher to accept uncritically any comment a student may make. In their zeal to encourage students to speak out, teachers may be tempted to dispense a dollop of positive reinforcement to every comment uttered by every student. Kuhn does not support this approach. As she puts it, "Everyone has a right to their opinion, but not all opinions are equally right."[47]

SES AND THE CIVIC READINESS GAP

In practice, students from disadvantaged backgrounds are less exposed to a strong civics curriculum than are other students. Regrettably, disadvantaged students are much less likely to have opportunities for robust discussions about political issues than other students. One study found that high-SES students were 80 percent more likely to have opportunities for classroom discussions and debates about political issues and twice as likely to take part in service learning projects. Similarly, African American students and Hispanic students and students not headed for a four-year-college were less likely to have such opportunities.[48]

The gap in exposure to civic education between disadvantaged and middle-class students is especially unfortunate because disadvantaged children benefit even more from such exposure than middle-class children. In a recent study, David Campbell found evidence to support this proposition, which he labeled the "compensation hypothesis." The basic idea is that low-SES students exposed to robust political discussions in the classroom can "compensate" for more limited political discussions at home. In an analysis of data on the civics or social studies class experiences of fourteen-year-olds from twenty-eight nations, Campbell found that low-SES students (which he measured by looking at expected education, because the two are correlated) are more appreciative of conflict and more likely to express an intent to vote if exposed to an "open classroom climate."[49] In contrast, this is not true for high-SES students.

Students in an inner-city school can benefit enormously from an in-depth, candid discussion of problems facing their community, including the grave issue of community violence. When I visited Lincoln Elementary School in Pittsburgh, I found third graders who had decided to explore neighborhood violence as a classroom project. Eventually, this mushroomed into a schoolwide event and a neighborhood rally against violence that got the students thinking and talking about crime and how to stop it (see "Seeds of Protest," pp. 151–153).

SOCIAL STUDIES COURSES AND PROGRAMS

If we work backward from the desired end result of a well-functioning deliberative democracy, it is natural to focus on social studies classes as a key vehicle for inculcating norms of good citizenship. Most states require students to take three or more semesters of social studies courses in high school, and most states require at least one semester of US government.[50] According to NAEP, 92 percent of students today have had a civics course or a US history course in high school.[51] This provides some basis for civics instruction.

In fact, there is relatively broad agreement (among parents, teachers, and school administrators) on what students in different grades need to know: fourth graders should understand the connection between the Constitution and the way our government works and should be able to give an example of a right protected by the Constitution; eighth graders should understand the concept of separation of powers and the role that slavery played in the history of the United States; twelfth graders should understand how immigration has shaped the United States at different points in history and should be able to compare and contrast the US economic system with those of other countries.[52] These understandings can and should be cultivated in social studies classes like history and civics. And they sometimes are.

If they wanted to, or were encouraged to do so, social studies teachers could also build an experiential component into their civics instruction, and school districts could assist with this. In Boston and in Lowell, Massachusetts, the public schools work in tandem with a nonprofit organization, Discovering Justice, to stage mock trials in which students participate. The culmination of weeks of preparation is a hearing before a real judge in a real courtroom.[53] Even first graders have been brought into the process—asked to resolve a case involving a missing teddy bear.[54] In Chicago, Illinois, 73 percent of Chicago Public Schools high school students participate in a program called the Mikva Challenge. After steeping themselves in local issues, students make concrete recommendations through an Education Council, a Teen Health Council, a Youth Safety Council, and an Out-of-School Council.[55] Also in Chicago, the Constitutional Rights Foundation sponsors public debates on current events.[56] These innovative programs exemplify the potential for hands-on civic instruction that is likely to have a lasting impact (see Table 6-1).

An excellent resource is also available at the national level. The iCivics program, launched by former Supreme Court Justice Sandra Day O'Connor, is an innovative way to engage students in interesting debates over government and public policy. By combining electronic games with hypothetical debates involving key government institutions, this program gets students to acquire more knowledge and to think critically about the merits of different policy positions, such as competing claims before the Supreme Court.[57]

BEYOND SOCIAL STUDIES

Habits of good thinking on important issues of the day do not begin or end in social studies classes. Science classes are great venues for improving civic readiness because in these classes students learn the nature of the scientific method—hypotheses that lead to tests that lead to conclusions. This cognitive template is valuable not just for thinking about obviously scientific debates (e.g., over global warming and how to deal with it) but also over any dispute in which scientific evidence is being contested (e.g., a debate over school vouchers).

TABLE 6-1   Programs that encourage civic readiness

PROGRAM	SITE	AGES	STRATEGY
iCivics	National	K–12	Combines electronic games with hypothetical debates involving key government institutions
Discovering Justice	Boston and Lowell, Massachusetts	Elementary and Middle School	Students participate in mock trials before a real judge in a real courtroom
The Mikva Challenge	Chicago, Illinois	High School	Students become experts on an issue and make policy recommendations through nonprofit organizations
The Constitutional Rights Foundation	Chicago, Illinois	K–12	Students debate current events in a public setting

James Youniss gives a splendid example of how a science class can contribute to civic skills and civic engagement.[58] Mr. Ibarra's seventh-grade science class, in West Branch, Iowa, investigated oil filters disposed in waste facilities and found they could leach toxic lead, cadmium, and arsenic into the groundwater. The students also found that 88 percent of the residual oil in filters was extractable, which is to say it could be recovered. After synthesizing these findings, they spoke with the local landfill director and conservation board and then to a state legislator. In May 2008, Governor John Culver signed a bill into law prohibiting the disposal of untreated oil filters in waste facilities. What a civics lesson!

Math teachers can also make valuable contributions to civic readiness. Many debates in American politics—on immigration, budget deficits, crime, poverty, and other issues—involve the use of numbers and statistics. When citizens encounter such information, will they process it objectively or through partisan lenses? A recent experiment, focusing on probation as an alternative to incarceration, found that numeracy enhances information processing. As Vittorio Merola and Matthew Hitt report, "Highly numerate subjects exhibited a significant persuasion effect whenever presented with strong information."[59] In contrast, low-numeracy subjects were less persuaded by information sponsored by the opposite party, more persuaded by information sponsored by their own party. By enhancing their students' numeracy, math teachers can help prepare future citizens for debates that feature contested statistics.

In English classes, students learn how to distinguish between good and bad sources, good and bad evidence, credible and implausible arguments. They also learn the difference between good and bad dialogue. These skills are valuable when citizens hear thirty-second political ads on television, when they watch a candidate debate, or when they try to draw inferences from the evening news. In fact, Sarah Stitzlein believes that the humanities are especially well suited to learning critical thinking, skepticism, empathy, and other perspectives that encourage dissent. [60]

Larry Cagle, who teaches AP English in Edison Preparatory High School in Tulsa, is a good example of an English teacher who cultivates good citizenship. Once a year, he organizes a symposium on a hot topic in the news, in which students get to hear from and confront community leaders. In 2015, the hot topic was police tactics (see "Can You Keep the Big Boys Honest?" p. 153–154).

As many English teachers know, a well-chosen work of fiction can be an excellent way to encourage respect for others, including greater cross-cultural awareness. Consider, for example, *The Great Wall of Lucy Wu*, by Wendy Wan-Long Shang.[61] Lucy Wu, a Chinese American sixth grader, loves basketball, good friends, and the prospect of having her own bedroom when her big sister heads off to college. She is crushed to learn that she will have to share her bedroom with her great-aunt Yi Po, from Shanghai, who unexpectedly comes to live with her family. In an act of defiance, Lucy rearranges the bedroom furniture so that a desk and bookcase create a "wall" between her great-aunt's side of the room and her own. As her great-aunt settles in, Lucy's bitterness grows: her room now reeks of Vicks Vapo Rub, a Chinese radio station blasts news reports and hokey music, and her great-aunt's nocturnal wanderings disturb her sleep. Also, her parents expect her to take Chinese language classes when she would rather be attending basketball practice. Lucy's frustrations boil over, and she behaves peevishly toward her great-aunt and her parents. Eventually, though, she comes to appreciate her great-aunt's old-fashioned ways and her own Chinese roots. The story does a brilliant job of showing young readers how cultural differences can be a source of pleasure rather than friction. The story also shows how empathy can grow, as Lucy identifies with her great-aunt's eagerness to be accepted and loved.

After students read this book, a teacher could probe for cultural differences that seem off-putting at first—for example, Yi Po's strong preference for fixing Chinese food, rather than American food, on special occasions like birthdays. Why did Lucy object to this? And how did she eventually come to appreciate the joys of home-made Chinese food? (Hint: When Lucy's teenage friends discovered how delicious Yi Po's dumplings were and joined in the fun as Yi Po made them, turning food preparation into a festive occasion.) Was Lucy's initial behavior toward her great-aunt disrespectful? How might she have conveyed her concerns without being rude? Have you ever been disrespectful and later regretted it? What were the circumstances? Why is mutual respect so important to a family? To a school? To a community?

Whose responsibility is it to promote mutual respect in private and public conversations? A lively discussion of these questions could help middle school students appreciate the need for mutual respect, even in difficult circumstances.

A work of fiction can also encourage citizen awareness, involvement, and activism. In recent years, John Grisham, the master of courtroom dramas, has written a series of mysteries for young adults featuring Theo Boone, "kid lawyer." In these books, Theo demonstrates his budding skills as an aspiring lawyer by defending the rights of his classmates, in school debates and elsewhere. In one of the Grisham books, Theo actually represents a client in court.[62] Well, it's animal court! Rocky, a schnauzer, has been impounded after wandering through town without a leash. Theo explains to the judge that the owners, who were out of town, took appropriate precautions but that Rocky managed to sneak out of the house through a pet door in the laundry room and burrow his way under the fence to freedom. The judge, impressed by Theo's command of the law, lets Rocky off with a stern warning. In another book, Theo and some of his pals make a two-minute video opposing the construction of a bypass that could contribute to air pollution near an elementary school and a soccer field.[63] The video goes viral, and Theo is asked to make a brief presentation to the county commissioners. He makes an eloquent plea, to loud applause. The final vote is 2–2, with one abstention, and the bypass motion is tabled. Not every child is as motivated or as articulate as Theo. And not every public official is as responsive to citizen input as the animal court and the county commissioners. Still, the Grisham books show how young people can make themselves heard in a positive way by mustering good evidence, by crafting coherent arguments, and by participating respectfully in the policy-making process.

Finally, it is important to note that the seeds of good citizenship can be planted very early in life—in fact, as early as first grade. This premise guided architects of a program known as Fast Track, which randomly assigned outgoing kindergarten students to an intervention that used a variety of techniques to teach children how to regulate their emotions and how to work well with others. The program continued through grade 10. Many years later, researchers found that individuals who participated in Fast Track as children voted at a rate

11–14 percentage points higher as adults—a 40 percent increase compared to their control group peers. Effects were especially dramatic for more disadvantaged students.[64] In short, a well-designed early childhood intervention, sustained over time, can teach students self-control, teamwork, and other valuable soft skills that encourage civic participation later in life.

WHAT POLITICIANS CAN DO

In principle, politicians ought to be fierce advocates for civic readiness and civic engagement. In practice, though, politicians have created a political environment and adopted public policies that nip civic skills and civic engagement in the bud.

Consider, for example, the gridlock that exists in Washington, DC, where the Congress has become largely unproductive and where the president and the Congress seldom agree on something as rudimentary as the government budget. If lawmakers are paralyzed, then why should citizens get involved? Citizens may tire of participating in politics if public officials seem incapable of governing. The evidence is not crystal clear on this point. Voter turnout in presidential elections has actually increased, from 51 percent (1948) to 59 percent (2016). However, voter turnout in midterm Congressional elections has decreased, from 41 percent in 1950 to 37 percent in 2010 and then to 36 percent in 2014.[65] The *Washington Post* recently reported a 20 percent decline in applications for a demonstration permit on Capitol Hill.[66] Apparently, many activists have given up on Congress, which seems incapable of legislating on any subject. As this perception worsens, or spreads to state capitals, we may see a decline in public dissent.

In more specific ways, politicians have made it less likely that schools will fulfill their potential in promoting civic readiness. Although thirty-nine states require high school students to take at least one course in American government or civics, most states require only one and it is often to be taken at twelfth grade. As Peter Levine notes, "By that time, senioritis has set in, and—worse—many students have dropped out of high school. The course is often too little and too late."[67] Also, the principal vehicle for civics instruction remains the textbook, which often emphasizes factual knowledge, as opposed to oral communication, deliberative skills, teamwork, or actual civic engagement.[68]

Although twenty or twenty-one states require civics testing, only eleven states require a high-stakes assessment—either a graduation requirement or a test that contributes toward a grade in a civics course that is required for graduation.[69] By taking advantage of variations and shifts over time in state requirements, David Campbell and Richard Niemi were able to assess the effects of high stakes civics requirements on the political knowledge of US youth. Using NAEP data, they found that high-stakes civics requirements have either modest positive effects on political knowledge (if one makes cross-sectional comparisons) or no effects at all (if one makes longitudinal comparisons). However, they also found that such requirements have strong positive effects on political knowledge for Hispanic students in particular, regardless of whether one makes cross-sectional or longitudinal comparisons.

Several states have taken bold steps to improve their civics instruction and assessment. Florida has mandated strong civics instruction in middle school and has linked that mandate to high-stakes testing.[70] Tennessee has required that students compile a civics portfolio before graduating from high school. Hawaii requires students to take a new high school course that focuses on solving important real-world problems.[71] Another variation on this same theme is character education, which can encourage students to care for others by participating in volunteer activities after school. For example, in Sierra Vista Middle School in Covina, California, students collect and distribute money, sheets, blankets, and towels for homeless veterans.[72]

It is never too early to get students thinking about problems in their community and the role that government can play in addressing those problems. However, it is important to think not just about government but also about nonprofit organizations, which make valuable contributions to every community. This perspective animated Pittsburgh's Environmental Charter School teacher, Deirdre Keller, when she invited her second-grade students to identify and write about community organizations that promote worthy social goals. Each student wrote about one local nonprofit. After reviewing the essays, an adult committee chose the best group, and the students raised funds to help support it (see "Charity Begins at School," p. 154–155).

STEPS TOWARD DELIBERATIVE DEMOCRACY

So, what have we learned about civic readiness? How might a stronger dose of critical thinking improve civic readiness? And what exactly should schools do to produce better citizens?

First, there are plenty of reasons to be discouraged. Even the basic building blocks for civic readiness—knowledgeable, informed voters who pay attention to politics—are shaky at best. In Milton Lodge and Charles Taber's words, the voters seem to prefer "rationalizing" to "rationality."[73] Nor does it look better down the road. Young people are less interested in politics than they used to be. They are less likely to engage in a wide range of civic activities than they used to be, with volunteering being a notable exception. Despite higher levels of education, their civic awareness has either decreased or remained basically the same.[74] Also, increasingly, both liberals and conservatives are shutting themselves off from uncomfortable and uncongenial political opinions. The ideological polarization of political elites, worrisome enough, has spilled over to the mass level, as ordinary citizens selectively expose themselves to a limited range of opinions. It follows from this that our citizens are poised to become less tolerant than they used to be. This makes it less likely that they will engage in critical thinking because critical thinking requires open-mindedness as a prerequisite.[75]

Our citizenry's knowledge of politics and public policy must improve and sharply. We need citizens who know basic facts about how government works, who today's public officials are, and what today's public policy controversies are. This in itself is not critical thinking. On the other hand, it is an essential prerequisite to it. Without such knowledge, citizens cannot weigh evidence and reach sound conclusions about the issues of the day.

Second, our citizens must be able to formulate good arguments, recognize bad arguments, and engage in reasoned debate. As Stephen Macedo and his colleagues have noted, a citizen must be able to "explain and justify one's opinions to others in civil dialogue."[76] Citizens must also be capable of "finding points of common agreement." A key habit of mind as citizens evaluate public officials and their proposed policies is a willingness to seriously consider alternative points of view. The popular philosopher Eric Hoffer put it this way: "The beginning of thought is disagreement—not only with others but also with ourselves."[77]

Third, our public schools need to teach students the A–B–Cs of reasoned argumentation. Many of our nation's high schools already do this, through Socratic seminars, in which students take sides in a debate over a contemporary controversy. But these debates can and should take place not just in social studies courses (including civics) but also in English classes, science classes, and other classes. Our public schools need to teach norms of tolerance and norms of collaboration. This is no small task, and it is not simply a matter of adding more time to civics instruction, important though that may be. In courses across the curriculum, teachers need to make students aware of alternative viewpoints and help them to appreciate them. In courses across the curriculum, teachers need to encourage collaboration, inside and outside the classroom. In courses across the curriculum, teachers need to emphasize the obligations inherent in being a member of a community and a citizen of a country.

We also need to begin civic education much earlier than we do. Given the right assignments, early elementary school students can easily grasp the role of nonprofit organizations and charities in making their community a better place. Given the right assignments, early elementary school students can articulate their fears about neighborhood safety and try to imagine a better world. Given the right assignments, early elementary school students can make connections between recycling and water quality, between biking and air quality. Our youngest children are bursting with curiosity, trying to make sense of the world around them. Politics, broadly defined, is a proper subject for early elementary education.

As we reconsider civics instruction, what should our goals be for the future? In Peter Levine's words, we must move beyond "negotiation" to "deliberation." As Levine explains, negotiation implies predetermined goals. This conception of the policy process has been embraced, explicitly or implicitly, by many political scientists, including the late

Harold Lasswell, who famously described politics as who gets what, when, and how. In contrast, deliberation implies that people's "goals, judgments, preferences, and values are open to change."[78] Deliberation requires active listening and a capacity to reconsider one's own initial position. It welcomes surprises and anticipates persuasion and compromise. These skills are vital for a democracy.

As a society, we also need to decide whether our ultimate goal, in Diana Mutz's words, is participatory democracy or deliberative democracy.[79] Do we want a society in which many citizens are joiners, many citizens vote, and many citizens contribute to political campaigns? What if such a society is marked by intense partisanship, highly selective media exposure, truculence, and intractability? Or might we prefer a society in which citizens critically examine competing perspectives, including their own? In such a society, we might see fewer extreme political views, more mutual respect, more compromise.

As Table 6-2 suggests, the path to deliberative democracy looks different from the path to participatory democracy. If deliberative democracy is our goal, then critical thinking, with its emphasis on tolerance and open-mindedness, is essential. If participatory democracy is our goal, then motivated reasoning, with its emphasis on passion and commitment, might suffice. If deliberative democracy is our goal, then schools might inculcate norms of teamwork and mutual respect. If participatory democracy is our goal, then schools should promote independence and self-confidence.

These options, are not mutually exclusive, of course. Some pedagogical strategies, like open classrooms, can promote both.[80] But it

TABLE 6-2 Pathways to citizenship

	PARTICIPATORY DEMOCRACY	DELIBERATIVE DEMOCRACY
Type of Thinking	Motivated reasoning	Critical thinking
Media Exposure	Narrow	Broad
Social Network	Homogenous	Heterogeneous
Classroom Activities	Essays, speeches	Socratic seminars, debates
Classroom Goals	Independence, self-confidence	Teamwork, mutual respect

would appear, at this point in American history, that what is conspicuously missing from our political culture is the capacity to bridge ideological divides, to engage in reasoned deliberation.

The situation today is not entirely bleak. According to one recent study, approximately one-fourth of all US adults engaged in at least one instance of face-to-face public deliberation during the previous year. Also, based on self-reports, these interactions with fellow citizens met some widely accepted criteria for rational civic discourse. As the authors put it, "Face-to-face deliberators consistently report that the forums they attended relied on expert information, reason-giving, and toleration."[81] If accurate, this is a good foundation on which to build. On the other hand, it applies to only one-fourth of the US population. In practice, that probably means citizens who are well educated, middle class, or wealthy.

Although much remains to be done, there is some additional good news. When David Campbell studied civic instruction in the schools, he found that schools differ in what he called their "civic ethos" or "norms encouraged, shared, and 'enforced ' within a school community."[82] He found that adolescents who had attended a high school with a strong civic ethos were more likely to be civically engaged (as measured by voting and volunteering) fifteen years after they graduated high school.[83] Thus, the effects of a strong civic ethos can be long lasting.

CONCLUSION

To sum up the preceding three chapters, college readiness, career readiness, and civic readiness are among the three most important goals of K–12 education. Each of them requires strong critical-thinking skills, though the operational embodiment of such skills varies across the three goals. In the context of college readiness, critical thinking is likely to feature textual analysis. In the context of career readiness, critical thinking resembles practical problem solving. In the context of civic readiness, critical thinking looks a lot like reasoned deliberation. The trick is not just to promote critical thinking but to promote different kinds of critical thinking in pursuit of different societal goals.

We have not devoted enough attention to critical thinking, but that is especially true of critical thinking harnessed to career readiness as a goal and critical thinking harnessed to civic readiness as a goal. Growing unease over the US economy (declining productivity, vanishing middle-skill jobs) and the US polity (rising partisanship, legislative gridlock) confirms that we face some serious challenges ahead. Although critical thinking cannot solve these deeply rooted systemic problems overnight, it is one of our best bets because it strengthens our country's single greatest resource, which is our human capital.

In chapter 7, I focus on one effort to inject a strong dose of critical thinking into K–12 education: the STEM education movement. I also devote considerable attention to its cousin, the STEAM education movement. STEM and STEAM are not just about critical thinking. In fact, they are more aptly described as efforts to promote blended thinking because they combine critical thinking, problem solving, and creative thinking in felicitous ways. The purpose of the next chapter, which takes a deep dive into these reforms, is to investigate the possibility that STEM and STEAM can transform our educational system for the better and improve the prospects of disadvantaged students in particular.

SEEDS OF PROTEST

In Pittsburgh's Larimer neighborhood, violence is an ever-present concern. As reporter Jeffrey Benzing has noted, "In Pittsburgh, only certain neighborhoods bleed." Unfortunately, Larimer is one of them.

Children at Lincoln Elementary, in the Larimer neighborhood, understand this very well. When English teacher Teresa Partee asked her third graders to brainstorm about big problems, they discussed bullying at school and harm to the environment, but they eventually settled on community violence as the biggest threat. Mary Anderson's third graders reached a similar conclusion after considering more prosaic school issues (school lunches, recess, etc.).

For at least one third-grade student, community violence was deeply personal. He had lost his uncle, a star athlete, to gun violence in 2008. When this student suggested a rally to end violence, other students reacted positively. "They were excited by the idea," Partee recalls. Teachers and administrators also responded favorably.

Students planned and organized the rally, with considerable help from teachers and other experts. A gym teacher, a rap artist himself, assisted students who wanted to write rap lyrics. A consultant from Apple helped other students develop a website. A math teacher worked with students to conduct a survey on neighborhood safety. Some students designed posters and placards, while others wrote "letters to bigwigs."

The rally took place just outside the school on a winter's day. Principal Virginia Hill kicked things off by explaining the connection between the rally and Lincoln's new STEAM initiative: "Through our STEAM initiative, we have embraced the maker movement to not just be things we make with our hands. We have embraced the maker movement as an ability to be makers of change and shapers of a brighter life." Next, a third-grade student spoke: "We're here today 'cause we want to make our neighborhood a better place. We want to ask our fellow citizens to end this senseless violence against one another. According to a recent Public Source article, 85 percent of Pittsburgh homicides have been a black victim. Many of those who were killed were innocent victims. One way to reduce the violence in our neighborhood is by decreasing poverty. . . . Also we need to make sure that we get a good education so we have better jobs. Another way to decrease violence is by having more police in our neighborhoods to protect us, police that we can trust."

A fifth grader, who lost a cousin to gun violence, also spoke at the rally: "I don't feel safe around here in my neighborhood or walking to school. . . . Every day we see people dying. . . . They kill each other for drugs, money, or just because they are sensitive or mad. Every other day, there's a funeral to go to. Why can't we have one day with no shootings or no violence on the news? If you have a problem with someone, don't take matters into your own hands . . . That's just going to get you arrested or killed."

Mayor Bill Peduto attended the rally, as did state representative Ed Gainey. Police Commander Jason Lando also came and conveyed a personal message: "If you ever feel like you're in danger or someone ever offers you drugs or wants you to do something you don't feel comfortable with, come find me."

Benzing, the reporter, who visited with the students prior to the rally, was impressed by their awareness: "They had a much broader understanding of neighborhood violence than you would expect from people that age." Jason Rivers, a Lincoln Elementary School parent whose family has been touched by violence, was impressed by the degree to which his son and his classmates got involved in planning and executing the protest. Rivers acknowledges some concern about exposing students to the raw realities of neighborhood violence at such a tender age. But he notes that "they can't live in a bubble." As he sees it, the school provided a forum for students to think critically about neighborhood violence and ask hard questions that need to be answered. "They did an amazing job," he said.

CAN YOU KEEP THE BIG BOYS HONEST?

Larry Cagle, who teaches AP English and AP Research at Edison Preparatory High School in Tulsa, wants his students to move up the ladder of Bloom's taxonomy, from memorizing facts to analyzing, synthesizing, and evaluating ideas. He doesn't use the phrase "critical thinking" all that often, but he frequently urges his students to be "independent thinkers." As one of his students puts it, "Cagle wants us to think for ourselves. . . . He wants us to take everything with a grain of salt."

Every year Cagle organizes a symposium on a hot topic in the news. In October 2015, that topic was police tactics. With recent headlines in mind, he and a fellow AP English teacher invited a diverse panel: a retired policeman, an assistant DA, a former state senator, an imam, and a black activist. At the public forum, students asked tough, probing questions of the panelists. One student asked the policeman whether police officers receive enough training to prevent them from discriminating against blacks. Another student, a Hispanic, asked the black activist whether the phrase "black lives matter" implies that Hispanic lives matter less.

Cagle recalls the evening and its aftermath with satisfaction: "We put everyone on the hot seat! And we invited the news media in. They did a news report. Then we took the news media to task! The kids produced thirty to fifty critical comments on the news reports." For example, one student wrote this: "It's subtle, but if you follow the news story closely it becomes clear that it's a white narrative. The students had concerns that the minority community was being mistreated and that police officers were too aggressive in treating citizens. However, the news report reads as though the students were concerned about people rioting and about police being misunderstood. The students wanted a minority narrative."

According to Cagle, when the reporter read the students' reactions, he said, "That's not true! I did not tell a white narrative story." So Cagle invited the reporter to come back and discuss his news story. "We raked him over the coals!" Cagle recalls. "But he realized this was a teaching moment. Kids learn to think independently, to think critically."

CHARITY BEGINS AT SCHOOL

One of the premises of Pittsburgh's Environmental Charter School is that children should use their "time, talent, and treasure" for the common good. The Lower School (grades K–3), like the Upper School (grades 4–8), emphasizes citizenship and community. With these goals in mind, second-grade teacher Deirdre Keller, with a boost from academic coach Melanie Cowherd, designed a project that would help students understand the goals, accomplishments, and inner workings of nonprofit organizations that seek to benefit the Pittsburgh community.

Keller's students began by listing some goals that a community organization might want to pursue, such as food security, clothing, education, and shelter. Keller then identified eight to nine local organizations that promote these goals in some way. Next, each student was assigned to a nonprofit. In groups of three, students looked at snippets of their nonprofit's website and met with a representative of that organization or with a teacher who knew something about it. Each student then wrote a paragraph aimed at persuading others that their nonprofit was worthy of financial support.

At this point, the paragraphs were reviewed by a grants committee, consisting of adults from the Lower School. The committee decided that the best of the groups was a new store in nearby Wilkinsburg, called the Free Store. Patterned after a similar store in Braddock, Pennsylvania, the Wilkinsburg Free Store gathers clothes, toys, household goods, and other items of value and gives them away. In short, it is Goodwill without a pricing system.

The students then embarked on a fundraising campaign. And they were asked to count the money they collected. The good news: they raised about $850. The bad news: they thought they raised about $650. So, the kids need to work on their math! Arithmetic aside, though, the students learned a great deal about community needs and how to help meet them through a local charity. They learned that some of their neighbors don't have enough money to meet their basic needs. And they learned how to persuade adults to give them something of value through written and spoken words. As one second grader put it, "You can make a big difference even if you are very small."

Sometime soon the students will visit the Free Store to see how their hard work is paying off.

Critical Thinking and the Technological Revolution

ALTHOUGH THIS BOOK is about critical thinking, I recognize that critical thinking is not the only valuable higher-order thinking skill. Problem solving and creativity also play a positive role in promoting college readiness, career readiness, and civic readiness. Nevertheless, critical thinking is a vital part of the mix. In this chapter, I discuss initiatives that promote blended thinking, through STEM or STEAM. I begin with a school district that might serve as a showcase for the rest of the nation—South Fayette Township, Pennsylvania—and then I ask whether this model can be replicated elsewhere. By burrowing inside several school districts, and by talking with teachers about robots, butterfly gardens, and even pots and pans, I try to understand how meaningful educational reform can be achieved.

CHOOSING AN ACRONYM

The term *STEM* (Science, Technology, Engineering, and Math) originated between 2001 and 2004.[1] Judith Ramaley, then at the National Science Foundation, preferred it as an alternative to the previous acronym, *SMET*. That's easy enough to understand. SMET sounds like an international spy ring trying to kill James Bond. In contrast, STEM evokes flowers, life, and the promise of a bountiful spring. As a term, it is far more appealing.

STEM is hot these days, though perhaps not hot enough. Overall, 40 percent of all bachelor's degrees earned by men and 29 percent of all bachelor's degrees earned by women are now in STEM subjects; 58 percent of all PhD degrees earned by men and 33 percent of all PhD degrees earned by women are in STEM subjects.[2] These changes reflect growing demand for jobs and higher wages in the STEM field.[3] On the other hand, we are still likely to face STEM shortages, given that few individuals without college degrees have the job skills employers are seeking.[4] Only 16 percent of high school seniors contemplate a future in a STEM field.[5]

To some, the STEM movement may not seem to exemplify critical thinking. It does not explicitly focus on the clash of ideas. It does not attempt to reconcile competing points of view. It does not plumb the depths of complex texts in a quest for deeper meaning. It does not lend itself to Socratic seminars in which students explain their reasoning and challenge other students to explain theirs. It does not manifest itself in debate tournaments or Model United Nations speeches.

However, some of the most interesting forms of thinking transcend traditional categories. By combining critical thinking and creative thinking, students can make new discoveries. By combining critical thinking and problem solving, students can cut production costs for new products. By combining critical thinking, creative thinking, and problem solving, students can catch a glimpse of their full intellectual potential.

One of the distinctive features of STEM is its strong emphasis on problem solving. The problem might be poor soil quality or poor water quality. The problem might be a balky robot that doesn't want to move backward on command. STEM helps students solve problems in ways that have considerable practical utility. No wonder that so many employers love STEM programs. They see STEM education as producing skilled workers for the future.

Some critics have wondered whether the term *STEM* gets in the way of the central ideas STEM is trying to promote. As writer Natalie Angier put it, "Mention the odious and increasingly pervasive term STEM education and instead of cheerleading gear . . . I reach for my pistil."[6] She complains, as does scientist Elizabeth Stage, that the term distracts us from the core skills STEM is trying to promote, such as problem solving, arguing from evidence, and reconciling conflicting views.

To other critics in the humanities and the social sciences, STEM seems a bit tedious and mundane. Where is the lift of a driving dream? Where is the poetry? Where is the magic? One answer to these questions is that there is considerable magic associated with a moon launch or the Golden Gate Bridge or even my Prius (if you can ignore the limited vision outside its rear window).

But another answer to these criticisms is STEAM, or Science, Technology, Engineering, Art, and Math. One of the distinctive features of STEAM is its strong emphasis on creativity. By urging students to combine science, engineering, and the arts, STEAM helps them integrate instrumental and expressive aspects of production.[7] The maker movement, which encourages engineers to find their inner muse and encourages artists to make something useful, breaks down conventional stereotypes and promotes blended thinking. As Erica Halverson and Kimberly Sheridan have argued, "Maker culture has become a way to express creative and communal drive."[8]

STEAM could be just what is needed to reach disadvantaged students, who may find STEM a bit too daunting. As Ruth Catchen has argued, the arts can serve as an "on-ramp" to STEM for underrepresented students.[9] Students who have done well in the arts but who have not yet excelled at STEM may be able to build on their artistic aptitudes and contribute something unique and valuable to a science project or an engineering project, thus easing their entry into this increasingly important world.

To learn more about the potential for STEAM education, I visited the South Fayette Township School District in McDonald, Pennsylvania, about twenty miles southwest of downtown Pittsburgh. South Fayette has a kind of Brigadoon quality to it: as you travel there, you can almost imagine it disappearing in the mist, like a phantom community. To get to South Fayette Township, you have to traverse some rural roads, with names like Thoms Run Road and Battle Ridge Road. It is easy to lose your way. In fact, I got lost coming and going. But it was worth the trip.

STEAMING INTO THE TWENTY-FIRST CENTURY

At South Fayette Township, students love to make things, and they benefit from an organizational culture that encourages them to do exactly that. South Fayette Township's school administrators call it STEAM, but it is really much more than that—a heady mix of problem-solving, project-based learning, and hands-on assignments that are extremely practical and lots of fun but also aimed at promoting some broader intellectual goals, including "computational thinking" and the development of certain "habits of mind."

It all begins in the early elementary school (K–2), where students learn the basics of computer programming (through Scratch Junior, a block-based computer program), and where they build their first robot—a creature with spindly legs (felt pens) and a sturdy backbone (a battery-powered toothbrush) that produces art (colorful squiggly lines) while shuffling amiably across a construction paper plaza. Usually, these activities take place in first grade. Also in first grade, students learn about "squishy circuits" by using Play-Doh, and they develop a rudimentary understanding of how electricity works. In second grade, they make musical instruments using Makey Makey, they learn which geometric designs are best for holding a bag of sand, and they learn about the planets, among other activities. On the day I visited, Melissa Unger's second-grade students were creating posters featuring their designated planet and three fun facts. For example, the sun team came up with this: "It is so hot here that we feel like we are going to die to death!" Throughout elementary school, students get to enjoy exhibits that the Carnegie Science Museum donated to the school, including a bridge specially equipped with steel arm supports that permit students to move their arms aerodynamically as a bird in flight would do. The principal, Laurie Gray, puts it this way, "It's amazing to watch first graders and second graders have a problem and solve it. They design, build, test, fix, and rebuild."[10]

In grades 3–5 (intermediate school), students develop more impressive computer programming skills, using Scratch rather than Scratch Junior, and eventually VEX IQ, which shifts them from block-based to text-based programming. On the day I visited, students in Stephanie DeLuca's fourth-grade STEAM class were busy producing different types of clouds, using construction paper, balloons, string, glue, and huge amounts of cotton. Their goal was to understand the water cycle. Earlier, they had built a terrarium to better understand evaporation and condensation.

Nearby, in a technology literacy class, Shad Wachter showed students how to make a snowman using a 3D printer. On the day I visited, Wachter was discussing proportions. If the snowman was too big, he might not fit on his base (which was twelve centimeters wide). So, students had to calculate appropriate proportions for the base, the middle, and the top before writing the code to produce the snowman.

Meanwhile, in DeLuca's fifth-grade class, students were troubleshooting their robots and their environments. One student, Aidan Burns, showed me a basketball court he and three classmates had designed. He also proudly introduced me to a robot that picked up a circular object and did its best to deposit it in a makeshift hoop. Aidan and his classmates used ROBOTC programming language to get the robot to move forward and backward, to turn, and to raise its arm. Failure is always an option; the robot was not yet NBA material. Also, as Aidan explained, "You have to design the basketball court perfectly, because if you don't, the robot wanders off."[11] Still, Aidan and his classmates were learning how to adapt, how to learn from their mistakes, and how to conjure up solutions to tricky problems—all valuable skills in the workplace and in life.

Looming behind these separate classes are 16 Habits of Mind, developed by Art Costa and Bena Calick—questioning and problem posing, thinking flexibly, listening with understanding and empathy, thinking interdependently, and so on.[12] These habits of mind, which include several that could easily be characterized as critical-thinking skills, are posted in most intermediate school classrooms. Some teachers focus on one habit of mind at a time, for emphasis. For example, DeLuca stressed thinking interdependently as the students embarked on their first group project. Other teachers are more spontaneous, allowing the habits to flow from the designated task. For example, if students are debugging a computer program, Wachter may ask, "What are the habits of mind you used while you were debugging?"[13] With scaffolding from their teachers, the students develop valuable metacognition skills.

In grades 6–8 (middle school), students build on the habits of mind they learned earlier to master principles of human-centered design. In a course for seventh graders struggling with reading, Frank Kruth (the STEAM coordinator) and Beth Solon (a reading specialist) used Curious George to motivate and inspire their students. Each student read a Curious George book and outlined the plot. Then each student chose a scene to animate, using a sturdy poster board. On one of these boards, you see Curious George wearing a chef's hat and holding a skillet. If you peek behind the poster board, you see a motor and sensors that permit George to flip the pancakes! The motor and sensors come from a Hummingbird Robotics kit, the brainchild of a Carnegie Mellon University spinoff, Birdbrain Technologies. In another course, cotaught by Kruth and arts teacher Diane Lally, students orchestrated a contemporary version of Snow White and the Seven Dwarfs, using the same Hummingbird robotics kits. For example, Bashful was programmed to blush when embarrassed. Kruth explains the rationale behind these projects, which integrated art, reading, and engineering: "It definitely required creative thinking, as well as critical thinking in getting it to work."[14] Creativity generated a playful idea for animation, while critical thinking yielded the programming needed to activate the motors and sensors.

Students also invent their own apps (like one that informs parents instantaneously when their child enters or leaves a school bus) and devise increasingly sophisticated assignments for robots. One student recalls both frustration and exultation as he programmed and reprogrammed his robot: "Some of the code is challenging, but I like it a lot. Once you figure it out, you feel like jumping up and down!"[15] As incredible as it may seem, several eighth graders actually built their own 3D printer, with considerable help from a team of experts from INVENTORcloud, based in Youngstown, Ohio. Having learned how to assemble a 3D printer, these students can help out when something goes wrong. As eighth-grade teacher A. J. Mannarino says, "They are my first line of defense if one of our 3D printers goes down."[16] The middle schoolers' interest in programming has spilled over beyond normal class hours. In 2015–2016, some high school students arranged a special class for middle school students who wanted to learn how to use Python. The class was standing room only.

In high school, students learn human-centered design principles at an even higher level. In Jeannie Scott's Game Design class, one student showed me a game called The Life of a Spoon, a variation on a popular card game, where you grab a spoon as quickly as possible when you have a winning hand (there's always one less spoon than there are players). After some experimentation and feedback from Scott, the game format improved over time. Adding a draw pile, for example, reduced clutter on the board and quickened the pace by making it less likely that a player would lose a turn. Another student designed a game called Swimming Down the Stream, based on Go Fish. The eureka moment here was when the students realized the need for cutthroat competition. As Scott explained, "Part of the fun for adult games is sabotaging other people!"[17] By adding the possibility of sending an opponent back to the beginning, the students added some excitement to their game. Along the way, they learned the value of experimentation, collaboration, and problem solving.

The culmination of the high school experience for a turbo-charged dozen or so students is the Innovation Studio, run by Brian Garlick, an engineer. In this class, students work with representatives of All-Clad Metalcrafters, a nearby company that produces widely admired cookware products such as pots and pans. In 2016 South Fayette students were assisting All-Clad with a variety of projects, such as how to redesign the packaging that houses All-Clad products. In the past, students have advised All-Clad on how to remove burrs or bumps created by robotic presses (a process known as deburring) and how to design a pot handle that is easier for senior citizens to hold. One year, All-Clad came to the Innovation Studio and told the students they wanted to refilter oil laced with particulates and reuse it again. Later that year, South Fayette's students were visiting a medical facility where they noticed the medical technicians cleaning blood with a centrifuge (a process known as blood-spinning, which separates plasma from other blood components). As Garlick recalls, this led to an epiphany: "Ding! Ding! Ding!" Students saw a connection between blood-spinning and their All-Clad problem assignment. With advice from the students, All-Clad implemented a centrifuge to clean its oil and recycle and use it. South Fayette also partners with other companies and organizations, including the Calgon Carbon Corporation (which removes odors and contaminants from liquids and gases), the University of Pittsburgh Medical Center (UPMC), the Carnegie Mellon University Computer Science Department (which has hired some South Fayette High School students as research assistants), the Luma Institute (which specializes in human-centered design), E-FAB (which manufactures thin metal parts for various industries), and Alcosan (the local sanitation authority).

ANATOMY OF SUCCESS

South Fayette Township has produced an extraordinary educational program, with STEAM as its focus. They have a coherent educational philosophy that guides them and that is faithfully implemented at all four of their schools. The seeds of that educational philosophy are planted early and nurtured, through both STEAM courses and regular courses. Coordination across grades and across subjects is remarkably tight. Student artifacts and products—robots, home-made apps, animated art—are tangible reminders of what young minds can accomplish when they are excited and engaged and when they have strong faculty support.

What explains South Fayette's success? Let's begin with money. South Fayette Township spends $15,172 per student, about average for the commonwealth of Pennsylvania ($15,215) but significantly higher than the United States as a whole ($11,927). Its teachers are well paid. The average teacher salary at South Fayette is $68,616, while the national average is $46,325.[18] In short, South Fayette has considerable financial resources at its disposal.

Second, South Fayette has vigorous and enlightened leadership, including a superintendent who actively promotes STEAM, staff members who are brimming with ideas, and a school board that strongly supports them. The latter is really important. As South Fayette Township Superintendent Bille Rondinelli puts it, "A superintendent can have all the greatest ideas in the world, but if the board doesn't support them, you can't do anything."[19] Len Fornella, who has served on the school board for thirty-six years, including several years as president, sums up his philosophy: "The curriculum is now integrated so that every subject matter has to include some STEAM. I leave it to the educators to work that out."[20] In other words, settle on a vision and then ease up on the throttle.

According to Fornella, South Fayette Township first promoted technology in a big way under Superintendent Linda Hippert. When Hippert stepped down in 2009, the School Board hired Rondinelli to succeed her. With enrollments bursting at the seams, Rondinelli and her team concluded that a new school would have to be built, and they settled on the idea of a new intermediate school. They also decided to ramp up their emphasis on STEAM. They hired Greg Wensell, who had a strong science and math background, to be the principal of the new school. Then Rondinelli and her team (including Wensell) decided to create three STEAM labs in the new school and asked Eckles Architecture and Engineering to draw up appropriate plans. The first floor (for third graders) would focus on environment and ecology. The second floor (for fourth graders) would focus on earth and space. The third floor (for fifth graders) would focus on robotics. STEAM labs were big enough to accommodate two groups of students. Rooms were painted with bright colors to attract students' attention. Charging stations were built. Cabinets were designed with open windows to prevent computers from overheating. Multiple design decisions reflected South Fayette's new commitment to STEAM education. After that, Rondinelli and her team sought to redesign the existing buildings to feature STEAM labs as well.[21]

One of Rondinelli's most adroit moves was to hire Aileen Owens to be director of technology and innovation in 2010.[22] Smart, skilled, enthusiastic, and entrepreneurial, Owens served for six years as instructional technology coordinator for the prestigious Mt. Lebanon School District, just outside Pittsburgh, before coming to South Fayette. According to Rondinelli, Owens is "the architect of the vertically aligned computational thinking framework that you see embedded at South Fayette." Owens worked at building relationships with teachers and students—coteaching classes at the middle school, initiating after-school mobile app labs in the high school, and hosting after-school Scratch clubs in the elementary school. She recruited and trained technology interns who are now employed as STEAM teachers at South Fayette. She also initiated an emerging innovation leaders team, guiding students to use their computer science skills to build software applications and products. Owens has become the public face of the maker movement at South Fayette, leading frequent tours, speaking with the press, and fighting to promote STEAM. She has also brought in over $350,000 in external grants for robotics, environmental literacy, creative entrepreneurship, and STEAM innovation. In Rondinelli's words, Owens "has been critical to our success."[23]

Third, South Fayette has the considerable advantage of an affluent, homogeneous student body which frees up resources for the STEAM initiative. Only 11 percent of its students qualify for a free or reduced price lunch—a striking difference from the national average of 51 percent.[24] Only 9 percent of South Fayette's students have an Individualized Education Program (IEP), as opposed to 13 percent nationally. Only 1 percent are English language learners, as opposed to 9 percent nationally.[25] South Fayette's demographics are not typical of the nation as a whole.[26]

In addition to these big factors, several smaller but significant factors also facilitate success. South Fayette is only twenty miles away from the city of Pittsburgh, which boasts several fine universities, including one with a world-class computer science department and a famed robotics program (Carnegie Mellon University), two with schools of education that offer special programs for students interested in STEM education (Pitt, Duquesne), and two with strong or solid engineering programs (CMU, Pitt). Pittsburgh also features a first-rate museum (with one of the most amazing dinosaur exhibits anywhere), an outstanding children's museum (featuring opportunities for woodworking, circuitry, textiles, and stop-motion animation activities), and a superb, highly interactive science center (including a STEM center funded by Chevron and several other corporations). Proximity to these regional treasures makes it easier for South Fayette to arrange field trips and guest lectures that are enriching and stimulating for students.

Another factor that facilitates success is the compactness of the South Fayette school enterprise. All four schools are located on the same twenty-two-acre campus, which makes it easier to coordinate. Take, for example, the student-driven after-school instructional program in Python. It's relatively easy for the high school student volunteers to visit the middle school, to tutor students and faculty there. In a more typical urban school district, where grade schools, middle schools, and high schools are miles apart, that would require a more heroic effort.

REPLICABILITY

Given important differences between South Fayette and the average school district in the United States, a key question is this: Can South Fayette's experiment in STEAM education be replicated elsewhere? Or, to ask a more universal question, can a school with limited resources and a disadvantaged student body successfully integrate STEAM or STEM into its curriculum, as South Fayette has done?

Let's begin with the good news: STEM and STEAM initiatives are alive and well in schools with limited financial resources and disadvantaged student bodies. In 2007 Alabama's Talladega County School District (with 74 percent of students receiving free or reduced-price lunches) decided to make technology a primary focus, with project-based learning as the tool of choice.[27] The timing was awkward, due to the recession, but the district has forged ahead, at least incrementally. Every student now has a laptop, and the school district has purchased two 3D printers. Elementary school students are learning to code, and high school students are being exposed to computer science and, to a lesser extent, engineering. Science and math teachers are receiving additional professional development.

At the Tulsa Public Schools (with 85 percent of students receiving free or reduced-price lunches), several middle schools offer engineering courses through Project Lead the Way: Will Rogers, Memorial, Edison, George Washington Carver, Hale, Thoreau Demonstration Academy, and Monroe. Two high schools (Memorial, Booker T. Washington) have robotics teams that have competed in national tournaments.

In 2013, the Union Public School District (with 66 percent of students receiving free or reduced-price lunches), which straddles Tulsa County and Broken Arrow, Oklahoma, established STEM as one of its four educational pillars (the others are early childhood education, community schools, and college and career readiness). Since then, Union has embarked on an ambitious proposal to introduce STEM concepts and teaching strategies to all elementary school teachers and more gradually to other teachers also. As of the summer of 2016, all elementary school teachers at Union had received some training in STEM.

In 2015, the Pittsburgh Public Schools (with 76 percent of students receiving free or reduced-price lunches) announced a new STEAM initiative that would transform five schools into STEAM magnets or partial magnets. At three of the schools (Lincoln Elementary, Woolslair Elementary, and Schiller Middle School), all of the teachers received some professional development in STEAM and project-based learning (during the summer of 2015). At two more schools (Perry High, Brashear High), a smaller number of teachers received similar instruction during the summer of 2016.

All of this is the tip of a much larger iceberg nationwide. For example, Project Lead the Way, which has developed a multifaceted STEM curriculum that encompasses engineering, computer science, and biomedical education, has formal ties with over 6,500 schools in fifty states. Many of these are inner city schools. In preparation for the 2014–2015 school year, Project Lead the Way trained a total of 6,137 teachers.[28]

A WHOLE LOT OF THINKING GOING ON

But do these STEM and STEAM initiatives promote critical thinking, problem solving, and creativity? Joe Clemmer, who taught engineering and science at Tulsa's Memorial Junior High through May 2016, certainly thinks so: "Our students learn to think out of the box . . . they have to analyze, figure things out, discuss stuff with other students, ask the right kinds of questions, plan and create."[29] And many of their creations are marvelous. For example, one of Clemmer's seventh graders made a pair of glasses with a little windshield wiper and a small motor. Another seventh grader built a contraption that could saw wood and grind grain. Several students, meeting with Clemmer after school, designed and built a catapult. Every year, dozens of students in Clemmer's science class build pop-bottle rockets, which they launch to an appreciative audience of students, after predicting how high they will go and after predicting whether an attached parachute will open. They are judged by how high and how far their rockets go. According to principal Ginger Bunnell, approximately one-third of all Memorial Junior High students take at least one engineering course. In Bunnell's words, "We're trying to get them interested in being researchers or engineers."[30]

Rustan Schwichtenberg, a retired Air Force colonel, who runs the Junior ROTC program at Booker T. Washington High School in Tulsa, agrees that critical thinking and STEM go well together. In his aerospace course, Schwichtenberg teaches students the A–B–Cs of flight. Although Schwichtenberg is very knowledgeable, he tries to avoid a didactic approach: "It's okay if you ask an engineering question and don't fill in the blanks for them. That's part of the critical-thinking process. One of the key lessons I learned as a STEM instructor is don't fill in the blanks! Stop talking, and when you don't talk, they talk to one another. When you let students talk to students, that's where the critical analysis occurs." After hours, Schwichtenberg helps students develop their STEM skills in a rocket club: "Kids had to make all the parts of the rocket. They had to understand engines, drag, weight, and thrust. It has been just a joy to watch the kids build really complex rockets." Schwichtenberg also started a cybersecurity club, which he calls HACCT (Hornet Academic & Cyber Competition Teams). In this club, students are given a challenge, like figuring out a password. They compete electronically with other teams from around the nation and around the world. In Schwichtenberg's words, "They learn problem solving, coding skills, problem analysis, R&D, and communications skills."[31] In 2016, Booker T.'s HACCT club made it to the state CyberPatriot competition, where teams receive a set of virtual images that represent operating systems and are asked to spot cybersecurity vulnerabilities and harden the system. HACCT students won second place in their first competition.

At some schools, students develop critical-thinking skills by building robots, either in class or after school. Some also participate in regional tournaments, and a smaller group participates in the prestigious world championship held annually. According to a survey of world championship robotics participants, 76 percent report strengthened communication skills, 93 percent report increased conflict-resolution skills, 95 percent report increased time-management skills, and 98 percent report improved problem-solving skills.[32] Pam Diaz, who heads up the robotics club at Tulsa's Booker T. Washington High School, summarizes the benefits of participation in such competitions: "During the competition students learn to think on their feet. They learn to make repairs and adjustments and redesigns fast. They learn communication skills and collaborative skills. They learn to be independent. They learn to talk to adults in interviews. I think this program is as near to 'orchestrated immersion' in a real-life situation as it gets."[33]

Two Tulsa high schools—Memorial and Booker T. Washington—participated in the World Robotics Championships in St. Louis in 2016. In both instances, students learned valuable critical-thinking and problem-solving skills, while facing intense deadline pressure. One of the teams even got to meet a fabled high-tech icon—Steve "Woz" Wozniak, co-inventor of the Apple computer (see "Storming the Castle," pp. 181–183).

At Pittsburgh Public Schools, the premise is that STEAM can promote critical thinking when combined with project-based learning. Nicole Findon, who teaches STEAM at Schiller Middle School, defines critical thinking succinctly as "students questioning themselves and their outcomes through reflection." She sees engineering as a way to promote that kind of critical thinking: "The engineering design process requires reflecting, fixing, and improving."[34] In collaboration with other Schiller teachers, Findon developed these skills in 2015–2016 through a drone-building exercise, dubbed "The Game of Drones." As Pittsburgh Public Schools STEAM coordinator Shaun Tomaszewski recalls, "Kids designed, fabricated, and iterated their own drone. They figured out the shape of the fuselage, where to put the propellers, how to attach the propellers to the drone." The process spanned multiple classrooms: "The science teacher taught them fluid dynamics. The English teacher had them writing and debating. The social studies teacher had them discussing the use of drones internationally. All of the middle school faculty got involved."[35]

At Lincoln Elementary School in Pittsburgh, another STEAM project has gained enough momentum to move from one or two classes to the entire school. In the summer of 2015, Mary Anderson, a third-grade science and math teacher, and Cary Allen, a fifth-grade science teacher, traveled to the University of Minnesota for a seminar on monarch butterflies. "They gave us all kinds of equipment and information," Anderson recalls. And their core message contained a challenge: "Our butterfly population is decreasing to alarming levels. What can we do to try to bring it back?" Excited and energized, Anderson applied for and obtained a $1,000 grant for planning a butterfly garden space— nectar-producing plants and milkweed so butterflies will return to the neighborhood. Next, she enlisted her students in the planning process. "We planned the garden together," Anderson recalls. Her math students used such concepts as perimeter and area to design the shell of the garden. Her science students investigated the botany side to determine which plants are most likely to attract butterflies. Mary Anderson is excited and so are her students: "Kids talk about spaces in the school as theirs. Third graders just *own* the garden. This is *our* garden!"[36] That fits in with the STEAM program's master plan, which is to give students a sense of agency and a sense that their dreams can become a reality by combining imagination, pluck, evidence, and hard work.

At around the same time, Lincoln Elementary launched a broader project, with support from the Pittsburgh Children's Museum and Grow Pittsburgh, which will transform a half acre of land into an outside maker space. That space will feature several gardens, including the butterfly garden, and some physical structures yet to be determined. Here, too, students participated significantly. They submitted sketches that depicted some very ambitious ideas: a pirate ship, a tree house, a river. Some of these ideas will have to be scaled back! But with a budget of $25,000 or more, there are still plenty of interesting possibilities. In the spring of 2016, students voted on several of the more promising ideas, and the winning proposals were forwarded to CMU's School of Architecture, which agreed to treat this as a design challenge. They consolidated some of the better ideas and sent recommendations to Pittsburgh Public Schools, which will move forward with some version of it. Shaun Tomaszewski, the STEAM coordinator, envisions that the new maker space will be beneficial not just for the school but for the community: "That neighborhood doesn't really have any community garden space. Ultimately, I want to see this become a sort of gathering place for the community as a whole."[37]

PERSONNEL CHALLENGES

It is not easy to recruit STEM or STEAM teachers. They are in great demand and are often gobbled up by school districts with bigger payrolls or school districts that benefit from close proximity to universities with STEM expertise or schools of education. Vicky Ozment, from Talladega County, puts it this way: "Our most difficult challenge in rural Alabama is finding engineers and computer programmers and people who are capable of teaching these subjects and willing to settle in Talladega County. We have those challenges already in math and science. We're struggling to find the math and science teachers as it is. Finding educators in these specialized areas will really be a challenge for us."[38]

Given recruitment problems and perennial budget shortfalls, some school districts have taken a different tack: enlisting regular teachers in the STEM or STEAM enterprise. Kathy Dodd, associate superintendent for Union Public Schools, explains: "At Union we use regular classroom teachers rather than dedicated teaching staff. All of our teachers are STEM trained in Project Lead the Way. If students are only taught problem-based learning in STEM class, what's happening the other four days? By making everybody a STEM teacher, it changes the way they teach their other courses."[39]

Retraining does not always follow a smooth path. When Pittsburgh launched its STEAM initiative, Tomaszewski was told that he could hire two new teachers but would mainly have to retrain the existing workforce. In July 2015, Tomaszewski conducted a two-week workshop on project-based learning for all teachers at three schools. "The elementary school teachers took to it immediately," he recalls. "But some of the middle school teachers reacted negatively."[40] Janet Jenkins, of Woolslair Elementary, was one of the skeptical teachers: "When I first heard about it, honestly, my first impression was that I wouldn't be able to give students what they need. I grew up in an era that was not strongly technology-based."[41]

Many of the affected Pittsburgh teachers, including Jenkins, have come to embrace STEAM. A key reason is that it has been implemented with sensitivity, with recognition that Rome wasn't built in a day, and with a very big carrot: STEAM school teachers have the freedom to deviate from the district's curricular requirements by embarking on a promising project. Lincoln Elementary School English teacher Teresa Partee puts it this way: "What I like the most is that we can step outside district rules prescribed for us as the curriculum. We can teach what *we* believe is most impactful, most meaningful. We could never have tackled the curse of violence in the community without the STEAM initiative. It allows us to work outside the traditional prescribed curriculum and do things differently. We can emphasize science and engineering and technology through field trips and speakers. It opens up things for kids that they don't always get to see because there's this belief that they can't do it. But they are capable. We can teach them! I love that we are a STEAM school and that we have these opportunities."[42] Jenkins agrees and now says she is thrilled that Woolslair has become a STEAM school. She also says she has learned that if you don't know as much as you might like about technology, some of your students can help you![43]

In my visits to school districts that have adopted STEM or STEAM initiatives, I asked whether these initiatives have met with resistance from teachers. Most of the time, administrators and coordinators reject the word *resistance*. At the same time, they acknowledge that some teachers take to STEM or STEAM more readily than others. Union School District's STEM coordinator Bill Murphy distinguishes between elementary school teachers, accustomed to teaching multiple subjects, and high school teachers, who specialize and not necessarily in STEM. For the latter, Murphy says, STEM may be a heavier lift: "I don't see resistance, but I do see a different level of anxiety and apprehension."[44] At Talladega County, the problem was more one of age. As Ozment recalls, "Some of our oldest teachers had the biggest learning curve."[45]

Even at South Fayette Township, acceptance of the STEAM initiative was not instant or universal. As South Fayette superintendent Rondinelli observes, "Anytime you do something different, there are three groups: those who are ready to jump in, those who are a little hesitant, and those who hang back. You need to start with people who are willing to jump in."[46] Trisha Craig, STEAM coordinator for the Fort Cherry School District, echoes this sentiment: "We start with the teachers who really want to learn."[47]

If recruitment and retraining are difficult, so too is retention. This is especially true when a school district faces cutbacks from the state. In Oklahoma, for example, the state legislature declined to raise taxes in 2016, despite shrinking oil revenue, resulting in huge cutbacks in education funding. For example, Tulsa Public Schools had to cut its budget by $8 million, and Union Public Schools had to cut its budget by $5.2 million.[48] Joe Clemmer retired in 2016, and Ginger Bunnell, principal of Memorial Junior High, was not sure she would be able to replace him.[49] Pam Diaz retired too, leaving the robotics team's future in doubt. As Nanette Coleman, principal of Booker T., said, "We're not sure we can afford robotics next year."[50]

Although few states have experienced budget cutbacks as severe as Oklahoma, other states have found that sustaining a STEM or STEAM program requires a combination of grit and ingenuity. This is especially true for underfunded school districts, like Fort Cherry in rural southwestern Pennsylvania. As Trisha Craig puts it, "We have to reinvent ourselves a lot because of budget cuts."[51] For example, the district hired a technology coach to help integrate technology and instruction several years ago, but that position was eliminated when the Pennsylvania legislature sharply cut education funding in 2011.

Despite these adversities, Fort Cherry remains committed to STEM education, and that commitment seems to be paying off. In 2016, Fort Cherry High school students won first prize in the Governor's STEM Competition for their invention: a device that helps disabled individuals and senior citizens use a computer despite limited manual dexterity (see "Grandpa Needs Help," pp. 183–185).

FUNDING CHALLENGES

Some of the STEM initiatives reviewed here have benefited enormously not just from enlightened school superintendents and supportive school boards but also from generous private foundations, which have fueled the growth in STEM activities. In the Pittsburgh area, the Grable Foundation has played a key role in supporting the STEAM initiatives of South Fayette Township, Fort Cherry, and the Pittsburgh Public Schools. In Tulsa, the George Kaiser Family Foundation has funded many local projects aimed at enhancing school quality, including the Union School district's STEM initiative. Union School District Superintendent Kirt Hartzler is deeply grateful for the private support his school district has received. But he worries about what will happen when these grants expire: "We're blowing up STEM—but how do we sustain it? If we don't have our philanthropists supporting us, we're in trouble."[52]

In Talladega County, it was a state agency grant, rather than a private foundation grant, that made a critical difference. Vicky Ozment recalls a visit to South Fayette Township in late 2015, when she and her school superintendent, Dr. Suzanne Lacey, observed a successful STEAM program in action: "We were so impressed by the fact that they seem to have a logical progression through high school. But we asked, 'How are we going to do this? We're broke!'"[53] Then manna appeared from heaven, in the form of a $300,000 grant from the Alabama Math Science and Technology Initiative (AMSTI) program. With these unexpected funds, Talladega County Public Schools were able to train some of their K–12 science and math teachers in STEAM concepts. They were also able to launch an engineering program at one of their schools (Childersburg). But who knows what will happen when the state grant expires?

DIVERSITY

Attracting girls has been a challenge for STEM programs from the beginning. Maker Academy, an Urban Assembly charter high school in New York City, which places a strong emphasis on STEM, has struggled to recruit girls. At the moment, two-thirds of the students are boys.[54] Principal Luke Bauer is trying to change that. One strategy is to use current students, including girls, as ambassadors and recruiters. Another strategy is to forge stronger links with middle school guidance counselors, who may recommend Maker Academy to female students.[55]

In Tulsa, girls are less likely to enroll in pre-engineering courses (known as gateway courses) than boys.[56] The same problem afflicts extracurricular activities in STEM. Of thirty-three robotics team members at Memorial High School in 2015–2016, seven were girls.[57] Of twenty-seven robotics team members at Booker T. Washington High School, five were girls.[58]

Attracting disadvantaged students and students of color to STEM courses and to STEM activities has also been a challenge. Part of the problem is that certain kinds of courses, like engineering courses, are less likely to be available at schools with higher poverty rates. Take Project Lead the Way, for example. Although PLTW offers its STEM courses at a wide variety of schools throughout the United States, high-poverty schools are less likely to offer such courses. In Pennsylvania, 33 percent of students who have access to PLTW courses are eligible for a free or reduced-price lunch, in a state where, on average, 54 percent of students are eligible for a free or reduced-price lunch.[59] In Oklahoma, 60 percent of students who have access to Project Lead the Way courses are eligible for a free or reduced-price lunch, in a state where, on average, 65 percent of students are eligible for a free or reduced-price lunch.[60] Presumably, these differences are due to the fact that high-poverty schools are less likely to be able to afford the annual fees required to affiliate with PLTW.

In Tulsa, students of color are less likely to enroll in pre-engineering courses, although that is purely a function of their lower SES. When one controls for school lunch eligibility, race and ethnicity are not related to enrollment in such courses, at least not in Tulsa.[61] Of thirty-three students on the robotics team at Memorial High in 2015–2016, three were black and four were Hispanic.[62] Of twenty-seven students on the robotics team at Booker T. Washington, one was black and six were Hispanic.[63] At Memorial High School, 34 percent of all students are black and 21 percent are Hispanic.[64] At Booker T. Washington High School, 36 percent of all students are black and 12 percent are Hispanic.[65]

The STEM diversity problem hits you over the head with a two-by-four if you visit regional and international robotics competitions. Bauer, who attended the World Robotics Competition in St. Louis, says it's "mostly white and Asian males."[66] Lane Matheson, who coached one of the teams, agrees: "Overall, it's still predominantly white male."[67] Ruthe Farmer of the National Center for Women & Information Technology sums up the problem succinctly. When it comes to STEM, she says, "We're not tapping 75 percent of the population."[68] The situation is equally discouraging for other elite STEM competitions, such as the International Math Olympiad, where no African American students and no Hispanic students and few girls have competed in the final event in its fifty-year history.[69] Tim Bajarin had a similar reaction when he visited a popular Maker Faire in San Mateo two years ago: he saw very few blacks and very few Hispanics among the one hundred twenty thousand attendees.[70]

On the bright side, schools with robotics teams often have policies in place that help disadvantaged students participate despite a lack of funds. At Booker T. Washington High School, if a student checks the box "financial assistance needed," the team absorbs the cost for that student. Also, the school tries to keep fees for traveling to robotics competitions as low as possible. For example, the school charged students $75 for a trip to Oklahoma City (including two nights of lodging and most meals) and $100 for a trip to St. Louis (including four nights of lodging and most meals).[71] At Memorial High School, a booster club pays for most expenses associated with the field trips. However, students can and do ask for financial assistance. Of twenty students attending the St. Louis competition in 2016, two asked for and received a scholarship to cover costs.[72] These scholarships are paid for by old-fashioned fundraising campaigns or by contributions from local foundations.

A CRITICAL LOOK AT STEM

There is so much to admire in STEM and STEAM that it seems almost churlish to raise objections. Yet, in a book on critical thinking, it would seem inappropriate not to do so. Like any promising education reform, STEM can fail to realize its full potential as a change agent.

One key question is this: if STEM is defined broadly enough to win over skeptical teachers, at what point does it stop being STEM? An ecumenical approach to STEM may both defuse the concept (by making it easier to accept) and dilute it (by transforming it into something that it is not). A common way to enlist teacher support and acceptance is to say, "You are probably doing something that is already close to STEM anyway." As a political tactic, this approach has much to commend it. But the danger is that STEM will lose its distinctiveness if it is defined broadly enough to include almost any innovation. One possible solution would be to be flexible initially (to win over skeptics) but more doctrinaire later (once teachers become more comfortable with something resembling STEM). But this course could be construed as disingenuous. Another possible solution would be to define STEM from the beginning as the shell, while defining project-based learning or critical thinking as the kernel within the shell. The advantage of this second approach is that it is both more honest and more consistent. A third approach would be to acknowledge that STEM competes with other worthy educational goals, thus justifying departures from STEM in pursuit of these other goals (building collaborative skills through project-based learning, promoting creativity through artistic self-expression, and so on). Whatever approach is taken, both teachers and students need frequent reminders that STEM at its best enhances a broad set of intellectual skills.

A second question for STEM advocates and coordinators is this: in our curricular and extracurricular assignments, are we focusing on the right STEM skills? Robots and rockets and drones have been great tools for motivating and enticing students, especially boys, to enlist in the STEM crusade. To design and redesign these movable objects requires coding skills, spatial-reasoning skills, hypothesis-testing skills, problem-solving skills, and collaborative skills, all of which are undeniably valuable. But other design projects may have even broader appeal—to students from disadvantaged backgrounds and to girls, for example. Music may be one of these, whether it takes the form of composing a tune on the computer or building a musical instrument from scratch. E-textiles, created, for example, by sewing batteries or LEDs or integrated circuits into garments, may be another, because it can appeal to students who care about fashion, dress, and personal appearance. Perhaps this is just another way of saying that STEAM has some advantages over STEM, because it integrates the more playful domain of the arts into the more practical domain of computer science and engineering. If it also creates sustained interest in STEM from a more diverse set of students, then that is a big bonus.

A third question to ponder is this: Should we be worried that only a relatively small number of students take full advantage of STEM offerings in the curriculum and after school? At the schools I visited, the number of students participating in STEM extracurricular activities after school is relatively small. For these students, STEM is exciting and empowering—a fantastic learning experience. But most students are not fully engaged in STEM. Even at South Fayette Township, which has unleashed a veritable STEAM revolution in its four schools, there is room for growth. For example, virtually every student participates in STEAM coursework to some degree, but only a dozen or so high school students a year sign up for the Innovation Studio, which offers a full range of work-focused engineering activities. This may change in the fall of 2017, when South Fayette High School unveils a new Fab Lab, which will be able to accommodate as many as eighty students at a time. It may change yet again when the first cohort exposed from the start to a STEAM curriculum comes of age. Still, it is a useful reminder that it takes awhile to radically transform the educational landscape, even under favorable conditions.

A final question to consider is this: Are STEM initiatives sustainable at a time when school budgets are so precarious? A viable STEM program requires both physical capital (computers, software, 3D printers, LEGOs, motors, sensors) and human capital (teachers and administrators). Many successful STEM programs owe a great deal to private foundations, which have provided vital financial support. As these programs mature and as other programs get started, where will the funds come to sustain them, to rejuvenate them, and to integrate them into the rest of the curriculum? There are limits to what foundations can accomplish. Without the strong and steady support of taxpayers, these and other STEM initiatives can easily lose their luster and become pale shadows of their former selves. In recent years, state funding for our public schools has faltered, with thirty-one states providing less funding in 2014 than before the Great Recession.[73] Clearly, the future of STEM depends on a school finance system that is robust, supple, and fair.

CONCLUSION

A big advantage of STEM or STEAM initiatives over some other educational reforms is that these initiatives promote the kinds of critical-thinking skills that are highly valued by employers, such as applied mathematics, adaptability, and teamwork. As I have argued repeatedly, our K–12 schools do not always emphasize such skills as much as they should. Much STEM activity involves problem solving, which helps students explore the valuable space in the Venn diagram where critical thinking and problem solving overlap. Much STEAM activity also involves creativity, which invites students to spread their wings artistically as they create products that are simultaneously useful and aesthetically appealing.

The future of STEM or STEAM is not equally bright in all school districts or all schools. Much depends on the presence of strong administrative leadership; a supportive school board; supportive taxpayers; public-spirited foundations, universities, museums, and corporations; a talented and flexible teaching staff; and students who are eager to learn. When all these ingredients are present, as in South Fayette Township, amazing learning experiences are possible. When they are not, the seeds of STEM or STEAM innovation may not take root.

One positive lesson from southwestern Pennsylvania is that school districts can accomplish much more when they work together as partners than when they toil in splendid isolation. With encouragement from the Grable Foundation, school districts in southwestern Pennsylvania have shared ideas and experiences in an effort to improve prospects for all students in the region. South Fayette Township has shared many ideas with Fort Cherry Township, and they have written successful grant proposals together. The Schiller Middle School in Pittsburgh has a good relationship with South Fayette, and the Lincoln Elementary School in Pittsburgh has an embryonic relationship with Chartiers Valley School District. In both instances, students from the two schools meet to share STEAM ideas and experiences. South Fayette regularly invites teachers and administrators from other school districts to come visit their STEAM labs. In the summer of 2015, they held a week-long professional development workshop for 100 teachers, charging only a nominal fee. In the summer of 2016, they expanded that workshop to 120 teachers and reduced the fee for teachers from disadvantaged school districts. South Fayette also participates in the League of Innovative Schools and shares ideas with their neighbors. Instead of thinking of themselves as islands, southwestern Pennsylvania's school districts have formed an archipelago, with lots of opportunities to share ideas and diffuse innovations.

Everyone benefits from such cooperation, in the short run and in the long run. As economist Tim Bartik has noted, an individual's wages depend not only on his or her education but also on the education levels of others in the labor market: "I can be the most skilled person in the world, but if everyone else in my firm lacks skills my employer is going to find it more difficult to introduce new technology, new production techniques. So, as a result, my employer is going to be less productive. They will not be able to afford to pay me as good wages."[74] In fact, Bartik argues that when someone gets a college degree, the spillover effects of this achievement on others in the labor market are actually greater than the direct effects on the person who earned the degree. At its best, STEM and STEAM programs produce multiplier effects that ripple throughout the regional economy.

It is exciting to see how schools can transform themselves to promote critical thinking, problem solving, and creativity. It is also exciting to see schools teach the kinds of skills that employers actually value—the ability to adapt, the ability to work with others, the ability to solve complex problems. When conditions are ripe, miraculous changes can occur. When some but not all of the most favorable conditions are present, meaningful changes are still possible. On the other hand, progress has been uneven. For some lucky students, STEM and STEAM initiatives have promoted both enjoyment and employment. But not all students have been so lucky. For many students, the American dream remains tantalizing but elusive.

STORMING THE CASTLE

A robotics competition can be a great way to encourage critical thinking, problem solving, and creative responses to new challenges. When designing a robot, students must apply principles learned in mathematics and engineering classes. When redesigning a robot, students must solve problems that surface when their robot tries to execute a given task. When competing with other robots, students must adapt to unexpected dilemmas, facing real deadlines.

Robotics begins at the school level, where students create their own robots, using aluminum or wood for the framing, wires, motors, sensors, wheels, and other materials. Schools with ambitious robotics programs compete in regional tournaments. A smaller group of schools are chosen to participate in the world championships, sponsored by an organization called FIRST (For Inspiration and Recognition of Science and Technology).

In April 2016, two Tulsa Public Schools high schools participated in the World Robotics Championships in St. Louis. Each team was assigned to two other partner teams at random. They had to decide who would do what in order to pursue their common goal. This year's game required the allies to storm a castle and assault it with boulders hurled by robots. To capture the tower, they had to overcome several barriers, including a moat and a drawbridge, among others.

Memorial High School's robotics team, coached by Lane Matheson, encountered a problem before the competition began. Safety advisors objected to the power strip (a relocatable power tap) that the team used in the pit to power their robot, contending that it was a daisy chain that violated the rules. The students conducted some quick research and determined that at most they were using 24 percent of the power strip's capacity, which should pose no threat of a fire. They then presented their findings to the safety advisors. Although the safety advisors insisted on applying the rule in this case, they praised the students for their research and for an articulate presentation. During the competition, Memorial's robot started to make sharp unscripted turns to the right, like a car whose wheels were out of alignment. The students investigated and identified the problem (something wrong with one of the gearboxes connected to the drive motors) but concluded that an immediate repair would take too much time. Of necessity, the fault went uncorrected.

It would be nice to report that these exercises in critical thinking and problem solving led the team to victory. Unfortunately, that was not the case. The Memorial High team's overall record was 2–8. However, the students did learn some valuable lessons—among them, how to cope with a problem without panicking, how to gather good evidence under severe time pressure, and how to "satisfice" given limited time and limited information. These skills may not have won the day in St. Louis, but they will help these students the next time they compete and also later in life.

Booker T. Washington High School's robotics team also coped with pressure in St. Louis. As coach Pam Diaz recalls, "We kept bending the aluminum wedges used to lift a sliding door. We had to take them to the machine shop and flatten them out." Between matches, the Booker T. team made the necessary repairs and their performance improved. One of the skills that students learn when they compete in a robotics tournament is collaboration. They must cooperate with two other teams, and they must divide the labor. In this year's game, normally, one robot had to breach barriers, while the other two teams got to shoot. The Booker T. team appraised the situation realistically and concluded that their allies had better shooters. They graciously acquiesced. As Diaz put it, "Our students . . . were the first to recognize that if someone else had a better shooter, their time was better spent breaching the barriers." These are the kinds of adaptive skills that employers value and that will help these students later in life. Ultimately, the team did pretty well, with a 5–5 record. Team members also rubbed elbows with high-tech royalty, when they met Steve "Woz" Wozniak, co-inventor of the Apple computer and one of the judges at the competition. What a story to tell their parents and what an inspiration for a future in STEM!

GRANDPA NEEDS HELP

Connor Ehrgood's grandfather loved to play fantasy football but had to stop when he fell and hurt himself. With weakened fine motor skills, he couldn't hit the keys on his keyboard well enough to type. That gave Connor, a sophomore at Fort Cherry High School, an idea: Why not connect a large joystick to a laptop so that people with disabilities could type commands and maneuver in different directions? The notion gained momentum when a fellow student, Emily Richard, invited Connor to join a small group of students interested in competing in the second annual Governor's STEM Competition. Connor's teammates and their faculty sponsor liked the idea, and together they started working on a prototype. They eventually called it SticKey.

As a first step, the students created outer cores for two joysticks, using a 3D printer. As Connor explained, "Two joysticks were much more efficient than one. With two joysticks, you should only need two clicks to get to the letter." They then connected the joysticks to a computer via USB devices. But much of this changed over time. The original joysticks were a bit cumbersome. As Connor recalled, "Some people couldn't grasp them." So they used Inventor (an Autodesk program that works with a 3D printer) to design a sphere, which was easier to handle. They also decided to use Bluetooth technology to connect the joysticks to the computer with wireless connections, thus enhancing maneuverability. Next, the students sought and received extensive feedback on SticKey, from technology experts, health professionals, disabled individuals, and others.

After developing a schematic, the students contacted Dr. Bambi Brewer from Birdbrain Technologies in Pittsburgh. She recommended that they eliminate a proposed pedal from the device because disabled persons might not have use of their legs. The students also met with a physical therapist at the Cameron Wellness Center (in nearby Washington, Pennsylvania), who suggested that the device could serve a broader purpose beyond just entertainment—as therapy for patients who suffered from manual disabilities. People at the New Horizon School (a special education school in Beaver County) also helped by recommending that the team use Dycem, a nonslip material, to keep the base from slipping.

With this valuable feedback, the students created an actual prototype. Then they visited Health South, a rehabilitation center in Sewickley, Pennsylvania, where health professionals suggested that the joysticks be attached to a wheelchair to make it more convenient for disabled patients to use them. The students also received valuable advice from Alpha Lab, Inventionland, and Tech Shop, on marketing, patenting, and related business activities.

Producing and improving SticKey was not smooth sailing. As the project became more and more demanding, some students withdrew. They just couldn't afford the time, because the project distracted them from class work or extracurricular activities. Both Connor and Emily recall that this was a discouraging time. In Emily's words, "That was a huge hurdle we had to overcome, but we did." Time management was a challenge for Connor and Emily too, but they persevered. Supportive teachers certainly helped, and the project itself was compelling. Despite a shrinking group and escalating time demands, Connor and Emily stuck with SticKey.

In February, the Fort Cherry team participated in a regional competition in LeMont Furnace, Pennsylvania, and beat seven other teams to win a coveted invitation to the state championships. In May, the Fort Cherry team attended the state championship tournament in Lancaster, Pennsylvania, along with twenty-four other teams. The atmosphere was friendly and supportive. Students seemed genuinely curious about other students' projects. Connor and Emily were both a little nervous, but they performed like pros when they had to. After two rounds, the judges announced the winners . . . and awarded first place to . . . the Fort Cherry team!

Looking back on the experience, Connor feels more self-confident: "I didn't think that I could bring this idea to fruition at first. But we did!" And Emily sharpened her organizational and communication skills: "I learned that people are willing to talk with you if you make a phone call. Sometimes just one phone call will get you the information you need." Trisha Craig, Fort Cherry's Director of Curriculum, who worked closely with the students from start to finish, was impressed by their tenacity and their adaptability: "Both kids had the courage to pursue their goals, try and fail, listen and act (or not act) on advice from others, not give up, visit new places, consider new ideas, speak their minds, ask difficult questions, and answer difficult questions."

A New Division of Labor

CRITICAL THINKING lies near the surface of many important debates over K–12 education in the United States. It is closely linked to what college admissions committees look for in prospective students and what college professors hope to develop in their students. It is routinely listed as one of the twenty-first century skills workers will need in the coming years, and it sometimes appears at the top of that list. It is one of the skills citizens require to be able to participate wisely in democratic deliberations over public officials and public policy. For better or worse, it is closely identified with the Common Core, with AP courses, and with SAT and ACT exams.

To recapitulate, critical thinking is an open-minded inquiry that seeks out relevant evidence to analyze a question or proposition. Critical thinking looks for flaws in other people's reasoning, as well as flaws in one's own reasoning. Critical thinkers follow good evidence where it leads them, even when the conclusions are unsettling. Contrary to Jack Nicholson's accusation in *A Few Good Men*, critical thinkers can handle the truth. In fact, the search for the truth is their primary mission.

Critical thinking did not suddenly emerge out of the ether. It has a proud heritage. Socrates had critical thinking in mind when he urged students to challenge his fundamental assumptions as well as their own.[1] Sir Francis Bacon had critical thinking in mind when he recommended that we formulate clear hypotheses and use good empirical evidence to confirm or refute them.[2] John Dewey had critical thinking in mind when he extolled the virtues of "reflective thinking."[3]

While highlighting the virtues of critical thinking, I have not asserted that it is the only useful form of higher-order thinking. On the contrary, I have emphasized the value of other forms of thinking, such as creative thinking and problem solving. In fact, I have argued that some of our most formidable intellectual breakthroughs occur at the nexus between critical thinking and creativity, or at the nexus between critical thinking and problem solving. When we manage to combine all three (critical thinking, creative thinking, and problem solving), marvelous discoveries and inventions are possible!

I have also stressed that other skills and habits of mind are important for success in school, success at work, and success in life. These skills include teamwork, or the capacity for fruitful collaboration with others. They include communications skills, such as reading, writing, and speaking with lucidity, coherence, and conviction. They include intellectual curiosity, tolerance, empathy, and an appetite for hard work. Substantive knowledge and expertise are also vitally important. Without substantive knowledge and expertise, critical thinking would be hopelessly abstract.

Critical thinking enhances these skills and habits of mind and vice versa. Critical thinking can be especially exhilarating and productive when conducted as a group activity. Critical thinking can promote and improve knowledge acquisition by providing strong conceptual scaffolding that facilitates retention and application. Critical thinking can enhance our prose so that it almost sounds like poetry, as in Lincoln's Gettysburg Address.[4] Critical thinking, like curry powder, can add spice to almost any intellectual endeavor. In many situations, it is not just an alternative to other forms of thinking but a crucial supplement or a helpful catalyst.

In this chapter, I review some cross-cutting themes on critical thinking that have been central to this book. They include the need to start early; the need to reach all children including disadvantaged children; and the need to adapt to a changing global economy, to new technology, and to new trends in politics and society. I also make some practical suggestions, for teachers and others, to advance the cause of critical thinking.

EARLY CHILDHOOD EDUCATION

A young child's brain is amazing in its complexity, its capacity, and its versatility. Children are capable of astonishing intellectual feats. As Alison Gopnik and her colleagues put it, a child's brain is "the most powerful learning machine in the universe."[5] Young children can be thought of as budding scientists who construct rough-and-ready theories that fit fragmentary evidence and then reconstruct new theories as additional evidence challenges earlier assumptions.[6]

The neuroscience literature seldom refers to critical thinking per se, but it often refers to fluid reasoning and executive functioning, which are closely related antecedents of critical thinking. That literature makes it abundantly clear that the conceptual scaffolding required for fluid reasoning, executive functioning, and critical thinking as adults is best acquired early. This has important implications for how we structure our educational curriculum, including pre-K and K–3 classes.

A constructivist approach to early childhood education is an excellent way to help young children develop rudimentary critical-thinking skills by exploring the world around them with help from a supportive adult. As Piaget and Vygotsky discussed, the constructivist approach posits that young learners need to be fully engaged and actively thinking for profound learning to occur; it also views teachers not as dispensers of knowledge but as facilitators and guides.[7]

One of the great benefits of a constructivist approach in early childhood education is that it promotes civic readiness. As Rheta DeVries and Betty Zan explain, a key goal of the constructivist approach is to create a "sociomoral atmosphere" in which "respect for others is practiced."[8] By minimizing the exercise of authority in relations with children, constructivist teachers help create conditions that facilitate deliberative democracy, including mutual respect and cooperation. The constructivist approach also promotes college readiness, by encouraging "active experimentation with all its necessary groping and error."[9] Finally, the constructivist approach has the potential to promote career readiness because it emphasizes real-world examples, which could easily include examples from the world of work. In short, the constructivist approach to early childhood education is a triple threat!

Another way to promote critical thinking would be to enroll students in a Montessori school, based on to the educational philosophy of Maria Montessori. Montessori was deeply committed to critical thinking, which she thought was best encouraged by teaching children to experience the world by using all five senses.[10] Although Montessori called for teachers to use "didactic materials," by which she meant physical objects that stimulate thinking, her pedagogy was anything but didactic. In fact, she lauded teachers who exercised self-restraint in the classroom: "It is necessary . . . that the teaching shall be guided by the principle of limiting to the greatest possible point the active intervention of the educator."[11] Montessori believed that students should learn from their mistakes and develop a "friendly feeling towards error."[12] She celebrated independent thinking and endorsed experiential learning.[13] More than four thousand Montessori schools in the United States promote these ideas.[14]

Specific curricula that stress understanding and comprehension rather than rote memorization can also be useful in laying the foundation for critical-thinking and problem-solving skills. The Building Blocks math curriculum, developed by Doug Clements and Julie Sarama, is a good example.[15] That curriculum helps young children make the connection between physical quantities (seven marbles), abstract symbols (7), and number words (seven). It helps them to "subitize," or count by sight. It introduces them to such concepts as cardinality (how many objects in a set) and one-to-one correspondence (matching groups of objects like cups and saucers).[16] In utilizing this curriculum and others like it, the teacher's attitude is important. Ideally, when students offer an answer, the teacher will ask: how do you know? Persistent probing helps ensure that the student truly understands what is going on.

EQUAL OPPORTUNITY

As with many educational deficits, disadvantaged children face a critical-thinking gap. It begins early in life, when at-risk children are more likely than other children to experience toxic stress. Children who suffer from toxic stress are less able to process new experiences and new information. They are less able to grow cognitively and socioemotionally. Because toxic stress adversely affects the brain's synapses, it contributes to a downward spiral over time.

Although toxic stress has many roots, poverty is the most fundamental. And poverty has big effects on brain development. As Kimberly Noble has noted, poor children have a smaller cortical surface area.[17] This helps explain developmental differences between low-income and higher-income children over time. In general, poor children also have weaker connections between the amygdala, the hippocampus, and other parts of the brain.[18]

Studies show that the executive-functioning skills of low-income children are relatively weak.[19] This is unfortunate because executive-functioning skills like self-regulation contribute to future learning and future success. The importance of saying no to a readily available marshmallow is one famous example of a broader phenomenon: if children learn to focus on long-term goals, to regulate impulsive behavior, and to manage their time well, they are more likely to be successful in school, at work, and in life. If children are easily distracted, have difficulty controlling their appetites, and can't discipline themselves, they are more likely to get into trouble later.

The educational achievement gap between high-income and low-income children has widened over the past twenty-five years, and by a substantial amount.[20] In fact, it now exceeds the achievement gap between blacks and whites. This raises questions about our self-image as an "equal opportunity" society. It also raises questions about whether states are discharging their constitutional responsibilities. Most state constitutions require a high-quality public education for *all* children.

Instead of reducing the critical-thinking gap, our public schools sometimes reinforce it, without intending to do so. More disadvantaged children are, in general, more likely to have teachers who use "didactic" or authoritative pedagogical techniques. This is true in pre-K, in early elementary education, in middle school, and in high school.[21] In contrast, more advantaged children are, in general, more likely to have teachers who use constructivist techniques.

More disadvantaged children are less likely to take AP courses, where they could get exposed to the Socratic method in classroom seminars. In contrast, more advantaged children are more likely to take such courses.[22]

More disadvantaged children are less likely to be exposed to enrichment activities, which help develop students' critical-thinking and problem-solving skills. Robotics clubs (and other STEM-related clubs), which offer fantastic learning opportunities to students, continue to enlist white, middle-class boys more often than other students.

The problem, in a nutshell, is that disadvantaged students are less likely to be exposed to teachers, to courses, and to extracurricular activities that will give them valuable critical-thinking skills.

TWENTY-FIRST CENTURY SKILLS

The futuristic world that Alvin Toffler described as "future shock" is already upon us.[23] We live in a global economy, at a time when middle-skill jobs are declining, and at a time when new technologies are rapidly changing how we acquire knowledge, how we work, how we communicate with one another, and how we make decisions. Critical thinking can be enormously useful in navigating such a world.

Critical thinking is an especially important skill today because it strengthens nonroutine thinking, for which there is growing demand. In recent years, we have witnessed a dramatic decline in jobs for secretaries, bank tellers, travel agents, and other middle-skill workers whose routine tasks can be performed reasonably well by computers.[24] In contrast, the demand for workers with strong analytical skills such as critical thinking has grown.[25]

In a global economy, we need to ask ourselves what our comparative advantage is, if we are to compete successfully with China, India, and other emerging powers. As President Obama has said, if we are to out-compete the rest of the world, we will need to out-educate the rest of the world.[26] And that is not simply a matter of producing more students with college degrees or more students who do well on standardized tests. Our advantages, when compared to other countries, include our entrepreneurial skills, our creativity (in both science and the arts), and, yes, our critical-thinking skills. When Chinese students apply to US graduate schools, their professors often praise their critical-thinking skills. That is not because Chinese students have such skills more than other students, but rather because their professors believe that *we* value such skills and that *we* are able to teach them.

RECOMMENDATIONS

If critical thinking is as important as I suggest, then what can we do to promote it and to embed it in our K–12 curriculum? Certainly, one answer to that question is that teachers can do a lot. However, the rest of us also can do a lot:

1. *What can pre-K teachers do?* They can help develop young children's executive-functioning skills, including self-regulation, working memory, and adaptability. They can ask lots of questions and invite young children to explain their reasoning. They can emphasize the importance of mutual respect.

2. *What can elementary school teachers do?* They can encourage a sense of excitement about learning. They can dig deeper into a narrower range of subjects. They can encourage students to solve problems themselves before offering an authoritative solution.

3. *What can middle school teachers do?* They can teach not only specific critical-thinking skills but also the concept of switching from one thinking style to another (e.g., by using de Bono's hats). They can require students to work collaboratively with other students on big projects (e.g., science projects and role-playing exercises).

4. *What can high school teachers do?* They can offer Socratic seminars in which students learn to challenge one another and their teacher respectfully. They can help students distinguish between evidence-based arguments and "blowing smoke." When students engage in sloppy thinking, they can say so, without being unpleasant. They can try to integrate workplace skills into their curriculum, through weekly (or even daily) examples that connect academic learning to authentic real-world problems that arise at work. They can declare a Media Awareness Day, in which students abandon their cell phones and their computers, to better appreciate the virtues of silence and face-to-face communication.

5. *What can schools of education do?* They can offer elective courses that show teachers how to teach critical thinking, how to

differentiate it from other forms of thinking, and how to assess it. They can include critical thinking as a subject in gateway courses required of all students. They can establish plausible connections between critical thinking and concepts such as inquiry and argument.

6. *What can principals do?* They can promote critical thinking but also the classroom environments and structures that are most conducive to critical thinking: open classrooms, project-based learning, collaborative projects, simulations and role-playing exercises. They can promote extracurricular activities that stress critical thinking, like Odyssey of the Mind and Destination Imagination. Above all, principals can ask whether their organizational culture promotes learning. It is easy to identify obvious problems like noise and the threat of violence that interfere with learning. It is more difficult to identify more subtle problems such as students who dutifully pursue better grades without really probing for deeper meanings and connections.

7. *What can school superintendents do?* They can develop strategic plans like the Fairfax County, Virginia Plan, Portrait of a Graduate, which emphasizes five Twenty-First Century Skills: Communicator, Collaborator, Global Citizen, Creative and Critical Thinker, and Goal-Directed and Resilient Individual.[27] They can support STEM and STEAM labs that simultaneously promote critical thinking, creative thinking, and problem solving through scientific research, applied engineering, and the arts. They can actively consider the possibility of a universal internship requirement, to help ensure that students have first-hand exposure to the intellectual, interpersonal, and logistical challenges of the world of work.

8. *What can guidance counselors do?* They can reallocate their time and their advising to place greater emphasis on career readiness and less emphasis on college readiness. Incidentally, they should do this for all students, not just for disadvantaged students. Middle-class students need to think about careers carefully too, and this should be a factor in their decisions about college.

9. *What can public officials do?* They can adopt the Common Core and require the use of assessment tools that evaluate critical-thinking skills, among other skills. They can ensure that all students (include disadvantaged students) have access to outstanding

teachers who stress critical thinking in their pedagogy. They can do this by authorizing programs that reward teachers for teaching in schools with challenging demographics. They can also actively consider establishing apprenticeship programs for high school students, such as those in place in Georgia and Wisconsin.[28] And they can make it easier for people with valuable business experience to teach in our classrooms.[29]

10. *What can journalists do?* They can continue to write about critical thinking but do more to explain through concrete examples what it actually looks like in practice. They can do a better job of highlighting workplace skills and career choices. They can seek out diverse opinions on controversial subjects, thus facilitating tolerance and deliberation. And when they screen opinion pieces for publication, they can insist that op-ed writers take evidence seriously. A bundle of strong opinions is not necessarily a strong opinion piece.

11. *What can Hollywood do?* Studios can produce movies that capture the excitement of intellectual discovery or problem solving, not just in the classroom (*Stand and Deliver, The Dead Poets Society*) but also in other settings (*Apollo 13, Lincoln, The Imitation Game*). They can also produce movies that illuminate the mysteries of the human brain (*Inside Out*).

12. *What can researchers do?* They can study and evaluate innovative critical-thinking programs and strategies. They can coax school districts to participate in some randomized experiments. And they can use rigorous quasi-experimental research designs when randomized control trials are not available.

13. *What can businesses do?* They can seek out opportunities to collaborate with schools and school districts. They can hire student trainees and interns, not for make-work projects but for meaningful assignments that illuminate the potential excitement of a particular occupation or profession. They can offer internships or jobs to high school students. They can follow the examples of Career Academies, P-Tech, and California's Linked Learning initiatives.

14. *What can nonprofits do?* Nonprofit organizations can provide after-school programs that build valuable critical-thinking

skills and that encourage empathy and mutual respect. They can reach out to underserved communities, including disadvantaged students and students of color. They can enlist parents as allies, by holding workshops that confirm the importance of critical thinking, whether through classwork or extracurricular activities.

15. *What can parents do?* They can teach critical-thinking skills at home. Instead of providing answers, they can ask better questions. Instead of offering information, they can provide conceptual scaffolding. They can give children meaningful choices to make and see how they respond. If your child has a blind spot, work on it.

16. *What can students do?* They can provide useful feedback to their teachers. They can let their teachers know which teaching strategies are most conducive to learning. They can come to school rested, well fed, and drug-free. If school is difficult for them, they can ask for help. If school is easy for them, they can offer help.

HOW HARD TO CHANGE?

Some of these changes will require substantial commitments of time, energy, and money. To establish new STEM or STEAM labs, for example, could require us to reconstruct some of our school buildings, restructure and realign our curricula across grades, recruit more highly qualified teachers who specialize in these subjects, and provide the funding for new equipment and new software. A system of apprenticeships comparable to what Germany and Switzerland have would require a new way of thinking, new resources, and new relationships between public schools and private businesses.

On the other hand, some changes are well within our grasp and would not require major alterations in either funding priorities or teachers' behavior. Take, for example, the most important of these changes, which would be for teachers to devote more attention to critical thinking, especially critical thinking aimed at career readiness and civic readiness.

That kind of change sounds daunting at first, but a little bit of effort—and greater self-consciousness about this enterprise—could go a long way. In some ways, it might be comparable to a small change that has revolutionized surgery in US hospitals: a simple two-minute checklist to make sure that certain basic steps have been taken to ensure a patient's safety.[30] It might be comparable to the sharp improvement in how we treat our military veterans, thanks in part to the now ubiquitous mantra, "Thank you for your service." Cultural changes take place by introducing powerful ideas and institutionalizing them.

Some years ago, I interviewed 104 child-care inspectors in four states, in an effort to understand their norms and practices as they inspected day-care centers and family day-care homes.[31] One of the things that struck me about their visits to child-care facilities is how narrowly they defined their jobs. To many child-care inspectors, their job was to look for code violations, report them, and try to eradicate them. This is undoubtedly a worthwhile objective, and it took a good deal of time to do this work and to do it well.

Other roles, however, were being neglected: as an informer (to let child-care providers know about government programs like the Child Care Food Program that could benefit their children); as a connector (to let child-care providers know about informal networks of providers who might help them improve their professional practices); and as an advisor (friendly tips to help them improve their pedagogy). A broader definition of the job of child-care inspector would not have required much additional time. It's easy enough to mention a social services program, leave a brochure with a contact person's name on it, or write a phone number for a support group on a slip of paper. It's also relatively easy to mention a strategy for dealing with a child who acts up on occasion or to coax a shy child to come out of his or her shell. The very best child-care inspectors defined their jobs broadly enough to include these additional roles, and it did not deter them from discharging their other responsibilities. On the contrary, it made them infinitely more valuable to the providers they regulated and to the children they were serving. Similarly, I would argue that the extraordinary success of the Nurse Family Partnership Program is due in part to the willingness of visiting nurses to define their role broadly.[32] For example, nurses routinely provide information on health care, child care, and job training opportunities as part of their regular visits to the homes of first-time mothers.[33]

My hope is that teachers will define their jobs a bit more broadly after reading this book. We need teachers to promote critical thinking, creative thinking, and problem solving. We need teachers to choose assignments and examples that promote college readiness, career readiness, and civic readiness. Is this unrealistic? Does it ask too much of teachers? Perhaps it does. None of us wishes to see teachers trying to mop up far too much water like Mickey Mouse in *Fantasia* or Lucille Ball trying to wrap too many chocolates on a rapidly accelerating assembly line.

But think instead of a painter who has more colors to work with, a musician who has Dorian and Mixolydian scales to choose from, a scientist who has more equipment in his or her lab, or a basketball coach who has more plays in his or her playbook. When teachable moments arise, I hope that teachers will think about critical thinking, regardless of what subject they teach and regardless of what grade they teach. Then, when critical thinking is on their radar screen, I hope that teachers will think about their students as future workers and future citizens. The mismatch between employers' expectations and workers' disappointing skills is one that teachers can help reduce. The mismatch between the norms of a deliberative democracy and our shrill, partisan political debates is one that teachers can help reduce. We need critical thinking more than ever. And teachers are our best bet to give it to us, and more particularly to our children.

I also hope that other sectors of society will provide teachers crucial support as they seek to sharpen and broaden our students' repertoire of critical-thinking skills. Employers can help by forging partnerships with schools, by offering internships to students, and by talking more concretely about the kinds of critical-thinking skills that are desperately needed in the workplace. Politicians can help by providing more funding to education, by allocating funds and deploying teachers more equitably, and by improving their own deliberative discourse, as a model for future citizens. Parents can help by asking good questions at the dinner table, by encouraging respectful disagreements at home and in public, and by weaning their children away from an excessive reliance on social media. The task of enhancing our students' critical-thinking skills belongs to all of us, and not just to teachers.

Schools Visited by Author

Booker T. Washington High School (Tulsa, OK)
City Charter High School (Pittsburgh, PA)
Edison Preparatory High School (Tulsa, OK)
Falk Laboratory School (Pittsburgh, PA)
Fort Cherry Elementary School (McDonald, PA)
Fort Cherry Junior/Senior High School (McDonald, PA)
George Washington Carver Middle School (Tulsa, OK)
Lincoln Elementary School (Pittsburgh, PA)
McAuliffe Elementary School (Broken Arrow, OK)
Memorial Junior High School (Tulsa, OK)
Schiller Middle School (Pittsburgh, PA)
South Fayette Elementary School (McDonald, PA)
South Fayette High School (McDonald, PA)
South Fayette Intermediate School (McDonald, PA)
South Fayette Middle School (McDonald, PA)
Swanson Middle School (Arlington, VA)
Urban Assembly Maker Academy (New York, NY)
Will Rogers College Junior High School (Tulsa, OK)
Woolslair Elementary School (Pittsburgh, PA)
Yorktown High School (Arlington, VA)

APPENDIX

Schools Visited by Author

NOTES

Introduction

1. Milton Lodge and Charles Taber, *The Rationalizing Voter* (Cambridge: Cambridge University Press, 2013).
2. Daniel Kahneman, *Thinking, Fast and Slow* (New York: Farrar, Strauss & Giroux, 2011).
3. Organization for Economic Co-operation and Development, *PISA 2012 Results in Focus* (Paris: OECD, 2014).
4. David Autor, "How Technology Wrecks the Middle Class," *New York Times*, August 25, 2013, 6.
5. Hart Research Associates, *It Takes More Than a Major: Employer Priorities for College Learning and Student Success* (Washington, DC: Association of American Colleges and Universities, April 10, 2013).

Chapter 1

1. Shane J. Lopez and Valerie J. Calderon, "Americans Say U.S. Schools Should Teach 'Soft' Skills," *Gallup*, August 21, 2013.
2. Louis Freedberg, "Teachers Say Critical Thinking Key to College and Career Readiness," *EdSource*, September 29, 2015, http://edsource.org/2015/teachers-say-critical-thinking-most-important-indicator-of-student-success/87810.
3. Motoko Rich, "As Graduation Rates Rise, Experts Fear Diplomas Come Up Short," *New York Times*, December 26, 2015, 1.
4. Emma Brown, "Fewer U.S. High-Schoolers Are Enrolling in College, but the Rate Dropped Sharply Among the Poorest Students," *Washington Post*, November 25, 2015, 2.
5. Rich, "As Graduation Rates Rise," 1.
6. Suzanne Mettler, *Degrees of Inequality*Paul Krugman, ic Books (2014).
7. Paul Krugman, "Jobs and Skills and Zombies," *New York Times*, March 30, 2014; Darren Dahl, "A Sea of Job-Seekers, but Some Companies Aren't Getting Any Bites," *New York Times*, June 28, 2012, 7.
8. Sarah E. Needleman, "Jobs Go Begging for Lack of Skills," *Wall Street Journal*, July 10, 2014, B5.
9. Michael Delli Carpini and Scott Keeter, *What Americans Know About Politics and Why It Matters* (New Haven: Yale University Press, 1996); Pew

Research Center, *Public Knowledge of Current Affairs Little Changed by News and Information Revolutions* (Washington, DC: Pew Research Center, April 15, 2007).

10. Charles Taber and Milton Lodge, "Motivated Skepticism in the Evaluation of Political Beliefs," *American Journal of Political Science* 50 (2006), 755–69; Milton Lodge and Charles Taber, *The Rationalizing Voter* (Cambridge: Cambridge University Press, 2013).

11. Natalie Jomini Stroud, *Niche News: The Politics of News Choice* (New York: Oxford University Press, 2011).

12. John Dewey, *How We Think* (Buffalo, NY: Prometheus Books, 1991), 6.

13. Alec Fisher, *Critical Thinking: An Introduction* (New York: Cambridge University Press, 2001).

14. O*Net, "Skills Search," https://www.onetonline.org/skills/.

15. Charlotte Danielson, "Framing Discussion About Teaching," *Educational Leadership* 72 (2015): 38–41.

16. Jacqueline King, interview by William Gormley, August 14, 2015.

17. Center for Teaching, "Bloom's Taxonomy," Vanderbilt University, https://cft.vanderbilt.edu/guides-sub-pages/blooms-taxonomy/.

18. Daniel Willingham, "Critical Thinking: Why Is It So Hard to Teach?," *American Educator* (Summer 2007): 8–19.

19. Ray MacGregor, "Fortune Smiled Upon Us," in *Total Gretzky: The Magic, The Legend, The Numbers*, ed. Steve Dryden (Toronto, Ontario: McClelland & Stewart Inc., 1999), 14–36.

20. Kellan McNulty, "How Kipp Teachers Learn to Teach Critical Thinking," *Edutopia*, YouTube video, 4:21, posted September 2011, https://www.youtube.com/watch?v=PtYABBs6LLc.

21. National Commission on Excellence in Education, *A Nation at Risk* (Washington, DC: US Department of Education, 1983).

22. Stephanie Simon, "Is Common Core Failing the Test?," *Politico*, July 13, 2013, http://www.politico.com/story/2013/07/common-core-academic-standards-094628.

23. David Kirp, "Rage Against the Common Core," *New York Times*, December 28, 2014, 18.

24. Farra Kober, "Randi Weingarten: Common Core Should Be a Guide not a Straightjacket," *MSNBC*, May 9, 2014, http://www.msnbc.com/all/you-asked-randi-weingarten-answered-common-core-standardized-testing.

25. Randi Weingarten, "Why I Support the Common Core Standards," *Diane Ravitch's blog*, May 10, 2013, http://dianeravitch.net/2013/05/10/randi-weingarten-why-i-support-the-common-core-standards/.

26. American Federation of Teachers, "AFT Members Pass Resolution to Fulfill Promise and Potential of Common Core, Lay Out Action Plan to Fix Botched Implementation," American Federation of Teachers, July 13, 2014, http://www.aft.org/press-release/aft-members-pass-resolution-

fulfill-promise-and-potential-common-core-lay.

27. Lyndsey Layton, "NEA President Calls for Core 'Course Correction,'" *Washington Post*, February 20, 2014, A15.

28. Michael Henderson, Paul Peterson, and Martin West, "The 2015 Education Next Poll in School Reform," *Education Next* 16 (Winter 2016): 9–20.

29. Diana Laboy-Rush, *Integrated STEM Education Through Project-Based Learning*, http://www.rondout.k12.ny.us/common/pages/DisplayFile.aspx?itemid=16466975.

30. Wendy Kopp, "TFA: Our 'Chance to Make History,'" *Education Week*, March 14, 2011, http://www.edweek.org/ew/articles/2011/03/16/24kopp_ep.h30.html.

31. Catherine Godbey, "Teach and Be Taught," *Teach for America*, http://tfadfw.org/2015/10/19/to-teach-and-be-taught/.

32. Edutopia, "Training Teachers to Teach Critical Thinking," *Schools That Work | Practice*, May 20, 2014, http://www.edutopia.org/stw-kipp-critical-thinking-professional-development-video.

33. Christopher Drew, "Rethinking Advanced Placement," *New York Times*, January 7, 2011, 24.

34. Toronto Catholic District School Board, "International Baccalaureate Program (IB)," https://www.tcdsb.org/programsservices/schoolprogramsk12/ib/Pages/default.aspx.

35. Jennifer Ruth, "Non-Critical Thinking in China," *Chronicle of Higher Education*, February 24, 2014, 6.

36. Erin Ryan, "When Socrates Meets Confucius: Teaching Creative and Critical Thinking Across Cultures Through Multilevel Socratic Method," *University of Nebraska Law Review* 92 (2013): 289–348.

37. Rob Gifford, "Chinese Top in Tests, But Educators Call for Reform," National Public Radio, December 29, 2010, http://www.npr.org/2010/12/29/132416889/chinese-top-in-tests-but-still-have-lots-to-learn.

38. Saga Ringmar, "Here's the Truth About Shanghai Schools: They're Terrible," *The Guardian*, December 28, 2013, http://www.theguardian.com/commentisfree/2013/dec/28/shanghai-china-schools-terrible-not-ideal.

39. Gifford, "Chinese Top in Tests."

40. Sumita Vaid Dixit, "Indian Education Doesn't Allow Critical Thinking," Rediff Get Ahead, April 12, 2010, http://www.rediff.com/getahead/slide-show/slide-show-1-achievers-raju-narisetti-indian-education-doesnt-allow-critical-thinking/20100409.htm.

41. "We Need Critical Thinkers," Editorial, *Times of India*, June 13, 2011, http://timesofindia.indiatimes.com/home/education/news/We-need-critical-thinkers/articleshow/8835271.cms.

42. David Coleman, "Bringing the Common Core to Life" (presentation, New York State Department of Education, Albany, NY, April 28, 2011).

43. Herbert Simon, *Administrative Behavior*, 3rd ed. (New York: Free Press, 1976).

Chapter 2

1. Ziva Kunda, *Social Cognition: Making Sense of People* (Cambridge, MA: MIT Press, 1999); Charles Taber and Milton Lodge, "Motivated Skepticism in the Evaluation of Political Beliefs," *American Journal of Political Science* 50 (2006): 755–69.

2. Daniel Kahneman, *Thinking Fast and Slow* (New York: Farrar, Strauss, & Giroux, 2011).

3. John Rawls, *A Theory of Justice* (Cambridge, MA: Belknap Press, 1976).

4. Eduardo Sacheri, *The Secret in Their Eyes* (Toronto: HarperCollins, 2011).

5. Keigo Higashino, *The Devotion of Suspect X: A Detective Galileo Novel* (New York: Minotaur Books, 2011).

6. Renee Dunlop, "The Making of Pixar's UP," *Techradar*, October 9, 2009, http://www.techradar.com/us/news/video/software/applications/the-making-of-pixar-s-up-603600.

7. Jonah Lehrer, *Imagine: How Creativity Works* (Boston: Houghton Mifflin Harcourt, 2012).

8. Jordan Ellenberg, *How Not to Be Wrong: The Power of Mathematical Thinking* (New York: Penguin, 2014); Manil Suri, "Book Review: 'How Not to Be Wrong: The Power of Mathematical Thinking,'" *Washington Post*, June 13, 2014, B7.

9. Atul Gawande, *Complications: A Surgeon's Notes on an Imperfect Science* (New York: Henry Holt, 2002).

10. William Gormley and David Weimer, *Organizational Report Cards* (Cambridge, MA: Harvard University Press, 2009).

11. Martha Derthick, *Up in Smoke: From Legislation to Litigation in Tobacco Politics*, 2nd ed. (Washington, DC: Congressional Quarterly Press, 2005).

12. Thomas Holford et al., "Tobacco Control and the Reduction in Smoking-Related Premature Deaths in the United States, 1964–2012," *Journal of the American Medical Association* 311, no. 2 (2014): 164–71.

13. David Levy, "Researchers Say 50 Years of Tobacco Control Extended Lives of 8 Million" [press release], Washington, DC: Georgetown University, January 7, 2014.

14. Robert Pear, "U.S. to Compare Medical Treatments," *New York Times*, February 15, 2009, 1.

15. Sylvia Burwell, "Next Steps in the Evidence and Innovation Agenda," [Memorandum to Department Heads and Agencies], Washington, DC: OMB, July 26, 2013; Ron Haskins and Greg Margolis, *Show Me the Evidence: Obama's Fight for Rigor and Results in Social Policy* (Washington, DC: Brookings, 2015).

16. Byron Auguste, Paul Kihn, and Matt Miller, *Closing the Talent Gap*, McKinsey on Society, (Washington, DC: McKinsey & Co., 2010).

17. Steven Brill, *Class Warfare: Inside the Fight to Fix America's Schools* (New York: Simon & Schuster, 2011).

18. Stephen Sawchuk, "TFA Alumni Groomed for Leadership Roles," *Education Week*, January 15, 2014, 1.

19. Paul Decker, Daniel Meyer, and Steven Glazerman, *The Effects of Teach for America on Students: Findings from a National Evaluation* (Princeton, NJ: Mathematica Policy Research Inc., 2004).

20. Melissa A. Clark et al., *The Effectiveness of Secondary Math Teachers from Teach for America and the Teaching Fellows Program* (Washington, DC: Mathematica Policy Research Inc., 2013).

21. Kevin Rector and Meredith Cohn, "Johns Hopkins Offers Unique Organ Donor-Pairing Program," *Washington Post*, December 31, 2013, B4.

22. UNOS, "Kidney Paired Donation Pilot Program to Begin Matching in October," *United Network for Organ Sharing*, October 5, 2010, https://www.unos.org/kidney-paired-donation-pilot-program-to-begin-matching-in-october/.

23. Somini Sengupta, "A Start-Up Bets on Human Translators Over Machines," *New York Times*, June 20, 2012, 3.

24. Gordon Wood, *The Creation of the American Republic, 1776–1787* (New York: W. W. Norton & Co., 1969); Jack Rakove, *James Madison and the Creation of the American Republic* (New York: Longman, 1990).

25. Wood, *The Creation of the American Republic*.

26. Rakove, *James Madison*.

27. Wood, *The Creation of the American Republic*.

28. Michael Zuckert, "Federalism and the Founding: Toward a Reinterpretation of the Constitutional Convention," *Review of Politics* 46 (1986), 166–210.

29. Thomas Kuhn, *The Structure of Scientific Revolutions* (Chicago: University of Chicago Press, 1962).

30. Ibid.

Chapter 3

1. Raymond Cattell, *Abilities: Their Structure, Growth, and Action* (Boston: Houghton Mifflin, 1971); Emilio Ferrer, Elizabeth O'Hare, and Silvia Bunge, "Fluid Reasoning and the Developing Brain," *Frontiers in Neuroscience* 3 (2009): 46–51.

2. Scott Kaufman, "Working Memory and Fluid Reasoning: Same or Different?" *Scientific American*, January 22, 2014, http://blogs.scientificamerican.com/beautiful-minds/working-memory-and-fluid-reasoning-same-or-different/.

3. Adele Diamond, "Executive Functions," *Annual Review of Psychology* 64 (2013): 135–68.

4. John Raven, "The Raven's Progressive Matrices: Change and Stability over Culture and Time," *Cognitive Psychology* 41 (2000): 1–48.

5. Adele Diamond, "Want to Optimize Executive Functions and Academic Outcomes?," in *Minnesota Symposia on Child Psychology*, vol. 37, ed. Philip Zelazo and Maria Sera (New York: John Wiley & Sons, 2014), 205–32.

6. Judy Willis, "Understanding How the Brain Thinks," *Edutopia*, June 13, 2011, http://www.edutopia.org/blog/understanding-how-the-brain-thinks-judy-willis-md.

7. Diamond, "Want to Optimize Executive Functions," 205–32.

8. Diamond, "Executive Functions," 135–68.

9. Raymond Bull and Gaia Scerif, "Executive Functioning as a Predictor of Children's Mathematics Ability: Inhibition, Switching, and Working Memory," *Developmental Neuropsychology* 19 (2001): 273–93.

10. Walter Mischel, Yuichi Shoda, and Monica Rodriguez, "Delay of Gratification in Children," *Science* 244 (1989): 933–38.

11. Clancy Blair and C. Cybele Raver, "School Readiness and Self-Regulation: A Developmental Psychobiological Approach," *Annual Review of Psychology* 66 (2015): 711–31.

12. Center on the Developing Child at Harvard University, "Building the Brain's 'Air Traffic Control System': How Early Experiences Shape the Development of Executive Function" (Working Paper #11, National Forum on Early Childhood Policy and Programs, Cambridge, MA, 2011), http://developingchild.harvard.edu/wp-content/uploads/2011/05/How-Early-Experiences-shape-the-Development-of-Executive-Function.pdf.

13. Emilio Ferrer, Elizabeth O'Hare, and Silvia Bunge, "Fluid Reasoning and the Developing Brain," *Frontiers in Neuroscience* 3 (2009): 46–51.

14. Diamond, "Want to Optimize Executive Functions," 205–32.

15. Scott Decker, Scott Hill, and Ray Dean, "Evidence of Construct Similarity in Executive Function and Fluid Reasoning Abilities," *International Journal of Neuroscience* 117 (2007): 735–48.

16. Kaufman, "Working Memory and Fluid Reasoning."

17. Joan Stiles and Terry Jernigan, "The Basics of Brain Development," *Neuropsychological Review* 20 (2010): 327–48.

18. Silvia Bunge and Samantha Wright, "Neurodevelopmental Changes in Working Memory and Cognitive Control," *Current Opinion in Neurobiology* 17, no. 2 (2007): 243–50.

19. David Dobbs, "Beautiful Brains," *National Geographic* (October 2011): 36–59.

20. Bunge and Wright, "Neurodevelopmental Changes," 243–50.

21. Beatriz Luna, Aarthi Padmanabhan, and Kirsten O'Hearn, "What Has fMRI Told Us About the Development of Cognitive Control Through Adolescence?," *Brain and Cognition* 72 (2010): 101–13.

22. Roper v. Simmons, 543 U.S. 551 (2005).

23. Amanda Schaffer, "Head Case: Roper v. Simmons Asks How Adolescent and Adult Brains Differ," *Slate*, October 15, 2004, http://www.slate.com/articles/health_and_science/medical-examiner/2004/10/head_case.html.

24. Philip Ackerman, "Adolescent and Adult Intellectual Development," *Current Dimensions in Psychological Science* 23 (2004): 246–51.

25. Allison Gopnik, Thomas Griffiths, and Christopher Lucas, "When Younger Learners Can Be Better (or at Least More Open-Minded) than Older Ones," *Current Directions in Psychological Science* 24 (2015): 87–92.

26. Christopher Lucas et al., "When Children Are Better (or at Least More Open-Minded) Learners Than Adults," *Cognition* 131 (2014): 284–99.

27. Deanna Kuhn, *Education for Thinking* (Cambridge, MA: Harvard University Press, 2005).

28. Daniel Krawczyk, "The Cognition and Neuroscience of Relational Reasoning," *Brain Research* 1428 (2012): 13–23.

29. Abby Marsh (associate professor, psychology, Georgetown University), interview by William Gormley, February 2, 2015; Chandan Vaidya (professor, psychology, Georgetown University), interview by William Gormley, February 25, 2015; Krawczyk, "The Cognition and Neuroscience of Relational Reasoning," 13–23.

30. Marsh, interview; Allyson Mackey, Allison Miller Singley, and Silvia Bunge, "Intensive Reasoning Training Alters Patterns of Brain Connectivity at Rest," *Journal of Neuroscience* 33 (2013): 4796–803.

31. Benedict Carey, "Studying Young Minds, and How to Teach Them," *New York Times*, December 21, 2009, 1.

32. "Teachers Tap into Brain Science to Boost Learning," *PBS NewsHour*, PBS (July 1, 2015), http://www.pbs.org/newshour/bb/teachers-tap-brain-science-boost-learning/.

33. G. Elliot Wimmer and Daphna Shohamy, "The Striatum and Beyond: Contributions of the Hippocampus to Decision Making," *Multiple Memory Systems of the Brain* (2011): 281–309.

34. Natalie Phillips, "Literary Neuroscience and History of Mind: An Interdisciplinary fMRI Study of Attention and Jane Austen," *The Oxford Handbook of Cognitive Literary Studies*, ed. Lisa Zunshine (New York: Oxford University Press, 2015), 55–81.

35. Ziva Kunda, "The Case for Motivated Reasoning," *Psychological Bulletin* 108 (1990): 480–98.

36. Drew Westen et al., "Neural Bases of Motivated Reasoning: An fMRI Study of Emotional Constraints on Partisan Political Judgment in the 2004 U.S. Presidential Election," *Journal of Cognitive Neuroscience* 18, no. 11 (2006): 1947–58.

37. Vincent Van Veen et al., "Neural Activity Predicts Attitude Change in Cognitive Dissonance," *Nature Neuroscience* 12 (2009): 1469–75.

38. Greg Duncan, Jeanne Brooks-Gunn, and Pamela Klebanov, "Economic Deprivation and Early Childhood Development," *Child Development* 65 (1994): 296–318.

39. Greg Duncan, and Katherine Magnuson, "The Long Reach of Early

Childhood Poverty," *Pathways* (Winter 2011): 23–27.

40. Charles Nelson and Margaret Sheridan, "Lessons from Neuroscience Research for Understanding Causal Links Between Family and Neighborhood Characteristics and Educational Outcomes," in *Whither Opportunity?*, ed. Greg Duncan and Richard Murnane (New York: Russell Sage Foundation, 2011), 27–46.

41. Kimberly Noble et al., "Family Income, Parental Education and Brain Structure in Children and Adolescents," *Nature Neuroscience* 18 (2015): 773–78.

42. Lyndsey Layton, "Study Influences Achievement-Gap Debate," *Washington Post*, April 16, 2015, 3.

43. Deanna Barch et al., "Effect of Hippocampal and Amygdala Connectivity on the Relationship Between Preschool Poverty and School-Age Depression," *American Journal of Psychiatry* (January 15, 2016): 625–33.

44. Marvin Minsky, *The Society of Mind* (New York: Simon & Schuster, 1986).

45. Center on the Developing Child at Harvard University, "Excessive Stress Disrupts the Architecture of the Developing Brain" (Working Paper #3, updated, Cambridge, MA, 2014).

46. Raymond Cattell, *Intelligence* (New York: Elsevier, 1987).

47. Allyson P. Mackey et al., "Differential Effects of Reasoning and Speed Training in Children," *Developmental Science* 14 (2011): 582–90.

48. Daniel Willingham, "Can Teachers Increase Students' Self-Control?" *American Educator* (Summer 2011): 22–27.

49. Diamond, "Want to Optimize Executive Functions," 205–32.

50. J. Elizabeth Richey et al., "Is the Link from Working Memory to Analogy Causal? No Analogy Improvements Following Working Memory Training Gains," *PLOS ONE* 9 (2014), e106616.

51. Jennifer Zuk et al., "Behavioral and Neural Correlates of Executive Functioning in Musicians and Non-Musicians," *PLOS ONE* 9 (2014): 6.

52. George Hicks, "How Playing Music Affects the Developing Brain," *wbur's CommonHealth* (Boston, MA: WBUR Radio, July 17, 2014), http://commonhealth.wbur.org/2014/07/music-language-brain.

53. Adele Diamond, "Activities and Programs That Improve Children's Executive Functions," *Current Directions in Psychological Science* 21 (2012): 335–41.

54. "Teachers Tap into Brain Science," *PBS NewsHour*.

55. Adam Green et al., "Connecting Long Distance: Semantic Distance in Analogical Reasoning Modulates Frontopolar Cortex Activity," *Cerebral Cortex* 10 (2010): 70–76.

56. Adam Green et al., "An Explicit Cue Improves Creative Analogical Reasoning," *Intelligence* 40 (2012): 598–603.

57. Sarah Sparks, "Classroom Lab Helps Researchers Study Learning in Natural Setting," *Education Week*, March 9, 2016, 1.

58. Herbie Hancock, *Possibilities* (New York: Viking, 2014).

59. Charles Limb and Allen Braun, "Neural Substrates of Spontaneous Musical Performance: An fMRI Study of Jazz Improvisation," *PLOS ONE* 3 (2008): 1–9.

60. Ryota Kanai et al., "Political Orientations Are Correlated with Brain Structure in Young Adults," *Current Biology* 21 (2011): 1–4.

Chapter 4

1. Kids Count, "Young Adults Ages 18 to 24 Enrolled in or Completed College," Annie E. Casey Foundation, 2014, http://datacenter.kidscount .org/data/Tables/77-young-adults-ages-18-to-24-who-are-enrolled-in-or-have-completed-college?loc=1&loct=1#detailed/1/any/false/36,868, 867,133,38/any/388,389.

2. National Center for Education Statistics, "Graduation Rates," Institute of Education Sciences, http://nces.ed.gov/fastfacts/display.asp?id=40.

3. Jolanta Juszkiewicz, *Recent National Community College Enrollment and Award Completion Data* (Washington, DC: American Association of Community Colleges, January 2014).

4. Ilyse Liffreing, *Advanced Placement Exams on the Rise for Public School Students: Report*, WNBC 4 New York (San Francisco: NBC, March 31, 2015); Stanley Kurtz, "The Next Great Education Debate," *Washington Post*, September 13, 2015, 21.

5. Erik Robelen, "Revised A.P. Physics, History Coming Soon," *Education Week*, October 4, 2012, http://blogs/edweek.org/edweek/curriculum/ 2012/10/the_college_board_today_announ.html.

6. Drew Christopher, "Rethinking Advanced Placement," *New York Times*, January 7, 2011, 24.

7. Alexandra Pannoni, "Discover the Difference Between AP and IB Classes," *U.S. News & World Report*, September 2, 2014, http://www .usnews.com/education/blogs/high-school-notes/2014/09/02/discover-the-difference-between-ap-and-ib-classes.

8. Peg Tyre, "The Writing Revolution," *Atlantic Monthly*, October 2012, 96–101.

9. David Coleman, Susan Pimentel, and Jason Zimba. "Three Core Shifts to Deliver on the Promise of the Common Core State Standards in Literacy and Math," State Education Standard, adjusted March 11, 2015, http://www.achievethecore.org/page/277/the-common-core-shifts-at-a-glance-detail-pg.

10. William Gormley Jr., "Would Shakespeare Have Unleashed His Sword to Fight Against Common Core?" *Fox News*, December 26, 2013, http:// www.foxnews.com/opinion/2013/12/26/would-shakespeare-have-unleashed-his-sword-to-fight-against-common-core.html; Tom Loveless, *Has Common Core Influenced Instruction?* (Washington, DC: The Brookings

Institution, Brown Center Chalkboard, November 24, 2015).

11. Eric Gorski, "At Smoky Hill High School, Common Core and Tests Not Always Easy to Sell," *Denver Post*, May 25, 2015, 1A.

12. Ross Brenneman, "Five-State Study Examines Teaching Shifts Under Core," *Education Week*, February 16, 2016, 16.

13. Catherine Gewertz, "State Solidarity Erodes on Standards Testing," *Education Week*, March 23, 2016, 1.

14. Jacqueline King, telephone interview by William Gormley, August 14, 2015.

15. Hart Research Associates, "Trends in Learning Outcomes Assessment," Association of American Colleges and Universities, February 17, 2016, http://aacu.org/sites/default/files/files/LEAP/2015_Survey_Report3.pdf.

16. Dan Berrett, "If Skills Are the New Canon, Are Colleges Teaching Them?" *Chronicle of Higher Education*, April 3, 2016, http://chronicle.com/article/If-Skills-Are-the-New-Canon/235948.

17. American Political Science Association, "Political Science: An Ideal Liberal Arts Major," 2016, http://www.apsanet.org/CAREERS/An-Ideal-Liberal-Arts-Major.

18. Marisa Kelly and Brian Klunk, "Learning Assessment in Political Science Departments: Survey Results," *Political Science and Politics* 36 (2003): 451–55.

19. "Why Study History," American Historical Association, 2013, https://www.historians.org/teaching-and-learning/why-study-history.

20. Suzanne Mettler, *Degrees of Inequality: How the Politics of Higher Education Sabotaged the American Dream* (New York: Basic Books, 2014).

21. Daniel DeVise, "U.S. Falls in Global Ranking of Young Adults Who Finish College," *Washington Post*, September 13, 2011, 4.

22. Liz Weston, "OECD: The US Has Fallen Behind Other Countries in College Completion," Reuters News Service, September 9, 2014, http://www.businessinsider.com/r-us-falls-behind-in-college-competition-oecd-2014-9; Madeline Will, "U.S. Trails in College Graduation in Global Study," *Education Week*, September 17, 2014, 7.

23. American Association of Community Colleges, "Remedial Courses at Community Colleges," *Data Points*, April, 2014.

24. Joy Resmovits, "And the World's Best Problem-Solvers Are . . . ," *Huffington Post*, April 1, 2014, http://www.huffingtonpost.com/2014/04/01/pisa-problem-solving_n_5066568.html.

25. Sean Reardon, "The Widening Academic Achievement Gap Between the Rich and the Poor: New Evidence and Possible Explanations," in *Whither Opportunity?*, ed. Greg Duncan and Richard Murnane (New York: Russell Sage Foundation, 2011), 91–116; Robert Putnam, *Our Kids: The American Dream in Crisis* (New York: Simon & Schuster, 2015); Jason

DeParle, "For Poor, Leap to College Often Ends in a Hard Fall," *New York Times*, December 22, 2012, 1.

26. Mettler, *Degrees of Inequality*.

27. Kyla Calvert, "Percentage of Americans with College Degrees Rises, Paying for Degrees Taps Financial Challenges," *PBS NewsHour*, PBS, April 22, 2014,http://www.pbs.org/newshour/rundown/percentage-americans-college-degrees-rises-paying-degrees-tops-financial-challenges/.

28. Tyre, "The Writing Revolution," 96–101.

29. Alvin Sanoff, "A Perception Gap Over Students' Preparation," *Chronicle of Higher Education*, March 10, 2006, B9–B14.

30. Miranda Cohen (Teach for America alumna), interview by William Gormley, April 10, 2015.

31. Eberly Center, *Why Are Students Coming into College Poorly Prepared to Write?* (Pittsburgh, PA: Eberly Center, Carnegie-Mellon University, 2008).

32. US Department of Education, *The Nation's Report Card: Writing, 2011* (Washington, DC: IES, National Center for Education Statistics, September 2012).

33. Kate Zernike, "White House Moves to Limit School Testing," *New York Times*, October 25, 2015, 1.

34. Brigid Barron and Linda Darling-Hammond, *Powerful Learning: What We Know About Teaching for Understanding* (San Francisco: Jossey-Bass, 2008).

35. Diane Marie Specht, "The Probe Method: A Project Based Learning Model's Effect on Critical Thinking Skills" (PhD dissertation, Dissertation Abstracts, Minneapolis, MN: Walden University, 2015).

36. Jo Boaler, "Open and Closed Mathematics: Student Experiences and Understandings," *Journal for Research in Mathematics Education* 29 (1998): 41–62.

37. Barron and Darling-Hammond, *Powerful Learning*.

38. Jasmine Mausner, "Study: Elementary School Science Education Neglected," *Daily Californian*, October 26, 2011.

39. Tony Murphy, "STEM Education—It's Elementary," *U.S. News & World Report*, August 29, 2011, 1.

40. Sarah Hulett, "Teaching Teachers to Teach: It's Not So Elementary," National Public Radio, October 24, 2015, http://www.npr.org/sections/ed/2015/10/24/437555944/teaching-teachers-to-teach-its-not-so-elementary.

41. Amanda Lenhart, "A Majority of American Teens Report Access to a Computer, Game Console, Smartphone, and a Tablet," *Teens, Social Media & Technology Overview 2015* (Washington, DC: Pew Research Center, April 9, 2015).

42. Common Sense Media, *Common Sense Census: Media Use by Tweens and Teens* (San Francisco: Common Sense Media, November 2015); Clive

Thompson, "The Minecraft Generation," *New York Times*, April 17, 2016, 48–83.

43. Matt Richtel, "For Better and for Worse, Technology Use Alters Learning Styles, Teachers Say," *New York Times*, November 1, 2012, 18.

44. Matt Richtel, "In Classroom of Future, Stagnant Scores," *New York Times*, September 4, 2011, 1.

45. Richtel, "For Better and for Worse," 18.

46. Sandra Calvert and Patti Valkenburg, "The Influence of Television, Video Games, and the Internet on Children's Creativity," in *The Oxford Handbook of the Development of Imagination*, ed. Marjorie Taylor (New York: Oxford University Press), 438–50.

47. Common Sense Media, *Common Sense Census*.

48. Yougov.com, "18% of Americans Veritable Potter-maniacs, 61% See at Least One Movie," July 18, 2011, https://today.yougov.com/news/2011/07/18/18-americans-veritable-potter-maniacs-76-seen-leas/.

49. Patricia Greenfield, "Technology and Informal Education: What Is Taught? What Is Learned?" *Science* 323 (2009): 71.

50. Common Sense Media, *Common Sense Census*.

51. Rachel Valentino, "Will Public Pre-K Really Close Achievement Gaps? Gaps in Prekindergarten Quality Between Students and Across States" (paper presented at the Annual Meeting of the Association for Education Finance and Policy, Washington, DC, February 27, 2015), http://cepa.stanford.edu/sites/default/files/Valentino%20RA_Quality%20Gaps%20Paper%2015_0515.pdf.

52. Roland Fryer and Steven Levitt, "The Black-White Test Score Gap Through Third Grade" (Working Paper #11049, NBER Working Paper Series, Cambridge, MA: National Bureau of Economic Research, January 2005).

53. Robert Putnam, *Our Kids: The American Dream in Crisis* (New York: Simon & Schuster, 2015).

54. Jacquelynne S. Eccles, and Bonnie L. Barber, "Student Council, Volunteering, Basketball, or Marching Band: What Kind of Extracurricular Involvement Matters?," *Journal of Adolescent Research* 14 (1999): 10–43; Nick Ronan, "Is Participation in High School Athletics an Investment or a Consumption Good?," *Economics of Education Review* 20 (2001): 431–42.

55. Julia Bryan et al., "School Counselors as Social Capital: The Effects of High School College Counseling on College Application Rates," *Journal of Counseling and Development* 89 (Spring 2011): 190–9; Patricia McDonough, *Counseling and College Counseling in America's High Schools* (Alexandria, VA: National Association for College Admission Counseling, 2005).

56. Emma Brown, "Pa. Tackles Chasm in School Funding Equality," *Washington Post*, April 23, 2015, 1.

57. Richard Mansfield, "Teacher Quality and Student Inequality," *Journal of Labor Economics* 33 (July, 2015): 751–88.

58. Tim Sass, Jane Hannaway, Zeyu Xu, David Figlio, and Li Feng, "Value Added of Teachers in High-Poverty Schools and Lower Poverty Schools," *Journal of Urban Economics* 72 (2012): 104–22.

59. Jeannie Oakes, *Keeping Track: How Schools Structure Inequality* (New Haven, CT: Yale University Press, 1985).

60. Becky Smerdon, David Burkam, and Valerie Lee, "Access to Constructivist and Didactic Teaching: Who Gets It? Where Is It Practiced?," *Teachers College Record* 101 (Fall 1999): 5–34.

61. Deborah Stipek, "Teaching Practices in Kindergarten and First Grade: Different Strokes for Different Folks," *Early Childhood Research Quarterly* 19 (2004): 548–68.

62. Valentino, "Will Public Pre-K Really Close Achievement Gaps?"

63. Murphy, "STEM Education," 1.

64. Doug Clements and Julie Sarama, "Math in the Early Years: A Strong Predictor for Later Success," *Progress of Education Reform* 14 (Denver, CO: Education Commission of the States, October 2013).

65. Doug Clements and Julie Sarama, "Play, Mathematics, and False Dichotomies," *Preschool Matters . . . Today!* (blog), National Institute for Education Research, March 3, 2013, http://preschoolmatters.org/2014/03/03/play-mathematics-and-false-dichotomies/.

66. Kelly Smith, "District Takes Science Ed Down to Preschool Level," *Minneapolis Star Tribune*, January 28, 2013, 1. See also Rheta DeVries and Christina Sales, *Ramps and Pathways: A Constructivist Approach to Physics with Young Children* (Washington, DC: National Association for the Education of Young Children, 2011).

67. Erin MacPherson, "STEM: It's Elementary!," *Early STEM Education* (blog), We Are Teachers, April 3, 2015, http://www.weareteachers.com/blogs/post/2015/04/03/stem-its-elementary.

68. Deborah Zaitchik, Yeshim Iqbal, and Susan Carey, "The Effect of Executive Function on Biological Reasoning in Young Children: An Individual Differences Study," *Child Development* 85 (2014): 160–75.

69. Sarah Sparks, "Common Standards Raise Questions on Questioning," *Education Week*, September 30, 2015, S8.

70. Lindsay Matsumura, Helen Garnier, and Jessica Spybrook, "Literacy Coaching to Improve Student Reading Achievement: A Multi-Level Mediation Model," *Learning and Instruction* 25 (2013): 35–48.

71. P. Karen Murphy et al., "Examining the Effects of Classroom Discussion on Students' Comprehension of Text: A Meta-Analysis," *Journal of Educational Psychology* 101 (2009): 740–64.

72. John Branford and Daniel Schwartz, "Rethinking Transfer: A Simple

Proposal with Multiple Implications," *Review of Research in Education* 24 (1999): 61–100.

73. C. Emily Festritzer, *Profile of Teachers in the U.S.* (Washington, DC: National Center for Education Statistics, 2011), 19.

74. Barbara Stengel (asssociate chair for teacher education, Department of Teaching and Learning, Vanderbilt University), telephone interview by William Gormley, March 22, 2016.

75. C. Stephen White (associate dean, College of Education and Human Development, George Mason University), telephone interview by William Gormley, February 8, 2016.

76. Philip Sadler and Gerhard Sonnert, "Understanding Misconceptions: Teaching and Learning in Middle School Physical Science," *American Educator*, 2016, http://www.aft.org/ae/spring2016/sadler-and-sonnert.

77. C. Samuel Micklus and Carole Micklus, *Odyssey of the Mind: 2015–2016 Program Guide* (Sewell, NJ: Creative Competitions, Inc., August 2015).

78. Anne Kitchens (retired librarian and OM coach, Johnson City School District, Tennessee), telephone interview by William Gormley, June 14, 2016.

79. Jay Greene, Brian Kisida, and Daniel Bowden, "The Educational Value of Field Trips," *Education Next* 14 (Winter 2014): 78–86; Jay Mathews, "Field Trips Declining Despite Their Value," *Washington Post*, January 30, 2014, T17.

80. Emily Richmond, "Why the Demise of Field Trips Is Bad News," *Atlantic Monthly*, December 9, 2014.

81. Envision Education, "Envision Education: Mission and History," 2012, http://www.envisionschools.org/mission-history.

82. Bob Lenz, "Transforming Schools Using Project-Based Learning, Performance Assessment, and Common Core Standards" (presentation at the American Youth Policy Forum, Washington, DC, March 11, 2015).

83. Ibid.

84. Matsumura, Garnier, and Spybrook, "Literacy Coaching to Improve Student Reading Achievement," 35–48.

85. Murphy, "STEM Education," 1.

86. Matsumura, Garnier, and Spybrook, "Literacy Coaching to Improve Student Reading Achievement," 35–48.

87. David Kanter and Spyros Konstantopoulos, "The Impact of a Project-Based Science Curriculum on Minority Student Achievement, Attitudes, and Careers: The Effects of Teacher Content and Pedagogical Content Knowledge and Inquiry-Based Practices," *Science Education* (2010): 855–87.

88. Ibid.

89. Ibid.

90. Ibid.

91. Shea Bennett, "Teens, Millennials Prefer YouTube to Facebook, Insta-gram to Twitter, " *SocialTimes, AdWeek,* February 24, 2014, http://www.adweek.com/socialtimes/teens-millennials-twitter-facebook-youtube/496770.

92. "4 Chord Song," YouTube video, 6:11, posted by "Axis of Awesome," July 20, 2011, https://www.youtube.com/watch?v=oOlDewpCfZQ.

93. Erika Patall, Harris Cooper, and Ashley Allen, "Extending the School Day or School Year: A Systematic Review of Research (1985–2009)," *Review of Educational Research* 80 (2010): 401–36; Amy Checkoway et al., *Evaluation of the Massachusetts Expanded Learning Time (ELT) Initiative: Year 5 Final Report* (Cambridge, MA: Massachusetts Department of Elementary and Secondary Education, February 2, 2012).

94. Marilyn Marshall, "20 Years: KIPP Schools Prepare Students for Success," *Houston Defender,* April 11, 2014, http://www.kipp.org/news/houston-defender-kipp-schools-prepare-students-for-success; Joshua Angrist, Susan Dynarski, Thomas Kane, Parag Pathak, and Christopher Walters, "Who Benefits from KIPP?" (Working Paper #15740, NBER Working Paper Series, Cambridge, MA: National Bureau of Economic Research, February 2010).

95. Diane Ravitch, *The Death and Life of the Great American School System* (New York: Basic Books, 2010).

96. "New Findings Show New York City's Small High Schools Boost College Enrollment Rates Among Disadvantaged Students" [MDRC press release], October 16, 2014, http://www.mdrc.org/news/press-release/new-findings-show-new-york-city-s-small-high-schools-boost-college-enrollment.

97. Bonnie Barber and Jacqueline Eccles, "Student Council, Volunteering, Basketball, or Marching Band?" *Journal of Adolescent Research* 14 (1999): 10–43.

98. Jacqueline Eccles and Jennifer Fredricks, "Is Extracurricular Participation Associated with Beneficial Outcomes?" *Developmental Psychology* 42 (2006): 698–713; Karin Kitchens and William Gormley, "The Hispanic-White Extracurricular Participation Gap in Middle School" (paper presented at the Annual Meeting of the Society for Research in Adolescence, Baltimore, MD, April 1, 2016).

99. Sandra Simpkins et al., "Socioeconomic Status, Ethnicity, Culture, and Immigration," *Developmental Psychology* 49 (2013): 706–21; Kitchens and Gormley, "The Hispanic-White Extracurricular Participation Gap."

100. Dixie Speer (principal, Clinton Middle School), telephone interview by William Gormley, April 25, 2014.

101. MDRC, "National i3 Evaluation of Diplomas Now" (Power Point presentation at Diplomas Now Summer Institute, Baltimore, MD, July 9, 2013).

102. National Center for Education Statistics, *High School Longitudinal Study*

of 2009 (Washington, DC: US Department of Education), http://www
.nces.ed.gov/surveys/hsls09.

103. Michael Hurwitz, and Jessica Howell, "Estimating Causal Impacts of School Counselors with Regression Discontinuity Designs," *Journal of Counseling and Development* 92 (2014): 316–27.

104. Patricia McDonough, *Counseling and College Counseling in America's High Schools* (Alexandria, VA: National Association for College Admission Counseling, 2005).

105. Alexandra Pannoni, "U.S. News Releases 2015 Best High Schools Rankings," *U.S. News & World Report,* May 12, 2015; Jay Mathews, "America's Most Challenging High Schools National Top 25 List for 2015," *Washington Post*, April 20, 2015, B2.

106. Fryer and Levitt, "The Black-White Test Score Gap"; Reardon, "The Widening Academic Achievement Gap Between the Rich and the Poor," 91–116.

107. Anat Zohar and Yehudit Dori, "Higher Order Thinking Skills and Low-Achieving Students: Are They Mutually Exclusive?," *Journal of the Learning Sciences* 12 (2003): 145–81; Deanna Kuhn, *Education for Thinking* (Cambridge, MA: Harvard University Press, 2005).

Chapter 5

1. Charles E. Lindblom, *Politics and Markets* (New York: Basic Books, 1977); Martin Gilens and Benjamin Page, "Testing Theories of American Politics: Elites, Interest Groups, and Average Citizens," *Perspectives on Politics* 12 (2014): 564–81.

2. Carl Van Horn, *Working Scared (or Not at All)* (Lanham, MD: Rowman & Littlefield, 2013).

3. Valerie Lee and Douglas Ready, "U.S. High School Curriculum: Three Phases of Contemporary Research and Reform," *The Future of Children* 19 (Spring 2009): 135–56.

4. Achieve, "College and Career Readiness," http://www.achieve.org/college-and-career-readiness.

5. Association for Career and Technical Education, *What Is 'Career Ready'?* (Alexandria, VA: n.d.).

6. Hart Research Associates, *It Takes More Than a Major: Employer Priorities for College Learning and Student Success* (Washington, DC: The Association of American Colleges and Universities, April 10, 2013), https://www.aacu.org/sites/default/files/files/LEAP/2013_EmployerSurvey.pdf.

7. Hart Research Associates, *Falling Short? College Learning and Career Success* (Washington, DC: The Association of American Colleges and Universities, January 20, 2015), https://www.aacu.org/sites/default/files/files/LEAP/2015employerstudentsurvey.pdf.

8. Ibid.

9. Marisa Taylor, "Schools, Businesses Focus on Critical Thinking," *Wall Street Journal*, September 12, 2010, http://www.wsj.com/articles/SB10 0014240527487038823045754661007733788806.

10. William C. Symonds, Robert Schwartz, and Ronald F. Ferguson, *Pathways to Prosperity: Meeting the Challenge of Preparing Young Americans for the 21st Century* (Cambridge, MA: Pathways to Prosperity Project, Harvard University Graduate School of Education, 2011).

11. P21, "Partnership for 21st Century Learning," http://www.p21.org/.

12. National Research Council, *Education for Life and Work: Developing Transferable Knowledge and Skills in the 21st Century* (Washington, DC: Author, 2012).

13. David Perkins and Gavriel Salomon, "Transfer of Learning," in *International Encyclopedia of Education*, 2nd ed., ed. T. Neville Postlethwaite and Torsten Husen (Oxford, England: Pergamon Press, 1994), 6452–57

14. Harry Holzer, *What Employers Want: Job Prospects for Less-Educated Workers* (New York: Russell Sage Foundation, 1996).

15. David Autor and Michael Handel, "Putting Tasks to the Test: Human Capital, Job Tasks, and Wages," *Journal of Labor Economics* 31 (2013): S59—S96.

16. Jeff Selingo, "How College Graduates Enter the Workforce Without Critical Skills," *Washington Post*, February 16, 2015.

17. On a 5-point Likert scale, with 1 being not important and 5 being extremely important, employees, on average, gave critical thinking a 3.52 rating, as opposed to complex problem solving (3.20) and originality (2.79), in describing the skills and abilities needed for their current job. Calculated by the author from O*NET data, 2014. Means were calculated from all occupational categories combined.

18. Office of Disability Employment Policy, "Problem Solving and Critical Thinking," in *Mastering Soft Skills for Workplace Success* (Washington, DC: US Department of Labor), http://www.dol.gov/odep/topics/youth/softskills/softskills.pdf.

19. O*Net OnLine, "Skills Search," https://www.onetonline.org/skills/.

20. Melissa Korn, "Bosses Seek 'Critical Thinking,' but What Is That?" *Wall Street Journal*, October 22, 2014, B2.

21. Marianne Bertrand and Sendhill Mullainathan, "Are Emily and Greg More Employable than Lakisha and Jamal? A Field Experiment on Labor Market Discrimination," *American Economic Review* 94 (2004): 991–1013; Joanna Lahey, "Age, Women, and Hiring: An Experimental Study," *Journal of Human Resources* 43 (2008): 30–56; Peter Riach and Judith Rich, "An Experimental Investigation of Sexual Discrimination in Hiring in the English Labor Market," *Advances in Economic Analysis & Policy* 6 (2006): 1–20; Dan-Olof Rooth, "Obesity, Attractiveness, and Differential Treatment in Hiring: A Field Experiment," *Journal of Human*

Resources 44 (2009): 710–35; Phillip Oreopoulos, "Why Do Skilled Immigrants Struggle in the Labor Market? A Field Experiment with Thirteen Thousand Resumes," *American Economic Journal: Economic Policy* 3 (2011): 148–71; Kory Kroft, Fabian Lange, and Matthew Notowidigdo, "Duration Dependence and Labor Market Conditions: Evidence from a Field Experiment," *Quarterly Journal of Economics* 128 (2013): 1123–67.

22. Cory Koedel and Eric Tyhurst, "Math Skills and Labor-Market Outcomes: Evidence from a Resume-Based Field Experiment," *Economics of Education Review* 31 (2012): 131–40.

23. Peter Hinrichs, "What Kind of Teachers Are Schools Looking For? Evidence from a Randomized Field Experiment" (unpublished manuscript, McCourt School, Georgetown University, Washington, DC, 2013).

24. Autor and Handel, "Putting Tasks to the Test," S59—S96.

25. Yujia Liu and David Grusky, "The Payoff to Skill in the Third Industrial Revolution," *American Journal of Sociology* 118 (2013): 1330–74.

26. Ibid.

27. William T. Gormley, Deborah Phillips, and Ted Gayer, "Preschool Programs Can Boost School Readiness," *Science* 320 (2008): 1723–24; Vivian Wong, Thomas D. Cook, W. Steven Barnett, and Kwanghee Jung, "An Effectiveness-Based Evaluation of Five State Pre-Kindergarten Programs," *Journal of Policy Analysis Management* 27 (2008): 122–54; Christina Weiland and Hiro Yoshikawa, "Impacts of a Prekindergarten Program on Children's Mathematics, Language, Literacy, Executive Functioning, and Emotional Skills," *Child Development* 84 (2013): 2112–30.

28. Steven W. Barnett, "Effectiveness of Early Educational Intervention," *Science* 333 (2011): 975–78.

29. James J. Heckman, Seong Hyeok Moon, Rodrigo Pinto, Peter Savelyev, and Adam Yavitz, "A New Cost-Benefit and Rate of Return Analysis for the Perry Preschool Program: A Summary" (NBER Working Paper Series, Cambridge, MA: National Bureau of Economic Research, July 2010); Arthur J. Reynolds, Judy A. Temple, Barry A. White, Suh-Ruu Ou, and Dylan L. Robert, "Age-26 Cost-Benefit Analysis of the Child-Parent Center Early Education Program," *Child Development* 82 (2011): 379–404; Timothy Bartik, William Gormley, and Shirley Adelstein, "Earnings Benefits of Tulsa's Pre-K Programs for Different Income Groups," *Economics of Education Review* 31 (2012): 1143–61.

30. Camille Farrington et al., *Teaching Adolescents to Become Learners: The Role of Noncognitive Factors in Shaping School Performance* (Chicago: University of Chicago Consortium on Chicago School Research, June 2012); James Heckman and Tim Kautz, "Hard Evidence on Soft Skills," *Labor Economics* 19 (2012): 451–64.

31. Karen Bierman et al., "Promoting Academic and Social-Emotional

School Readiness: The Head Start REDI Program," *Child Development* 79 (2008): 1802–17.

32. Carol Dweck, *Self-Theories: Their Role in Motivation, Personality, and Development* (Philadelphia: Psychology Press, 1999).

33. Mike Rose, *The Mind at Work: Valuing the Intelligence of the American Worker* (New York: Viking, 2004).

34. Theresa Brown, *Critical Care: A New Nurse Faces Death, Life, and Everything in Between* (New York: Harper, 2010).

35. Center on the Developing Child at Harvard University, *Key Concepts: Executive Function* (Cambridge, MA: Harvard University, 2011), http://developingchild.harvard.edu/about/.

36. Celia Hoyles, Richard Noss, Phillip Kent, and Arthur Bakker, *Improving Mathematics at Work: The Need for Techno-Mathematical Literacies* (London: Routledge, 2010).

37. Elizabeth Green, "(New Math)—(New Teaching) = Failure," *New York Times*, July 27, 2014, 22.

38. Sandra Laursen, Marja-Liisa Hassi, Marina Kogan, and Timothy Weston, "Benefits for Women and Men of Inquiry-Based Learning in College Mathematics: A Multi-Institution Study," *Journal for Research in Mathematics Education* 45 (2014): 406–18.

39. Emily Badger, "A Flat Tire for Bike Sharing in the Big Apple?," *Washington Post*, April 8, 2014, 8.

40. Herbert Simon, *Administrative Behavior*, 4th ed. (New York: Free Press, 1997).

41. Catherine Rampell, "Open Jobs and Good Candidates, but Employers Won't Commit," *New York Times*, March 7, 2013, 1.

42. David Autor, "How Technology Wrecks the Middle Class," *New York Times*, August 25, 2013, 6.

43. David Autor, Lawrence Katz, and Melissa Kearney, "Trends in U.S. Wage Inequality: Revising the Revisionists," *Review of Economics and Statistics* 90 (2008): 300–23.

44. Harry Holzer, *Job Market Polarization and U.S. Worker Skills: A Tale of Two Middles* (Washington, DC: Brookings Institution Economic Studies Policy Brief, April 2015).

45. David Deming, "The Growing Importance of Social Skills in the Labor Market" (Working Paper #21473, NBER Working Paper Series, Cambridge, MA: National Bureau of Economic Research, August 2015).

46. Damon Jones, Mark Greenberg, and Max Crowley, "Early Social-Emotional Functioning and Public Health: The Relationship Between Kindergarten Social Competence and Future Wellness," *American Journal of Public Health* 105 (2015): 2283–90.

47. "The Receptacles of Doom," YouTube video, 1:56, posted by "ETC On Film," July 27, 2013, https://www.youtube.com/watch?v=qVPF

hml-3O4.

48. Alex Pentland, "The New Science of Building Great Teams," *Harvard Business Review* 90 (April 2012): 60–70.

49. National Center for Education Statistics, "High School Longitudinal Study of 2009," http://www.nces.ed.gov/surveys/hsls09.

50. Patricia McDonough, *Counseling and College Counseling in America's High Schools* (Alexandria, VA: National Association for College Admission Counseling, 2005).

51. Michael Woolley et al., "Advancing Academic Achievement Through Career Relevance in the Middle Grades: A Longitudinal Evaluation of Career Start," *American Educational Research Journal* (2013): 1–27.

52. Fred Newman, Gudelia Lopez, and Anthony Bryk, *The Quality of Intellectual Work in Chicago's Schools* (Chicago: Consortium for Chicago School Research, October 1998).

53. David Stern, "Career Academies: A Proven Strategy to Prepare High School Students for College and Careers" (working paper, Career Academy Support Network, Berkeley, CA: University of California, Berkeley Graduate School of Education, 2010).

54. Harry Holzer, "Not Your Father's Shop Class: The Promising Revival of Career and Technical Education," *Washington Monthly* 45 (2013): 56–57.

55. Alesha Boyd and Michelle Gladden, "Reading, Writing, Marine Biology; Career Academies Find Seats in Schools," *USA Today,* May 28, 2013, 1B.

56. James Kemple, *Career Academies: Long-Term Impacts on Work, Education, and Transitions to Adulthood* (New York: MDRC, June 2008).

57. Stern, "Career Academies: A Proven Strategy."

58. David Stern, "Expanding Policy Options for Educating Teenagers," *The Future of Children* 19 (Spring 2009): 211–39.

59. Christopher Wu, "Thinking Through New Vocationalism" (PhD dissertation, Education in Mathematics, Science, and Technology Program, University of California-Berkeley, 2005); Christopher Wu, telephone interview by William Gormley, May 2, 2014.

60. David Stern (professor, Graduate School of Education, UC-Berkeley), telephone interview by William Gormley, April 30, 2014.

61. James Kemple, "Using Career Academies to Help Disadvantaged Students," interview by Andy Feldman, February 13, 2015.

62. Gilberto Conchas, *The Color of Success: Race and High-Achieving Urban Youth* (New York: Teachers College Press, 2006).

63. Bob Wise, "Linked Learning Helps Students Succeed," *Sacramento Bee*, November 7, 2014, http://www.sacbee.com/opinion/op-ed/soapbox/article3650692.html.

64. Roneeta Guha et al., *Taking Stock of the California Linked Learning District Initiative: 5th Year Evaluation Report, Executive Summary* (Menlo Park, CA: SRI International, December 2014).

65. Al Baker, "At Technology High School, Goal Isn't to Finish in Four Years," *New York Times*, October 22, 2012, 17.

66. Howard Bloom and Rebecca Unterman, "Can Small High Schools of Choice Improve Educational Prospects for Disadvantaged Students?," *Journal of Policy Analysis and Management* 33 (2014): 290–319.

67. Richard J. Murnane and Greg J. Duncan, "Restoring Opportunity," The Brookings Institution, March 14, 2014, http://www.brookings.edu/events/2014/03/19-restoring-opportunity.

68. Alexis Goldberg (Director of Instruction, Urban Assembly), telephone interview by William Gormley, December 3, 2015.

69. Robert Lenz, "Transforming Schools" (talk at American Youth Policy Forum, Washington, DC, March 11, 2015).

70. Harold Sirkin, "What Germany Can Teach the USA About Vocational Education," *Bloomberg News*, April 29, 2013, http://www.bloomberg.com/bw/articles/2013-04-29/what-germany-can-teach-the-u-dot-s-dot-about-vocational-education.

71. Robert Schwartz and Nancy Hoffman, "Career Pathways" (paper presented at Education for Upward Mobility Conference, Thomas Fordham Institute, Washington, DC, December 2, 2014).

72. Robert Lerman, "Career Apprenticeships and Youth Development" (paper presented at Education for Upward Mobility Conference, Thomas Fordham Institute, Washington, DC, December 2, 2014).

73. Schwartz and Hoffman, "Career Pathways."

74. Sirkin, "What Germany Can Teach the USA."

75. John Bishop and Ferran Mane, "The Impacts of Career-Technical Education on High School Labor Market Success," *Economics of Education Review* 23 (2004): 381–402.

76. Schwartz and Hoffman, "Career Pathways."

77. Robert Lerman and Arnold Packer, *Youth Apprenticeship: A Hopeful Approach for Improving Outcomes for Baltimore Youth* (Chevy Chase, MD: Abell Foundation, April 2015)

78. Anthony Carnevale, "College Is Still Worth It," *Inside Higher Education*, January 14, 2011, http://www.insidehighered.com/views/2011/01/14/carnevale_college_is_still_worth_it_for_americans; Neil Shah, "College Graduates Earn Nearly Three Times More Than High School Dropouts," *Wall Street Journal*, April 2, 2013, http://blogs.wsj.com/economics/2013/04/02/college-grads-earn-nearly-three-times-more-than-high-school-dropouts/.

79. Robert Schwartz, personal interview by William Gormley, February 6, 2015.

80. Jaison Abel, Richard Deitz, and Yagin Su, "Are Recent College Graduates Finding Good Jobs?," *Current Issues in Economics and Finance* 20 (2014): 1–8.

81. Lerman, "Career Apprenticeships and Youth Development"; Nancy

Cook, "Should the U.S. Adopt the German Model of Apprenticeships?," *National Journal*, April 11, 2014, http://www.nationaljournal.com/ next-economy/solutions-bank/should-u-s-adopt-german-model-apprenticeships; Joseph Perilla, Jesus Trujillo, and Alan Berube, *Skills and Innovation Strategies to Strengthen U.S. Manufacturers: Lessons from Germany* (Washington, DC: Brookings Institution, Metropolitan Policy Program, 2015).

82. Uri Berliner, "In South Carolina, A Program That Makes Apprenticeships Work," National Public Radio, November 6, 2014, http://wuwf .org/post/south-carolina-program-makes-apprenticeships-work.

Chapter 6

1. Kathleen Hall Jamieson, "The Challenges Facing Civic Education in the 21st Century," *Daedalus* (Spring 2013): 65–83.

2. Constance Flanagan, *Teenage Citizens: The Political Theories of the Young* (Cambridge, MA: Harvard University Press, 2013).

3. Molly Hunter, *State Constitution Education Clause Language* (Newark, NJ: Education Law Center, 2011).

4. Peter Levine et al., *The Civic Mission of Schools* (New York: Carnegie Corporation, February, 2003).

5. David Campbell, "Civic Education in Traditional Public, Charter, and Private Schools," in *Making Civics Count*, ed. David Campbell, Meira Levinson, and Frederick Hess (Cambridge, MA: Harvard Education Press, 2012), 229–46.

6. Sidney Verba, Kay Schlozman, and Henry Brady, *Voice and Equality: Civic Voluntarism in American Politics* (Cambridge, MA: Harvard University Press, 1995).

7. Diana Mutz, *Hearing the Other Side: Deliberative versus Participatory Democracy* (New York: Cambridge University Press, 2006).

8. Ibid.

9. Michael McDonald, "2012 November General Election Turnout Rates," *U.S. Elections Project*, http://www.electproject.org/2012g.

10. Editorial Board, "The Worst Voter Turnout in 72 Years," *New York Times*, November 11, 2014.

11. US Elections Project, "2016 November General Election Turnout Rates," http://www.electionproject.org/2016g.

12. Constance Flanagan and Peter Levine, "Civic Engagement and the Transition into Adulthood," *The Future of the Children* 20 (Spring 2010): 159–79.

13. The Center for Information and Research on Civic Learning and Engagement, "The 2014 Youth Vote," *Youth Voting*, November 2014, http://civicyouth.org/quick-facts/youth-voting/.

14. Charles Taber and Milton Lodge, "Motivated Skepticism in the

Evaluation of Political Beliefs," *American Journal of Political Science* 50 (2006): 755–69; Milton Lodge and Charles Taber, *The Rationalizing Voter* (New York: Cambridge University Press, 2013).

15. Lodge and Taber, *The Rationalizing Voter.*

16. Ibid.; David Redlawski, "Hot Cognition or Cool Consideration? Testing the Effects of Motivated Reasoning on Political Decision Making," *Journal of Politics* 64 (2002): 1021–44.

17. Michael Delli Carpini and Scott Keeter, *What Americans Know About Politics and Why It Matters* (New Haven, CT: Yale University Press, 1996).

18. Richard Niemi, "What Students Know About Civics and Government," in *Making Civics Count*, ed. David Campbell, Meira Levinson, and Frederick Hess (Cambridge, MA: Harvard Education Press, 2012), 1–13.

19. Pew Research Center, *Public Knowledge of Current Affairs Little Changed by News and Information Revolutions: What Americans Know: 1989–2007* (Washington, DC: Pew Research Center, April 15, 2007); Delli Carpini and Keeter, *What Americans Know About Politics.*

20. Annenberg Public Policy Center, *Americans Know Surprisingly Little About Their Government, Survey Finds* (Philadelphia, PA: University of Pennsylvania, September 17, 2014).

21. Delli Carpini and Keeter, *What Americans Know About Politics.*

22. James Madison, "The Alleged Danger from the Powers of the Union to the State Government Considered," *The Federalist*, http://avalon.law.yale/edu/18th_century/fed45.asp.

23. Gary Mucciaroni and Paul Quirk, *Deliberative Choices: Debating Public Policy in Congress* (Chicago: University of Chicago, 2006), 181.

24. James Fishkin and Robert Luskin, "Experimenting with a Democratic Ideal: Deliberative Polling and Public Opinion," *Acta Politica* 40 (2005): 284–98.

25. Campbell, "Civic Education," 229–46.

26. Amy Smith, "Do Americans Still Believe in Democracy?," *Washington Post*, April 9, 2016, https://www.washingtonpost.com/news/monkey-cage/wp/2016/04/09/do-americans-still-believe-in-democracy/.

27. Mutz, *Hearing the Other Side.*

28. Natalie Stroud, *Niche News: The Politics of News Choice* (New York: Oxford University Press, 2011).

29. Amy Mitchell et al., *Political Polarization and Media Habits* (Washington, DC: Pew Research Journalism Project, October 21, 2014).

30. Natalie Stroud and Alexander Curry, "The Polarizing Effects of Partisan and Mainstream News," in *American Gridlock*, ed. James Thurber and Antoine Yoshinaka (New York: Cambridge University Press, 2015), 337–54.

31. Gary Jacobson, "Partisan Media and Electoral Polarization in 2012" in *American Gridlock*, ed. James Thurber and Antoine Yoshinaka (New York: Cambridge University Press, 2015), 259–86.

32. Pew Research Center, "Partisanship and Political Animosity in 2016," June 22, 2016, http://www.people-press.org/2016/06/22/partisanship-and-political-animosity-in-2016/.

33. Mitchell et al., *Political Polarization*.

34. Eytan Baksy, Solomon Messing, and Lada Adamic, "Exposure to Ideologically Diverse News and Opinion on Facebook," *Science* 348 (2015), 1130–32.

35. Pew Research Center, "Teaching the Children: Sharp Ideological Differences, Some Common Ground," September 18, 2014, http://www.people-press.org/2014/09/18/teaching-the-children-sharp-ideological-differences-some-common-ground/.

36. Catherine Rampell, "Stop Saying Only Democrats Are Politically Correct. Republicans Also Favor Censorship," *Washington Post,* August 12, 2015, 15.

37. Mutz, *Hearing the Other Side*.

38. James Youniss, "How to Enrich Civic Education and Sustain Democracy," in *Making Civics Count,* ed. David Campbell, Meira Levinson, and Frederick Hess (Cambridge, MA: Harvard Education Press, 2012), 115–33.

39. Mark Lopez et al., "Schools, Education Policy, and the Future of the First Amendment," *Political Communication* 26 (2009): 84–101.

40. Youniss, "How to Enrich Civic Education," 115–33.

41. John Hibbing and Elizabeth Theiss-Morse, "Civics Is Not Enough: Teaching Barbarics in K–12," *PS: Political Science and Politics* 29 (1996): 57–62.

42. Campbell, "Civic Education," 229–46.

43. Peter Levine et al., *The Civic Mission of Schools* (New York: Carnegie Corporation, February 2003).

44. Campbell, "Civic Education," 229–246.

45. Deanna Kuhn and Wadiya Udell, "The Development of Argument Skills," *Child Development* 74 (2003): 1245–60.

46. Constance Flanagan, *Teenage Citizens: The Political Theories of the Young* (Cambridge, MA: Harvard University Press, 2013).

47. Deanna Kuhn (professor, Teachers College, Columbia University), telephone interview by William Gormley, March 25, 2016.

48. Joseph Kahne and Eileen Middaugh, *Democracy for Some: The Civic Opportunity Gap in High School* (College Park, MD: CIRCLE, 2008).

49. David E. Campbell, "Voice in the Classroom: How an Open Classroom Climate Fosters Political Engagement Among Adolescents," *Political Behavior* 30 (2008): 437–54.

50. Anna Saavedra, "Dry to Dynamic Civic Education Curricula," in *Making Civics Count,* ed. David Campbell, Meira Levinson, and Frederick Hess (Cambridge, MA: Harvard Education Press, 2012), 135–59.

51. Peter Levine (Professor of Citizenship & Public Affairs, Tufts University), telephone interview by William Gormley, February 2, 2015.

52. Hall Jamieson, "The Challenges Facing Civic Education," 65–83.

53. Saavedra, "Dry to Dynamic Civic Education Curricula," 135–59.

54. Levine, telephone interview.

55. Saavedra, "Dry to Dynamic Civic Education Curricula," 135–59.

56. Levine, telephone interview.

57. MacArthur Award, "iCivics, 2015 MacArthur Award Recipient," *MacArthur Foundation*, 3:50, February 4, 2015, https://www.macfound.org/videos/466/.

58. Youniss, "How to Enrich Civic Education," 115–33.

59. Vittorio Merola and Matthew Hitt, "Numeracy and the Persuasive Effect of Policy Information and Party Cues," *Public Opinion Quarterly* 80 (2016): 554–62.

60. Sarah Stitzlein, *Teaching for Dissent: Citizenship Education and Political Activism* (Boulder, CO: Paradigm Publishers, 2012).

61. Wendy Wan-Long Shang, *The Great Wall of Lucy Wu* (New York: Scholastic Press, 2011).

62. John Grisham, *Theodore Boone: Kid Lawyer* (New York: Puffin Books, 2010).

63. John Grisham, *Theodore Boone: The Activist* (New York: Dutton Children's Books, 2013).

64. John Holbein, *Marshmallows and Votes? Childhood Skill Development and Adult Political Participation* (Durham, NC: Sanford School of Public Policy, Duke University, 2015).

65. Editorial Board, "The Worst Voter Turnout in 72 Years"; Drew Desilver, "Voter Turnout Always Drops Off for Midterm Elections, but Why?," *Fact Tank*, Pew Research Center, July 24, 2014, http://www.pewresearch.org/fact-tank/2014/07/24/voter-turnout-always-drops-off-for-midterm-elections-but-why/.

66. Ben Terris, "A Congress Too Pathetic to Picket," *Washington Post*, July 22, 2014.

67. Peter Levine, "What We Need to Do About Civic Education," *Huffington Post*, October 11, 2012, http://www.huffingtonpost.com/peter-levine/what-we-need-to-do-about-_b_1957948.html.

68. Saavedra, "Dry to Dynamic Civic Education Curricula," 135–59.

69. David Campbell and Richard Niemi, "Testing Civics: State-Level Civic Education Requirements and Political Knowledge," *American Political Science Review* (forthcoming).

70. Levine, telephone interview.

71. Peter Levine and Kei Kawashima-Ginsberg, *Civic Education and Deeper Learning* (Boston, MA: Jobs for the Future, 2015).

72. Kathleen McCleary, "Operation Good Citizen," *Parade*, August 2, 2015,

6–8.

73. Milton Lodge and Charles Taber, *The Rationalizing Voter* (Cambridge, MA: Cambridge University Press, 2013).

74. Delli Carpini and Keeter, *What Americans Know About Politics*.

75. Campbell, "Civic Education," 229–46.

76. Stephen Macedo et al., *Democracy at Risk* (Washington, DC: Brookings Institution Press, 2005).

77. Kathleen McCartney, "Is Free Speech at Risk at Our Universities?," CNN, updated September 3, 2014, http://www.cnn.com/2014/09/04/opinion/mccartney-college-students-free-speech/

78. Peter Levine, *We Are the Ones We Have Been Waiting For* (New York: Oxford University Press, 2014).

79. Mutz, *Hearing the Other Side*.

80. David Campbell, "Civic Education," 229–46.

81. Lawrence Jacobs, Fay Cook, and Michael Delli Carpini, *Talking Together: Public Deliberation and Political Participation in America* (Chicago: University of Chicago Press, 2009).

82. Campbell, "Civic Education," 229–46.

83. David Campbell, *Why We Vote: How Schools and Communities Shape Our Civic Life* (Princeton, NJ: Princeton University Press, 2006).

Chapter 7

1. Eleanor Chute, "STEM Education Is Branching Out," *Pittsburgh Post Gazette*, February 10, 2009.

2. Allie Bidwell, "More Students Earning STEM Degrees, Report Shows," *U.S. News & World Report*, January 27, 2015, http://www.usnews.com/news/articles/2015/01/27/more-students-earning-degrees-in-stem-fields-report-shows.

3. Anthony Carnevale et al., *STEM, Executive Summary* (Washington, DC: Center on Education and the Workforce, McCourt School of Public Policy, Georgetown University, 2011).

4. US Department of Education, "Science, Technology, Engineering, and Math: Education for Global Leadership," http://www.ed.gov/stem.

5. D. T. Max, "A Whole New Ball Game: The Rolling Robot That Teaches Kids to Code," *New Yorker*, May 16, 2016, 40–46.

6. Natalie Angier, "STEM Education Has Little to Do with Flowers," *New York Times*, October 4, 2010.

7. Anne Jolly, "STEM v. STEAM: Do the Arts Belong?," *Education Week Teacher*, November 18, 2014, http://www.edweek.org/tm/articles/2014/11/18/ctq-jolly-stem-vs-steam.html.

8. Erica Halverson and Kimberly Sheridan, "The Maker Movement in Education," *Harvard Educational Review* 84 (2014): 495–504.

9. Jolly, "STEM v. STEAM."

10. Laurie Gray (principal, South Fayette Elementary School), informal remarks at South Fayette Elementary School, February 24, 2016.
11. Visit to fifth-grade class, Stephanie DeLuca, February 24, 2016.
12. Arthur Costa and Bena Kallick, *Learning and Leading with Habits of Mind* (Alexandria, VA: Association for Supervision and Curriculum Development, 2008).
13. Shad Wachter (teacher, South Fayette Intermediate School), interview by William Gormley, February 24, 2016.
14. Frank Kruth (STEAM coordinator, South Fayette Middle School), interview by William Gormley, March 18, 2016.
15. South Fayette School District, informal student remarks to visitors, February 24, 2016.
16. A. J. Mannarino (teacher, South Fayette Middle School), interview by William Gormley, March 11, 2016.
17. Jeannie Scott (teacher, South Fayette High School), interview by William Gormley, March 7, 2016.
18. "South Fayette Township School District," Niche, https://k12.niche.com/d/south-fayette-township-school-district-pa/.
19. Bille Rondinelli (superintendent, South Fayette Township School District), interview by William Gormley, May 18, 2016.
20. Len Fornella (school board member, South Fayette Township School District), interview by William Gormley, May 17, 2016.
21. Rondinelli, interview.
22. Ibid.
23. Bille Rondinelli, personal communication, September 28, 2016.
24. "South Fayette Township School District," Niche.
25. US Department of Education, "English Language Learners," National Center for Education Statistics, http://www.nces.ed.gov/programs/coe/indicator_cgf.asp.
26. Only 3 percent of South Fayette's students are Hispanic, as opposed to 16 percent black and 25 percent Hispanic nationally. See National Education Statistics, "Racial/Ethnic Enrollment in Public Schools," Institute of Education Sciences, 2013, http://www.nces.ed.gov/programs/coe/indicator_cge.asp.
27. Vicky Ozment (coordinator, instruction, Talladega County Schools), telephone interview by William Gormley, April 25, 2016.
28. Project Lead the Way, "Project Lead the Way Continues Record Growth" [press release], Indianapolis, IN, September 23, 2014.
29. Joe Clemmer (teacher, Memorial Junior High School, Tulsa), telephone interview by William Gormley, April 13, 2016.
30. Ginger Bunnell (principal, Memorial Junior High School, Tulsa), interview by William Gormley, December 11, 2015.
31. Rustan Schwichtenberg (teacher, Booker T. Washington High School,

Tulsa), interview by William Gormley, April 27, 2016.

32. FIRST, "First Impact," http://www.firstchampionship.org/first-impact.

33. Pam Diaz (teacher, Booker T. Washington High School, Tulsa), personal correspondence with William Gormley, May 6, 2016.

34. Nicole Findon (teacher, Schiller Middle School, Pittsburgh), interview by William Gormley, May 16, 2016.

35. Shaun Tomaszewski (STEAM administrator, Pittsburgh Public Schools), interview by William Gormley, May 16, 2016.

36. Mary Anderson (teacher, Lincoln Elementary School, Pittsburgh), interview by William Gormley, May 24, 2016.

37. Tomaszewski, interview.

38. Ozment, telephone interview.

39. Kathy Dodd (associate superintendent, Union Public Schools), interview by William Gormley, April 27, 2016.

40. Tomaszewski, telephone interview.

41. Janet Jenkins (teacher, Woolslair Elementary School, Pittsburgh), telephone interview by William Gormley, May 23, 2016.

42. Teresa Partee (teacher, Lincoln Elementary School, Pittsburgh), interview by William Gormley, May 16, 2016.

43. Jenkins, telephone interview.

44. Bill Murphy (STEM curriculum specialist, Union Public Schools), interview by William Gormley, April 28, 2016.

45. Ozment, telephone interview.

46. Rondinelli, interview.

47. Trisha Craig (director of curriculum, Fort Cherry School District), interview by William Gormley, May 18, 2016.

48. Andrea Eger, "TPS Plan: Cut 142 Teachers," *Tulsa World,* April 28, 2016, 1; Andrea Eger, "Budget Cuts: Broken Arrow, Union and Bixby School Boards Approve Reductions," *Tulsa World,* May 10, 2016, http://www.tulsaworld.com/news/education/budget-cuts-broken-arrow-union-and-bixby-school-boards-approve/article_1fae2a95-c5d2-57c4-bcfc-01b928728c53.html.

49. Ginger Bunnell (principal, Memorial Junior High School, Tulsa), telephone interview by William Gormley, April 11, 2016.

50. Nanette Coleman (principal, Booker T. Washington High School, Tulsa), telephone interview by William Gormley, April 20, 2016.

51. Craig, interview.

52. Kirt Hartzler (superintendent, Union School District), interview by William Gormley, April 27, 2016.

53. Ozment, (telephone interview.

54. Luke Bauer (principal, Urban Assembly Maker Academy, New York City), telephone interview by William Gormley, May 2, 2016.

55. Bauer, personal interview by William Gormley, May 26, 2016.

56. Center for Research on Children in the U.S. *Tulsa Public Schools data* (William Gormley, p.i.) (Washington, DC: CROCUS, Georgetown University, 2016).

57. Lane Matheson (teacher, Memorial High School, Tulsa), telephone interview by William Gormley, May 4, 2016.

58. Center for Research on Children in the U.S. *Tulsa Public Schools data*.

59. Calculations by Nghia-Piotr Le, for William Gormley, using data from Project Lead the Way, Niche, and Pennsylvania Department of Education, June 1, 2016.

60. Calculations by Nghia-Piotr Le, for William Gormley, using data from Project Lead the Way, Niche, and Oklahoma Department of Education, June 1, 2016.

61. Center for Research on Children in the U.S. *Tulsa Public Schools data*.

62. Matheson, telephone interview.

63. Center for Research on Children in the U.S. *Tulsa Public Schools data*.

64. Memorial High School, http://k12.niche.com/memorial-high-school-tulsa-ok.

65. Booker T. Washington High School, http://k12.niche.com/booker-t-washington-high-school-tulsa-ok.

66. Bauer, telephone interview.

67. Matheson, telephone interview.

68. Max, "A Whole New Ball Game," 40–46.

69. Liana Heitin, "Elite Math Competitions Struggle to Diversify Their Talent Pool," *Education Week,* May 18, 2016, 1.

70. Tim Bajarin, "Why the Maker Movement Is Important to America's Future," *Time,* May 19, 2014, http://www.time.com/104210/maker-faire-maker-movement.

71. Diaz, personal correspondence.

72. Matheson, telephone interview.

73. Michael Leachman, Nick Albares, Kathleen Masterson, and Marlana Wallace, *Most States Have Cut School Funding, and Some Continue Cutting* (Washington, DC: Center on Budget and Policy Priorities, January 25, 2016).

74. Tim Bartik, "The Economic Case for Preschool," 15:45. TEDvideo, Posted May 6, 2013, https://www.ted.com/talks/timothy-bartik-the-economic-case-for-preschool.

Chapter 8

1. W. K. C. Guthrie, *Socrates* (London: Cambridge University Press, 1971).

2. Byron Steel, *Sir Francis Bacon: The First Modern Mind* (Garden City, NY: Doubleday, 1930).

3. John Dewey, *How We Think* (Buffalo, NY: Prometheus Books, 1991).

4. David Hirsch and Daniel Van Haften, *Abraham Lincoln and the Structure*

of Reason (New York: Savas Beatie, 2010).

5. Alison Gopnik, Andrew Meltzoff, and Patricia Kuhl, *The Scientist in the Crib* (New York: William Morrow, 1991), 1.

6. Ibid.

7. Ozgur Ozer, "Constructivism in Piaget and Vygotsky," *Fountain Magazine*, 48 (2004), http://www.fountainmagazine.com/Issue/detail/CONSTRUCTIVISM-in-Piaget-and-Vygotsky.

8. Rheta DeVries and Betty Zan, *Moral Classrooms, Moral Children: Creating a Constructivist Atmosphere in Early Education* (New York: Teachers College Press, 2012): 1.

9. Ibid., 5.

10. Adam Cooney and Samantha Jones, "The Educational Theory of Maria Montessori," New Foundations, August 18, 2011, http://www.newfoundations.com/GALLERY/Montessori.html; Elizabeth Hainstock, *The Essential Montessori* (New York: New American Library, 1986).

11. Maria Montessori, *The Montessori Method* (Cambridge, MA: Robert Bentley, Inc., 1965): 231.

12. Cooney and Jones, "The Educational Theory of Maria Montessori."

13. Hainstock, *The Essential Montessori*, 46–92.

14. American Montessori Society, "Montessori Schools," http://www.amshq.org/Montessori-education/Introduction-to-Montessori/Montessori-Schools.

15. Douglas Clements and Julie Sarama, "Effects of a Preschool Mathematics Curriculum: Summative Research on the Building Blocks Project," *Journal for Research in Mathematics Education* 38 (2007): 136–63.

16. Benedict Carey, "Studying Young Minds, and How to Teach Them," *New York Times*, December 20, 2009.

17. Kimberly Noble et al., "Family Income, Parental Education, and Brain Structure in Children and Adolescents," *Nature Neuroscience* 18 (2015): 773–8.

18. Deanna Barch et al., "Effect of Hippocampal and Amygdala Connectivity on the Relationship Between Preschool Poverty and School-Age Depression," *American Journal of Psychiatry* (January 15, 2016): 625–33.

19. Gwendolyn M. Lawson et al., "Associations Between Children's Socioeconomic Status and Prefrontal Cortical Thickness," *Development Science* (2013): 1–12.

20. Sean Reardon, "The Widening Academic Achievement Gap Between the Rich and the Poor," in *Whither Opportunity?*, ed. Greg Duncan and Richard Murnane (New York: Russell Sage Foundation, 2011), 96–116; Jane Waldfogel, "Translating Policy Analysis into Action" (SREE presidential address at Society for Research on Educational Effectiveness, Washington, DC, March 4, 2016).

21. Rachel Valentino, "Will Public Pre-K Really Close Achievement Gaps?" (paper presented at the Annual Meeting of the Association for

Education Finance and Policy, Washington, DC, February 27, 2015); Deborah Stipek, "Teaching Practices in Kindergarten and First Grade," *Early Childhood Research Quarterly* 19 (2004): 548–68; Deanna Kuhn, *Education for Thinking* (Cambridge, MA: Harvard University Press, 2005); and Joseph Kahne and Ellen Middaugh, "Democracy for Some: The Civic Opportunity Gap in High School" (Working Paper #59, CIRCLE, College Park, MD, February 2008).

22. Catherine Gewertz, "More Low-Income Students Taking AP Classes," *Ed Week*, February 4, 2009, http://www.edweek.org/ew/articles/2009/02/04/21ap.h28.html; also see Ronald Hallett and Kristan Venegas, "Is Increased Access Enough?," *Journal for the Education of the Gifted* 34 (2011): 468–87.

23. Alvin Toffler, *Future Shock* (New York: Random House, 1970).

24. David Autor, Frank Levy, and Richard Murnane, "The Skill Content of Recent Technological Change: An Empirical Exploration," *Quarterly Journal of Economics* 118 (2003): 1279–1334.

25. Yujia Liu and David Grusky, "The Payoff to Skill in the Third Industrial Revolution," *American Journal of Sociology* 118 (2013): 1330–74.

26. Barack Obama, "Remarks by the President on Higher Education and the Economy at the University of Texas at Austin," White House (University of Texas at Austin, August 9, 2010), https://www.whitehouse.gov/the-press-office/2010/08/09/remarks-president-higher-education-and-economy-university-texas-austin.

27. Fairfax County Public Schools, "Portrait of a Graduate," 2014, http://www.fcps.edu/supt/portrait.

28. Robert Lerman and Arnold Packer, *Youth Apprenticeship: A Hopeful Approach for Improving Outcomes for Baltimore Youth* (Chevy Chase, MD: Abell Foundation, April 2015).

29. Moriah Balingit, "Virginia Governor Moves to Upend Traditional High School," *Washington Post*, May 12, 2016.

30. Atul Gawande, *The Checklist Manifesto: How to Get Things Right* (New York: Metropolitan Books, 2010).

31. William Gormley, "Regulatory Enforcement: Accommodation and Conflict in Four States," *Public Administration Review* 57 (1997): 285–93; William Gormley, "Regulatory Enforcement Styles," *Political Research Quarterly* 51 (1998): 363–83.

32. David Olds et al., "Long-Term Effects of Nurse Home Visitation on Children's Criminal and Antisocial Behavior: 15-Year Follow-Up of a Randomized Controlled Trial," *Journal of the American Medical Association* 280 (1998): 1238–44.

33. King County, "Nurse-Family Partnership; Providing Babies with the Best Start in Life," http://www.kingcounty.gov/depts/health/child-teen-health-nurse-family-partnership.aspx.

ACKNOWLEDGMENTS

Writing a book about critical thinking is more like writing a book about time or space or love than it is like writing a book about, let's say, the politics of public utility regulation. Because the subject is so vast, my debts, commensurately, are enormous. Although I am happy to acknowledge many specific debts, many must go unacknowledged because people who helped did so by challenging or provoking me not during the time I worked on this specific project but well before that. They lit a spark that helped to illuminate my path as I wrote this book.

I would like to begin by thanking Paul Manna and Brook Manville, who read and critiqued the book from stem to stern. Their incisive comments on each chapter were exceptionally wise and constructive. I would also like to thank Dick Murnane for his early confidence in the critical thinking project and for asking some tough questions that I have tried to answer. When I finally decided on Pittsburgh as one of my research sites, my sister Nancy Pfenning and my brother-in-law Frank Pfenning were enormously helpful in suggesting specific schools and "deep throat" informants. On the ground in Tulsa, Andy McKenzie and Steven Dow were indispensable guides and connectors.

Several research assistants at Georgetown University, in addition to gathering and analyzing data, took an active interest in the project and served as sounding boards for my ideas. I am grateful to Kristin Blagg, Ben Lockshin, Piotr Le, and Esther Owolabi for their many contributions to the manuscript. Also at Georgetown, I would like to thank Harry Holzer, Jane Hannaway, John Glavin, Elise Cardinale, Chandan Vaidya, Abby Marsh, and Adam Green for giving me a more subtle understanding of programs, concepts, and thought processes that contribute to good thinking. In addition, I am deeply grateful to David Wakelyn, Deanna Kuhn, Caroline Hendrie, Erik Robelen,

Jack Shonkoff, Terry Rhodes, Karin Kitchens, Anne Kitchens, Carl Van Horn, Bob Schwartz, David Stern, Chris Wu, Mike Petrilli, Betsy Brand, David Campbell, Scott Keeter, Peter Levine, Tom Sander, Kim Schwadron, Charlie Wilson, David Kosbie, and Lindsay Matsumura for their sage advice on specific topics.

I owe a special thank you to Nancy Walser of the Harvard Education Press, who agreed that I could write a book on X after she proposed a book on Y and who offered tough but excellent suggestions at a critical stage. I would also like to thank Sumita Mukherji and Laura Cutone Godwin for helping to whip the manuscript into shape.

Much of what this book has to offer is thanks to many teachers and principals who allowed me to visit their classrooms and who gave me a glimpse of the magic that can transform students from reluctant dragons into eager beavers. For me, these classroom visits were pure gold—they inspired me and convinced me that many of our children are in good hands. At the same time, I appreciate those school officials who reminded me that many disadvantaged children do not have easy access to transformative teachers or the skills that enable them to take advantage of such teachers.

My wife Rosie and my daughter Angela endured many dinner table conversations in which the topics of this book were prominently featured. At times they must have wondered whether being a critical thinker means having a one-track mind. I thank them for their patience, love, and support.

Finally, I would like to dedicate this book to the many teachers who have helped me to distinguish between ordinary and extraordinary thinking. They include teachers whom I observed for this project, teachers who actually taught me in class, and my very first teachers, Bill and Elena Gormley. This book is for all of them.

ABOUT THE AUTHOR

WILLIAM T. GORMLEY, JR. is University Professor at Georgetown University. He is also a Professor of Public Policy and Government and co-director of the Center for Research on Children in the U.S. (CROCUS). Dr. Gormley is the author or coauthor of several books, including *Everybody's Children: Child Care as a Public Problem* (Brookings, 1995), *Organizational Report Cards* (Harvard University Press, 1999), and *Bureaucracy and Democracy* (Congressional Quarterly Press, 2003, 2007, 2011). His book *Voices for Children: Rhetoric and Public Policy* was published by the Brookings Institution Press in 2012. Dr. Gormley is a Fellow of the National Academy of Public Administration and a past president of the Public Policy Section of the American Political Science Association.

For the past fifteen years, Dr. Gormley has directed the Oklahoma pre-K project, which has evaluated the state-funded pre-K program in Tulsa, Oklahoma. He and his research team have documented substantial gains in prereading, prewriting, and premath skills for children enrolled in the school-based pre-K program in Tulsa. These findings have appeared in the *Journal of Human Resources*, the *Policy Studies Journal*, *Developmental Psychology*, the *Social Science Quarterly*, *Child Development*, *Science*, and elsewhere. The successes of Tulsa's pre-K program have been featured in the *New York Times*, the *Wall Street Journal*, NPR, the PBS NewsHour, and the CBS Evening News.

At Georgetown, Dr. Gormley served as Interim Dean of Public Policy for two years and was one of the founding members of Georgetown's day-care center, Hoya Kids.

INDEX